ENCYCLOPEDIA OF

Hydrangeas

ENCYCLOPEDIA OF

Hydrangeas

C. J. VAN GELDEREN

D. M. VAN GELDEREN

TIMBER PRESS

Portland ~ Cambridge

Published in 2004 by

Timber Press, Inc.   Timber Press
The Haseltine Building   2 Station Road
133 S.W. Second Avenue, Suite 450   Swavesey
Portland, Oregon 97204-3527, U.S.A.   Cambridge CB4 5QJ, U.K.

www.timberpress.com

Printed in China

Library of Congress Cataloging-in-Publication Data

Gelderen, C. J. van (Cornelis Johannes), 1960-
  Encyclopedia of hydrangeas / C.J. van Gelderen, D.M. van Gelderen.
      p. cm.
  Includes bibliographical references (p.   ).
  ISBN 0-88192-622-1 (hardcover)
  1. Hydrangeas--Encyclopedias. 2. Gardening--Encyclopedias. I.
Gelderen, D. M. van. II. Title.
  SB413.H93G45 2004
  635.9'3372--dc22   2003019741

A catalog record for this book is also available from the British Library.

Half-title page: *Hydrangea macrophylla*, Trebah Garden.
Frontispiece: *Hydrangea macrophylla*, Sir Harold Hillier Gardens and
                Arboretum.
Contents: *Hydrangea macrophylla*, Trebah Garden.

to FELICE

Contents

Hydrangea macrophylla, Trebah Garden.

Hydrangea macrophylla (Hortensia Group) 'Altona', Royal Horticultural Society Garden Wisley.

Preface

When we were first asked to write a book on the genus *Hydrangea*, we were immediately filled with skepticism. How were we going to write a book on such a limited subject? We realized that there were some species we could write about, that *H. macrophylla* had some cultivars—blue and pink or even white mopheads, and a few lacecaps—but an entire book? How ignorant we were!

Our study showed that hydrangeas are superb garden plants with an enormous diversity from evergreen climbers, to small deciduous trees with splendid masses of flowers, to lovely alpine shrubs no taller than 1.5 meters (5 ft.) but covered in delicate flowers, with excellent fall colors, and all of them displaying outstanding qualities. As a group, hydrangeas are summer flowering, easy to grow and maintain, suitable for all kinds of soils, and practically disease-free. They come in a wide range of flower colors and shapes, and flower time lasts at least six weeks but often much longer. What more could a gardener wish for?

So, after having researched and photographed hydrangeas, we have changed our minds entirely. We now believe this genus is very underestimated, in spite of its popularity, and offers much to be discovered. We hope this book will communicate our enthusiasm for this deserving genus of plants.

Acknowledgments

We want to thank everyone who helped us with the creation of this book. One of the most enchanting aspects of working on this project was meeting so many people who share our enthusiasm for hydrangeas. It is impossible to name all of you, but we know that without your help, this book would have been completely different. In addition to helping us write this book, you helped us enjoy hydrangeas even more by sharing your anecdotes, knowledge, and passion.

We would like to recognize certain individuals for their assistance: Philippe and Cathérine Quesnel, whose hospitality during our visit to France was very much appreciated; Madame Princess Sturdza, in whose garden, called Le Vastérival, we spent a very enjoyable few days; Mark Bulk, who generously shared his collection of hydrangeas with us so that we could study the plants at our own place; Maurice Foster, who helped us plan our tour of Great Britain and find additional information on many interesting hydrangeas; Erik van den Ham, who shared not only his knowledge but also his many slides of hydrangeas. A special thanks to Herbert Plokker, who accompanied us on our photographing missions, taking notes, removing labels, holding an umbrella over the camera when it rained, and sharing a good glass of wine in the evening as we discussed the day's events. We thank Dr. Ben J. M. Zonneveld for his DNA research, which is new in the genus *Hydrangea* and which proved to be important for the classification of the species. We also thank Mrs. H. J. J. van Gelderen-Esveld, who as wife and mother of the authors endured endless discussions about hydrangeas and helped select the slides.

Many thanks to all of you whom we had the pleasure of meeting over hydrangeas in the past few years.

Hydrangea macrophylla, Le Clos du Coudray, courtesy Arborealis.

Hydrangea or Hortensia?

Hydrangea macrophylla is by far the most well-known species in the genus, and from it hundreds of named cultivars have been selected or developed over the years throughout the world. The common name for cultivars of *H. macrophylla* is "hortensia," a name used by several botanists until the end of the 19th century, when it lost its taxonomic basis and the genus became known as *Hydrangea.* Gardeners and growers continued, however, to call the plants by the name with which they were most familiar, "hortensia." A similar situation developed with the name "azalea," which was once used by botanists for a certain group of rhododendrons, but was sunk in synonymy by G. Don in 1834. Again, horticulturists continued to use "azalea" as a popular name.

The origin of the name hortensia is vague and many explanations have been given. French botanist Philibert Commerson first used the name in 1771 for a plant found in the East Indies by astronomer Lengentil de la Galaisiere. The discoverer suggested calling it Lepautia, after Mrs. Lepaute, wife of a celebrated clockmaker and herself an astronomer of merit (Coats 1992). Commerson instead called it "hortensia." He had just returned from a botanical expedition (1766–1769) with Louis-Antoine de Bougainville, his mistress Jeanne Barré, and the Prince of Nassau, also a distinguished botanist. The most likely explanation is that he named the plant after the Prince's daughter, Hortense.

Another explanation is that the name hortensia refers to the garden origin of the plants found on Mauritius and send by Commerson to Paris. In Latin the word *hortensis* means "from the garden." Hortensia is certainly not named after Queen Hortense, daughter of empress Joséphine de Beauharnais. This queen had not been born when Commerson died in 1773.

Distribution of the Genus

Hydrangeas are plants of the Northern Hemisphere, scattered throughout eastern Asia, especially China and Japan, but found in many other countries in that region including Vietnam. They also inhabit large parts of the Americas, from the U.S. Northeast via Central America in countries such as Mexico and Costa Rica down to the Andes in Ecuador and Peru. They only touch the equator in Indonesia. Hydrangeas are not found in nature in Europe; however, Europeans seem to compensate for that by planting them at large in their gardens.

Some species can develop into huge trees in their habitat. One such example is *Hydrangea heteromalla* in the Chinese province of Sichuan. Among the species native to Japan, *H. macrophylla, H. paniculata,* and *H. serrata* are probably the most important to horticulture. *Hydrangea aspera* shares its vast distribution area, which covers a large part of Southeast Asia including Indonesia, with *H. heteromalla, H. scandens* and its allies, and *H. anomala.* Not surprisingly, therefore, these species show a large variability, giving botanists cause over the years to create a vast array of subspecies, varieties, and formas, not to mention synonyms. The exact divisions between the various expressions of the *H. scandens* complex, for example, will always be disputable, a matter of interpretation rather than an exact science. Although we largely follow Elizabeth McClintock's view, especially regarding the *H. scandens* complex, we can understand how the natural variability of these plants is so enormous that recognizing more subspecies or varieties seems defendable.

In Mexico and further south in Central America the members of section *Cornidia* are at home, all evergreen woody climbers or shrubs, quite often epiphytic. Last but certainly not least are two species in southeastern North America: *Hydrangea arborescens* and *H. quercifolia.*

Hydrangea Collections

To compile a representative survey of *Hydrangea* species and cultivars in cultivation as well as those lost to cultivation, we have tried to visit all the important collections in Europe and to study the literature on this genus. At gardens and nurseries in Belgium, France, England, and Wales, and Netherlands, we exchanged information about the collections with the people behind them. Although we gained much information by consulting and checking many books and publications, some more than 100 years old, we sometimes found the actual knowledge about certain plants could be obtained only by picking people's brains. This gave us a good excuse to communicate with the very diverse and interesting group of people who share a passion for hydrangeas. Thanks to their help we were able to make this survey of hydrangeas. We realize, however, that additional information and interesting details remain hidden and that some of them will surface as soon as we have finished our manuscript. So be it.

In researching hydrangeas we were intrigued by their diverse uses in the landscape. We expected that the collections and gardens we visited might start looking alike after a while, but not so. At the risk of offending some reader by not mentioning his or her favorite hydrangea garden, we want to point out a few gardens that impressed us on our tour of Europe. The "lake" of blue-flowering mopheads at the bottom of the valley in the Cornish garden of Trebah has a completely different look than the woodland garden style used by Maurice Foster in his private garden in Kent, where a variety of often wild-collected Asian hydrangeas flourish in conditions similar to that of their habitat. In Normandy, France, the well-known garden of Le Vastérival has a lovely setting of large groups of *Hydrangea macrophylla* in the English landscape style. We also encountered some small gems. In the pouring rain we visited Le Thuit Saint-Jean, a private French garden where hundreds of different hydrangeas were literally planted on top of each other, all of them looking surprisingly good for being packed together. In Netherlands, at Planten Tuin de Oirsprong, a long border is planted with more than 175 cultivars of *H. macrophylla* in strict alphabetical order, giving a good impression of the diversity this species offers. Each garden that we visited gave us something unique to remember it by. For a complete list of these gardens, see "Photographic Locations."

The hundreds of photographs we took throughout Europe show clearly that the differences between many cultivars are often minor, especially in *Hydrangea macrophylla* and *H. serrata*. This does not mean we think those cultivars are identical; however, we do wonder if naming another pink-flowering mophead isn't pointless. Instead, hybrids and selections could be made in other species, and even in *H. macrophylla* many new and interesting, easily distinguishable cultivars have been introduced recently.

In gardens and collections with inaccurately labeled plants, we did not take photos, preferring to leave out doubtful identifications than perpetuate mistakes. We cannot rule out, however, that errors do occur. Sometimes written sources seem to contradict each other or even our experience with a particular plant. A good example is *Hydrangea serrata* 'Impératrice Eugénie': Haworth-Booth (1984) describes it as a mophead, but we have never seen it other than a lacecap. At our own nursery, Firma C. Esveld in Boskoop, we have collected and planted more than 350 different *Hydrangea* species and cultivars, and our collection is still growing. We continue to study certain taxa more

Hydrangea macrophylla, Trebah Garden.

Hydrangea macrophylla, Parc des Moutiers, courtesy Arborealis.

closely, as we try to get some clarity about the sometimes-confusing nomenclatural or taxonomical matters. And we would not be nurserymen if we did not propagate our plants to share with others.

Flower Color

Another major problem when making a pictorial book on hydrangeas is selecting the "right" flower color for the cultivars of *Hydrangea macrophylla*. What color is typical for a given cultivar? It is well known that many hortensias change their flower color very easily depending on soil conditions. For most cultivars the natural flower color is pink, even on slightly acidic soil. The key factor in flower color is not the acidity of the soil, but a plant's accessibility to aluminum sulfate. A hydrangea growing in an acid soil without aluminum sulfate will not bear blue flowers. Neither will a hydrangea turn blue if the soil it grows in has aluminum sulfate but is extremely basic or alkaline; the calcium of soils with a high pH will bind the aluminum sulfate so that it is not available to the plant.

A further consideration when photographing hydrangea flower color is the cultivar itself. Some cultivars easily turn blue under the right conditions, others do not. When cultivars of *Hydrangea macrophylla* are planted in neutral soil—one with no extremes forcing them to choose color, such as lots of or no available aluminum sulfate—the natural diversity of flower colors can be seen and admired. In such common circumstances, it becomes obvious that each hortensia has a preferred color. This natural color preference should be a guide to gardeners in selecting a certain flower color. For our book we have tried to locate and photograph plants growing in neutral soil, to give our readers an honest picture of the flower color most likely to occur on their plants. We took numerous photographs in collections like the one at the Research Station for Nursery Stock in Boskoop, where more than two hundred cultivars were planted in a slightly acid soil, with a natural pH of 4.2. We realize, however, that flower color is a tricky subject, and that one's personal experience with hortensias in the garden will always be the best guide for what to expect.

Having said all this, it is possible to grow a hortensia with blue flowers, even in non-acidic soil with a natural pH above 4.5, by adding aluminum sulfate to the soil. It is equally important to choose a cultivar that turns blue easily, such as 'Blaumeise', 'Bodensee', 'Enziandom', 'Frillibet', 'Générale Vicomtesse de Vibraye', 'Madame Faustin Travouillon', 'Nikko Blue', 'Otaksa', 'Queen Elizabeth', or 'Renate Steiniger'. Forget about sticking rusty nails in the ground! Although a soil with iron is good, one with available aluminum sulfate is far more important. Do not use water containing calcium, but always rainwater. Do not put manure around hydrangeas between July and March; however, shortly after winter ends, it is ok to give hydrangeas old cow manure and some peat. When a hortensia produces blue flowers spontaneously, you can be sure that the soil is really acid.

If you want to add some aluminum sulfate to your soil, do so in September. Aluminum sulfate can easily be purchased at a drugstore and is simple to distribute. The quantity of aluminum sulfate required depends on the size of the plant and is usually 15–50 grams (0.5–1.7 ounces) per plant. The safest way to give the powder is to dissolve it in water, but try not to touch the foliage when applying the mixture. When a hortensia does not stay blue in spite of your efforts, the only remedy is to dig holes around the plant, remove the soil, and then replace it with soil whose pH is below 4.5.

In most gardens it is far easier to settle for a hortensia border with primarily pink flowers, although the inhabitants of Madeira (off Portugal) will disagree with us: we did not see a single pink-flowered cultivar of *Hydrangea macrophylla* on this volcanic island. Haworth-Booth (1984) writes that hortensias are naturally blue in their native habitat on acid soils. This may be true in Japan. In Europe, Mrs. Bertrand, a French researcher, has studied *H. macrophylla* for more than twenty years. She also confirms that a soil with a low pH of 4.5 is insufficient by itself to guarantee blue flowers; aluminum sulfate remains an essential element.

As a rule, red cultivars remain red or purple-red, never turning true blue. Most mopheads produce pink flowers in neutral soil, and several will only very reluctantly turn blue, even if fed with aluminum sulfate. It also is possible for a plant to display flowers of more than one color at a time or for the color of the flowers to change as the season progresses.

Efforts have been made to record flower colors using the RHS Color Chart. We doubt whether this is really useful, given how unstable hydrangea flower colors are.

White-flowering cultivars usually retain their color, but the white sepals become speckled with tiny pink or red dots, especially later in the flowering season. This should be regarded as fall color, a phenomenon that almost every hydrangea shows to some extent. The white-flowered cultivars of *Hydrangea paniculata* or *H. serrata* can change dramatically to lovely shades of pink or red in the fall. Unlike color changes that occur during the flower period, those that occur in fall are not particularly influenced by the soil conditions. A site in shade slows down fall coloring, especially in cultivars of *H. serrata*.

Hydrangea macrophylla (Hortensia Group) 'Générale Vicomtesse de Vibraye', Stourton House Flower Garden. Despite its "blue" reputation, this cultivar is pink in alkaline soils.

Hydrangea macrophylla (Hortensia Group) 'Générale Vicomtesse de Vibraye', Rein and Mark Bulk nursery. This cultivar easily turns light blue in acidic soil.

Moisture and Hardiness

In dry conditions, most hydrangeas need to be watered. Only *Hydrangea arborescens* seems untouched by drought. Although most hydrangeas begin to wilt immediately when the temperature is too warm for them or when they lack sufficient water, they almost always recover just as fast when the temperature drops or sufficient water is given. Structural damage to plants is very rare. In a warm spring many hydrangeas can develop new growth too early, so that late spring frosts injure the young growth. Again, the plants usually recover surprisingly well, although they will produce flowers less freely.

Severe winters can damage plants, but much damage can be avoided by protecting plants with straw and other comparable materials. Some species from Asia and Central America prove to be tender in many parts of the temperate zone and need more extensive protection in winter. Evergreen climbers and shrubs especially need extra care, but they can be a very welcome addition to the existing palette of evergreens, so that this care will generously be given by the proud owners of such a plant. Polyethylene sheets usually do not offer hydrangeas much protection and often increase damage to the plants. It is better to use natural materials for protection.

Although most *Hydrangea* species and cultivars are reasonably hardy, all plants need help in adapting to the local conditions. It makes a great difference whether your garden is located in southern England or in Bavaria. Knowledge of local conditions is best obtained through personal experience in a garden, sometimes by trial and error. Knowing the natural habitat of a given species is also a great source of information about the chances a plant has in your garden.

In general, hydrangeas can be grown successfully in U.S. Department of Agriculture Hardiness Zone 6, where the average minimum temperature in winter ranges from -23° to -18° Celsius (-10° to 0° Fahrenheit). The evergreen species are far more tender, as is *Hydrangea scandens* and its subspecies. It is a challenge for gardeners to find out what plants are successful in their gardens.

Pruning

Whenever we lecture on hydrangeas, we meet enthusiastic groups of people who recognize the enormous value these plants have for every garden as summer-flowering shrubs with great diversity of flower color, shapes, and habit for temperate climate. Most of the questions asked during these lectures focus on pruning and flower color. It would be easy to say that hydrangeas don't need to be pruned. After all, they survive in nature without pruning. For most gardeners, however, pruning hydrangeas seems to be a very compelling concept, even though only a few species respond well to this treatment.

Hydrangea macrophylla is one of the species that does not respond as well to pruning as is generally believed. It produces flowerbuds on second-year stems, so when the plant is pruned on a yearly basis, it rarely bears flowers. If you feel that pruning your plant is absolutely necessary, because of the size or shape of the plant, be prepared to loose the majority of flowers in the subsequent season. It is better to prune only a few branches almost to the base. Doing this once a year will rejuvenate the plant without being too radical and may result in slightly larger flowers. Nonetheless, the best shows of flowers we have seen on plants of *H. macrophylla* were in gardens where the secateurs remained in the workshed.

An exception in the genus should be made for *Hydrangea paniculata*, a species that responds remarkably well to annual pruning, by producing much larger flowerheads on vigorous-growing stems. The method of pruning is similar to that used on a rose bush: cut the stems back to two or three buds just after winter has ended. Although *H. paniculata* responds well to pruning, it does not require it. When left unpruned, plants of this species form impressive shrubs with lovely displays of hundreds of flowers. Individually the flowers of unpruned bushes may be a bit smaller than their counterparts on pruned specimens, but they compensate by their numbers.

Old flowers can be cut off, a practice known in horticulture as dead-heading, or they can be left on the plant. Again, in nature no one removes the old flowers, so it does not harm the plants to leave them on. Some people even suggest that leaving old flowers on the plant diminishes the risk of frost damage to flowerbuds for next year's flowers, but we did not see any significant differences between treated and untreated plants. Perhaps in other climates one might be able to tell the difference. As usual, your own garden experience is the best guideline.

Pests and Diseases

Hydrangeas are seldom bothered by pests and diseases, at least none specific to them. Like all plants, hydrangeas are susceptible to common insects such as aphids, capsid bugs, scale insects, thrips, vine weevils, and whitefly. While these insect pests may attack the plants, they do not consider hydrangeas a favorite plant. Well-established plants usually shrug off these insects and are unharmed.

Only honey fungus (*Armillaria mellea*) can attack hydrangeas, on rotting wood, and then it poses a real threat, as it is difficult to get rid of. Carefully digging out the damaged plant and destroying it is usually the best way.

Sometimes mildew can damage hydrangea foliage. Although mildew can spoil the plant's appearance, it never kills the plant. Removing fallen leaves in autumn is a good means to control this illness, but you should also regard the presence of mildew as an indicator that your plant is not as vital and happy as it should be. The plant may have been transplanted recently, over- or under-fertilized, or it may be reacting to exposure to heat or drought. No matter what agent is behind your plant's susceptibility to mildew, find and correct it.

In this book we do not recommend particular chemicals for two reasons. First, there are no lethal hydrangea diseases that could easily be cured by the use of chemicals. Second, the regulations for the use of pesticides and insecticides are becoming increasingly strict in many countries for environmental reasons and thus it is important for gardeners to learn what is or is not acceptable in their region.

Propagation

Almost all hydrangeas are easy to propagate by softwood cuttings. A greenhouse is not needed for most cuttings of *Hydrangea macrophylla* and *H. serrata,* although putting the cuttings under glass speeds up the rooting process. Softwood cuttings are usually taken in midsummer, July to August, but the best time can vary with local circumstances. It is important that the shoots have stopped growing and started to ripen off a little, but they should not have turned brown and woody yet.

In general, hydrangeas are easy to root, and cuttings with two pairs of buds give the best results. The pair at the bottom of the cutting is inserted in the rooting medium, while the higher pair with two leaves is left exposed. If the leaves are large, they should be pruned to half the blade. This practice helps to decrease the respiration of the cuttings.

Single cuttings are usually inserted in 7-cm (ca. 3-inch) pots or in trays with prefabricated little pots. Well-rooted cuttings can be potted in 3-liter (ca. 0.5 gallon) pots in March, and these usually grow into plants with two to three branches and few flowers. For a good display of flowers, the cuttings need to grow another year. Weak cuttings are potted in 9-cm (ca. 4-inch) pots and left in the frame or greenhouse. It is possible to start cuttings in the open field instead of pots, again depending on the climate. In the middle of the 20th century almost all hydrangeas for garden use were grown in the open field. It was only toward the end of the century that pot-grown plants took over.

Professional growers of potted hydrangeas use a more complicated method, pruning the plants mechanically or chemically in various stages of their development, cooling them in slightly refrigerated warehouses to make sure that the plants will develop at least three to five flowers and remain reasonably compact. These treatments are necessary to ensure a crop that flowers reliably on a predictable date in a predictable fashion, but they are not necessary to ensure good and healthy plants. On the contrary, plants treated in this manner, especially those grown indoors, have a more difficult time becoming established in the garden than those grown in the old-fashioned way outdoors. Yet, the retail market demands a visually attractive product that can easily lure consumers into buying a hortensia, so growers choose to grow plants indoors even though the average gardener is better served by an outdoor-grown nonflowering plant.

Growing potted hydrangeas by the newer, more complicated method limits the number of cultivars that can be grown. Few plants respond well to such treatment, especially among cultivars of *Hydrangea macrophylla*. Many cultivars do not reliably produce enough flowers when young, so commercial growers ignore the beautiful ones among them to satisfy their customers' needs for flowering plants.

In addition to softwood cuttings, gardeners use other methods to propagate hydrangeas. Layering gives plants of good quality, but only in very limited quantities. Some hydrangea cultivars root from hardwood cuttings, taken in December or January and grown in a greenhouse. Unfortunately, this method produces unreliable results, so few professional growers use it. Finally, it is possible to grow plants from seed. These seedlings are very variable and not suitable for commercial purpose, except maybe in the case of wild-collected seeds from rare species. Seedlings, especially from seed of garden origin, can produce novelties, but careful selection and trials are essential, as there are so many beautiful named cultivars already.

Hydrangeas in the Garden

The enormous diversity of *Hydrangea* species, from small multistemmed trees *(H. heteromalla)* to evergreen climbers *(H. seemannii)* to small shrubs flowering in midsummer *(H. serrata)* and others with brilliant fall color and beautifully shaped leaves *(H. quercifolia)*, results in many opportunities for using hydrangeas in the garden. Anyone who has seen a mixed border with a rich display of different *H. macrophylla* cultivars in full bloom wonders why all gardeners don't aim to establish these plants in their gardens. Hydrangeas are relatively easy to grow, free of pests and diseases, and not very particular about type of soil. Their only requirement is enough water.

The history of hydrangeas in European and later American gardening is a true success story, thanks to the plants' remarkable quality of an extremely long flowering period from midsummer until early winter. Furthermore, the flowers constantly change color, from the bright and uplifting summer tones to the more diffused shades of fall. Some species, in particular *Hydrangea quercifolia*, even smell sweet when they are in flower. The flowers of a climbing hydrangea, especially on a north-facing wall, are irresistible and improved only by planting them near a close relative, *Schizophragma hydrangeoides*. The way *H. aspera* in a walled city garden always seems to create an air of naturalness is unsurpassed by many other plants.

When Japanese hydrangeas were first introduced in Netherlands, they became popular so quickly that most people are surprised to learn the plants are not native. Hydrangeas are successful garden plants also in China and Japan. The Chinese common name for a mophead hortensia is *xiuqiu*, meaning "embroidered globe" and indicating one use of the plant in a garden. Before Europeans arrived in Asia, the Japanese produced crosses with Chinese cultivars. Looking at the hybrids developed by Japanese, European, and American breeders, it is obvious that Japanese taste for hydrangeas differs from European or American tastes. Where European breeders, especially in the earlier ages of selecting and hybridizing, tried to develop cultivars from *Hydrangea macrophylla* with even bigger and brighter colored inflorescences, the Japanese developed or selected many cultivars from *H. serrata* with much smaller flowers and far more subdued colors.

Today we are fortunate to be able to enjoy the fruits of these earlier labors and to grow hydrangeas suitable for every taste and almost every application in the garden. Many of the original Chinese cultivars have not made the voyage through history to our gardens, so it is uncertain what hidden treasures may yet come out of that country.

Dried Flowers

The flowers of several cultivars are suitable for drying and use in winter decorations. Elizabeth Bullivant, keeper of a fine collection of hydrangeas at Stourton House Flower Garden in England, has found in her experience with numerous cultivars of *Hydrangea macrophylla* and other species that their suitability for drying is diverse. The best time for cutting the flowers for drying can be heard as well as seen. You look at the flower color, and you listen to the flower when you gently squeeze it. If the flower has turned brown, you are too late, and if you do not hear a rustling sound when you squeeze it, you are too early. Make sure that you are not observed by other people when you press your ear to the flower and squeeze it, for people will make fun of you. It is important to remove all the foliage as it will disturb the drying process.

Some hydrangeas suitable for drying are mentioned here. The list is by no means complete. Cultivars of *Hydrangea macrophylla* suitable for drying include 'Altona', 'Deutschland', 'Europa', 'Enziandom', 'Générale Vicomtesse de Vibraye', 'Hamburg', 'Lanarth White', 'Madame Emile Mouillère', 'Maréchal Foch', 'Mariesii Lilacina', 'Mariesii Perfecta', 'Renate Steiniger', 'Soeur Thérèse', and 'Veitchii'. From other species we recommend *H. serrata* 'Grayswood' and 'Preziosa' and *H. paniculata* 'Grandiflora' and 'Unique'. We did not obtain good results when we dried flowers of *H. arborescens* 'Annabelle', perhaps because we did something wrong, like not listening carefully to the flowers. The lovely light green autumn color of the flowers seems inviting enough to keep trying. The best cultivar of *H. villosa* is the bright colored 'Anthony Bullivant', but choosing the right moment is important for any cultivar of this species.

Leaves as Tea or Medicine

The foliage of some hydrangeas can be dried and used to make tea. Most hydrangeas, however, should not be used for this purpose as their leaves contain hydrangin, a toxin related to cyanide. The "safe" hydrangeas belong to the *Hydrangea serrata* Amacha Group. The names of all the cultivars in this group include the word *amacha*, literally meaning "sweet tea." Although the leaves of this group of hydrangeas have long been used as a natural sweetener, no mass cultures of these plants are known. One member of this group, *H. serrata* 'Yae no amacha', meaning "double sweetened tea," has an interesting double flowerhead. This most peculiar form is worth trying as a garden plant as well as a tea plant.

In Japan *Hydrangea paniculata* is used in the production of a high-quality paper. A gluelike substance, called *nori* in Japan, is derived from the fiber and used to reinforce the very thin sheets of paper.

Native Americans of the Cherokee tribe used *Hydrangea arborescens* to treat a variety of ailments. They regarded the plant, especially its roots and bark, as a very effective medicine for diverse maladies, from kidney stones to burns.

Taxonomy

Taxonomy is the study of relationships between naturally occurring groups of plants. Each such group of plants is known as a taxon (plural taxa). The hierarchy of taxa in the genus *Hydrangea* is stated in the synopsis that follows this section.

The genus *Hydrangea* was established when Swedish botanist Carl Linnaeus published *Species Plantarum* in 1753. The name is derived from the Greek word *hydro* (water) and *angeion* (vase or vessel). Dutch botanist Johann F. Gronovius used this name for the first time in 1739 in his *Flora Virginica*. Linnaeus adapted the name for the same plant, *Hydrangea arborescens*, later followed by *H. radiata* and *H. quercifolia*.

Hydrangea arborescens, the first species of the genus to come into cultivation in Europe, was introduced from Pennsylvania in 1736, collected by John Bartram, the first American botanist. Bartram and his son William later discovered *H. quercifolia* in Georgia. Many of the plants John Bartram discovered on his field trips were sent to London merchant Peter Collinson, who introduced many plants from the New World to Europe.

The Chinese species were introduced to Europe much later, and as we will see later, they were confused with Japanese species, the plants collected being of garden origin. Hydrangeas were cultivated in both Asian countries long before they were known in Europe. Native to China, *Hydrangea anomala*, *H. aspera*, and *H. heteromalla* were discovered in the eastern Himalayas by Francis Buchanan-Hamilton and Nathaniel Wallich in the first half of the 19th century and described by David Don in *Prodomus Florae Nepalensis* in 1825.

The first species from South America were classified as a separate genus, *Cornidia*, and later included as a section in *Hydrangea*.

The history of the introduction of the Japanese species to the West is mainly a Dutch story. Japan closed its borders to all foreigners in 1639, after banning Catholic missionary priests earlier in 1587. The only exceptions were for two trading posts. For these the Japanese chose the Dutch and the Chinese because neither of them had sent missionaries to Japan earlier. The history of the relationship between the V.O.C. (United East Indies Company) and Japan is fully described in several publications.

The V.O.C. sent to Japan a succession of physicians who, because they were skilled in botany, studied the Japanese flora. The first of these, Engelbert Kaempfer, discovered and described Asian hydrangeas for the first time in the West, although he included them in the genus *Sambucus*.

Nearly a hundred years later Swedish botanist Carl Peter Thunberg, who lived for a short time on Deshima, the Dutch trading post on an artificial island just offshore from Nagasaki, described the first mophead hydrangeas. On the pretext of collecting fodder for the goat he kept, Thunberg was allowed to send his servants to collect greenery and hay on the mainland. There they found two hydrangeas which Thunberg did not recognize as garden plants in spite of their sterile inflorescences. Unfortunately, he described the two in his book *Flora Japonica* (1784) as *Viburnum macrophyllum* and *V. serratum*. Although Thunberg made the same mistake in other genera (for example, *Rhododendron*, *Kerria*, *Prunus*), he can easily be forgiven when we realize the difficult circumstances under which he made his early plant collections and the little information he had.

Another doctor, Philipp Franz von Siebold, who was in Japan between 1823 and 1829 and later again from 1859 until 1862, also sent plants to Europe, including garden plants that were described as species. Many of the plants he

Hydrangea macrophylla, Boering Garden.

collected in Japan were further propagated around 1859 in his nursery in the village of Leiderdorp, near Leiden, Netherlands. From this nursery the plants were distributed to many botanical gardens, nurseries, and private collections. Among his introductions is *Hydrangea macrophylla*, the first plant coming from Japan named "otaksa," after Siebold's Japanese wife Sonogi Kusumoti, also called Otaki. This is the plant Thunberg described earlier as *Viburnum macrophyllum*.

Another "otaksa" came from China under the auspices of Joseph Banks, named as *Hydrangea hortensis* Smith. The Chinese plant is fairly loose and slender, whereas the Japanese plant is smaller. The Chinese plant is a strong-growing shrub, with coarse, shining green leaves and enormous greenish yellow flowerheads that turn to pale pink. Botanists did not immediately recognize in the early days of the introduction of *H. macrophylla* that plants originating in Japan could also be found in China thanks to the long history of gardening in both countries and the trade relations between them. In other cases plants native to China were attributed to Japan by Siebold when he found them in Japanese gardens.

Today the Japanese otaksa is called *Hydrangea macrophylla* 'Otaksa' and the Chinese otaksa is properly named *H. macrophylla* 'Joseph Banks'. Both plants come from coastal regions of Japan and were referred to by Haworth-Booth (1984) as *H. maritima*, a name rejected by McClintock and subsequently sunk in synonymy.

This kind of confusion made the initial classification of hydrangeas uncertain, and the taxonomy of the genus was not established until the beginning of the 20th century, culminating with the publication of *Monograph of the Genus Hydrangea* by Elizabeth McClintock in 1957. In our book we follow McClintock's taxonomy with two exceptions: we use *H. serrata* instead of *H. macrophylla* subsp. *serrata*. We feel that the *H. scandens* complex as well as the *H. heteromalla* complex are so diverse that further study of these species is necessary.

Most cultivars belong to *Hydrangea macrophylla* and *H. serrata*. These two species, with *H. paniculata*, are horticulturally the most important in this genus. DNA research proved that H. villosa deserves its earlier status as a species (see appendix 1).

Synopsis of the Genus Hydrangea

Genus *Hydrangea* Linnaeus 1753
  Section 1 *Hydrangea* Linnaeus 1753
    Subsection 1 *Hydrangea* (Americanae)
      Species *H. arborescens* Linnaeus subsp. *arborescens* 1753; type of the genus
      H. arborescens subsp. *discolor* Seringe 1956
      H. arborescens subsp. *radiata* (Walter) McClintock 1956
      H. quercifolia Bartram 1791
    Subsection 2 *Asperae*
      Species *H. sikokiana* Maximowicz 1887
      H. involucrata Siebold & Zuccarini 1839
      H. aspera D. Don subsp. *aspera* 1825
      H. aspera subsp. *strigosa* (Rehder) McClintock 1956
      H. aspera subsp. *robusta* (Hooker f. & Thomson) McClintock 1956
      H. aspera subsp. *sargentiana* (Rehder) McClintock 1956
      H. villosa Rehder 1911
    Subsection 3 *Calyptranthae*
      Species *H. anomala* D. Don subsp. *anomala* 1825
      H. anomala subsp. *petiolaris* (Siebold & Zuccarini) McClintock 1956
    Subsection 4 *Petalanthae*
      Species *H. hirta* (Thunberg) Siebold 1828
      H. scandens Seringe subsp. *scandens* 1830
      H. scandens subsp. *chinensis* (Maximowicz) McClintock 1956
      H. scandens subsp. *liukiuensis* (Nakai) McClintock 1956
      H. scandens subsp. *kwangtungensis* (Merrill) McClintock 1956
    Subsection 5 *Heteromallae*
      Species *H. paniculata* Siebold 1829
      H. heteromalla D. Don 1825
    Subsection 6 *Macrophyllae*
      Species *H. macrophylla* (Thunberg) Seringe subsp. *macrophylla* 1830
      H. macrophylla subsp. *stylosa* (Hooker f. & Thomson) McClintock 1956
      H. macrophylla subsp. *chungii* (Rehder) McClintock 1956
      H. serrata (Thunberg) Seringe

  Section 2 *Cornidia*
    Subsection 1 *Monosegia*
      Species *H. seemannii* Riley 1924
      H. asterolasia Diels 1941
      H. integrifolia Hayata 1906
      H. oerstedtii Briquet 1919
      H. peruviana Moricand 1830
      H. diplostemona (Donnell Smith) Standley 1921
      H. preslii Briquet 1919
      H. steyermarkii Standley 1940
    Subsection 2 *Polystegia*
      Species *H. serratifolia* (Hooker & Arnott) Philippi 1881
      H. tarapotensis Briquet 1919
      H. jelskii Szyszylowicz 1895
      H. matthewsii Briquet 1919

Although McClintock divides the genus *Hydrangea* into 23 species and 7 subspecies, altogether 30 taxa, in this book we discuss more than 100 species names which have been used by various authorities. As mentioned previously, we have adopted McClintock's taxonomy with two exceptions. First, we consider *H. serrata* a valid species, as do almost all modern-day authors. This view is based on the DNA research of Ben J. M. Zonneveld (see appendix 1). Second, another species has been restored, *H. villosa*. Here too the research of Zonneveld shows clearly that there is a constant difference between *H. villosa* and *H. aspera*. A few formas have been restored instead of sinking the species in synonymy. These are formas from *H. scandens* subsp. *chinensis* and are fully discussed at the appropriate place in the text.

The genus *Hydrangea* belongs to the family Hydrangeaceae. Other genera in that family are *Carpenteria*, *Decumaria*, *Dichroa*, *Fendlera*, *Jamesia*, *Kirengeshoma*, *Pileostegia*, *Platycrater*, and *Schizophragma*, among others. Most of these are monotypic. Other genera such as *Deutzia* and *Philadelphus* are sometimes alternatively classified in the family Philadelphaceae, but that family is not mentioned in Cronquist's (1988) classification.

Another issue is the matter of the family to which genus *Hydrangea* belongs. In all older studies, and in McClintock's monograph of 1957, the family name is Saxifragaceae. Other and often newer publications, such as Krüssmann (1976–1978), Bean (1991), and the *RHS Encyclopaedia of Gardening*, use the newer name Hydrangeaceae. Haworth-Booth (1984) in his book on hydrangea does not even mention the family, and Lawson-Hall and Rothera (1995) use Saxifragaceae. This illustrates that some authors seem not to have been aware of the classification of Magnoliophyta published in 1988 by Cronquist.

Following Cronquist's authoritative classification, the genus *Hydrangea* is classified as follows. Note that it no longer belongs to Family 18, Saxifragaceae, but to Family 9, Hydrangeaceae.

Division Embryophyta (Seed plants)
    Subdivision Magnoliophyta (Flowering plants)
        Class Magnoliopsida (Dicotyledons)
            Subclass 5 Rosidae
                Order 1 Rosales
                    Family 9 Hydrangeaceae
                        Genus *Hydrangea*
                            Species *Hydrangea arborescens*
                                Subspecies *Hydrangea arborescens* subsp. *radiata*
                                    Variety *Hydrangea macrophylla* subsp. *macrophylla* var. *normalis*
                                        Forma *Hydrangea scandens* subsp. *chinensis* f. *obovatifolia*

Nomenclature

Plant populations often show variability. Where to draw the line between one taxon and the next is part of the science of taxonomy and, as different methods are used, different classifications may emerge over time. Assigning the correct names to the taxa recognized is also part of taxonomy. Rules governing the choice of the correct name for natural taxa are provided by the International Code of Botanical Nomenclature (ICBN). Genus and species names, for example, must be written in italics.

The naming of cultivated plants is governed by the International Code of Nomenclature for Cultivated Plants (ICNCP). The most important rule for cultivars names since 1959 is that they must be written in a modern language, begin with an initial capital letter, and be set off by single quotation marks. Examples are *Hydrangea arborescens* 'Annabelle' or *H. aspera* 'Pink Cloud'. These conventions prevent confusing cultivar names with names of natural taxa. Many older cultivars, however, have Latinized names. The ICNCP requires that such names be written as cultivar names. Two examples are *H. paniculata* 'Grandiflora' and *H. heteromalla* 'Xanthoneura'.

Trademarks are not cultivar names nor are they a part of a cultivar name. They should be written in uppercase letters, without quotation marks. An example is *Hydrangea arborescens* WHITE DOME, the trademarked name for the cultivar *H. arborescens* 'Dardom'. A list of plants protected by trademarked names follows:

CITY-LINE: Introduced by Rampp Jungpflanzen, Pfaffenhausen, Germany. Includes 'Amsterdam', 'Athen', 'Berlin', 'Côte d'Azur', 'Hamburg', 'Heidelberg', 'Helsinki', 'Nizza', 'Odense', 'Oslo', 'Paris', 'Prag', 'San Remo', 'Venedig', 'Wien', and 'Zürich'.

DUTCH LADIES: Introduced by D. van der Spek of Sidaco nursery, Nootdorp, Netherlands. Includes 'Sandra', 'Selina', 'Selma', 'Sheila', 'Sonja', 'Soraya', and 'Stella'.

HOVARIA: Introduced by K. and W. Hofstede of Wilko Hofstede BV, Huissen, Netherlands. Includes 'Hobella', 'Hobergine', 'Holibel', 'Homigo', 'Hopaline', 'Love You Kiss', 'Mirai', and a selection of *H. quercifolia*.

LADY (series): Produced by Japanese nurseryman Hiroshi Ebihara and trademarked by Mr. van Rijswijk, Vianen, Netherlands. Includes 'Frau Fujiyo', 'Frau Katsuko', 'Frau Mariko', 'Frau Nobuko', and 'Frau Taiko', among others. Although the names with "lady" in them are trademarked, German versions of the name which include the word "frau" can be used by anyone.

RIVER-LINE: Introduced by Rampp Jungpflanzen, Pfaffenhausen, Germany. Includes 'Amazonas', 'Berliner Spree', 'Colorado', and 'Rio Grande'.

STAR-LINE: Introduced by Rampp Jungpflanzen, Pfaffenhausen, Germany. Includes: 'Blue Earth', 'Mars', and 'Orion'.

Cultivar names should not be translated from one modern language to another and used in place of the original plant name. 'Buntspecht', for example, means "woodpecker" and is one of many German bird names assigned to cultivars introduced by the Federal Research Institute for Horticulture (Eidgenössische Forschungsanstalt) in Wädenswil, Switzerland. While English speakers may refer to this hydrangea as 'Woodpecker', such usage is incorrect. A translation can be used with the original cultivar name but not as a substitute for it.

Only names written or published in a different alphabet, such as Cyrillic, Greek, Chinese, or Japanese, should be transliterated (but not translated) in the Roman alphabet. A telling example is *Hydrangea macrophylla* 'Hanabi', a cultivar of Japanese origin, which is often found in the trade as 'Firework', 'Vuurwerk', or 'Feuerwerk', all of them translations of the Japanese name where a transliteration would have been correct. Again, it is acceptable to add a transla-

Hydrangea macrophylla, Holehird Gardens.

tion after a registered cultivar name in a foreign language, as in this example: *H. macrophylla* 'Hanabi' ("firework"), but not as a substitute for it. The German word *teller,* meaning "saucer," is often combined with a color and used as a cultivar name (for example, 'Red Teller', 'Blue Teller'). This practice should be discontinued immediately.

According to the most recent rules of the ICNCP, groups of similar cultivars can be established. What this means for hydrangeas is that lacecaps can be designated, by adding (L) after the cultivar name, for Lacecap Group, and mopheads can be designated by adding (H), for Hortensia Group.

About the Book

The plant descriptions are arranged in alphabetical order by scientific name and then, when given, cultivar name. The many cultivars of *Hydrangea macrophylla* are divided into two groups on the basis of the shape of the flower head. The first group, called *Hydrangea macrophylla* Hortensia Group, includes plants with globose-headed flowers, known also as mopheads, while the second group, *Hydrangea* Lacecap Group, lists cultivars with flat or slightly domed flowerheads.

Valid plant names are written in **boldface.** The lists are complete until the end of 2002. Few new cultivars have been introduced in recent times, but several old cultivars have been re-introduced to horticulture.

Several sources were most helpful in compiling the lists of cultivar names. Mrs. H. Bertrand compiled a preliminary checklist of hydrangea names, hereafter referred to as "Checklist." Her list did not include descriptions, but was edited by the National Institute of Horticulture in Angers, France. The invaluable work of Haworth-Booth (1984) made it possible to include the names of many old and mostly forgotten cultivars, which most likely are now lost to cultivation. Nevertheless, we include those names here so they are registered and not used again for newer forms. A third source, the *Repertoire de l'Association Shamrock,* hereafter referred to as "Shamrock list," was very useful too.

For the cultivars, we attempted to track down the names of the breeders, the year of origin, and the country of origin, but we were not always successful. Unfortunately, the existing literature is full of gaps and far from complete. Furthermore, most breeders were not scientists and did not document their newly introduced and named plants.

All references to the original sources of the plant names have been recorded by the authors. Readers wanting to know the sources of these data are invited to ask for information.

Photographic Locations

Agapanthe Jardin, Crigneuseville, France
Arboretum Kalmthout, Kalmthout, Belgium
Jardin Bellevue, Beaumont-le-Hareng, France
Mr. Boering (garden), Groningen, Netherlands
Branklyn Garden, Perth, Scotland, United Kingdom
Rein and Mark Bulk nursery, Boskoop, Netherlands
Crûg Farm Nursery, Caernafon, Gwynedd, Wales, United Kingdom
Darthuizer Nurseries, Leersum, Netherlands
Arboretum de Dreijen, Agricultural University of Wageningen, Netherlands
C. Esveld Nurseries, Boskoop, Netherlands
Floriade 2002 (international horticultural exhibition), Netherlands
Maurice Foster garden, Sevenoaks, Kent, England, United Kingdom
Hemelrijk Tuinen, Essen, Belgium
Sir Harold Hillier Gardens and Arboretum, Ampfield, England, United Kingdom
Holehird Gardens, Windermere, England, United Kingdom
Hydrangeum (association), Destelbergen, Belgium
Jardin de Valloire, Argoules, Frances
Jardin du Mesnil, Monterolier, France
G. A. van Klaveren garden, Hazerswoude, Netherlands

Kruidtuin, Leuven, Belgium
National Arboretum, Meise, Belgium
H. J. van Paddenburgh garden, Amersfoort, Netherlands
Plantarium (international horticultural trade show), Netherlands
Planten Tuin de Oirsprong, Oirschot, Netherlands
Research Station for Nursery Stock, Boskoop, Netherlands
Rokko Alpine Botanical Garden, Kobe, Japan
W. A. M. Rutten, Leende, Netherlands (Dutch National Collection of Hydrangeas)
Spinners Garden, Lymington, England, United Kingdom
Stourton House Flower Garden (Elizabeth Bullivant), Wiltshire, England, United Kingdom
Le Thuit Saint-Jean (garden), Saint-Jean-du-Cardonnay, France
Trebah Garden, Mawnan Smith, near Falmouth, England, United Kingdom
Trelissick Garden, Feock, near Truro, England, United Kingdom
Jardin de Valérianes, Ennecuit, Bosc-Roger-sur-Buchy, France
Von Gimborn Arboretum, Doorn, Netherlands
Le Vastérival, Jardin Botanique de France, Varengeville-sur-Mer, France
Royal Botanic Garden, Edinburgh, Scotland, United Kingdom
Royal Horticultural Society Wisley Garden, Woking, England, United Kingdom

Hydrangea macrophylla, Trebah Garden.

Hydrangea macrophylla, Trebah Garden.

Hydrangea

DESCRIPTIONS

Hydrangea anomala, Crûg Farm Nursery.

Hydrangea anomala subsp. *glabra*, C. Esveld Nurseries.

Hydrangea anomala, courtesy Klaas Verboom.

Hydrangea anomala subsp. *petiolaris*, C. Esveld Nurseries.

H. anomala D. Don subsp. *anomala* 1825

A climbing plant resembling *H. anomala* subsp. *petiolaris*, but less vigorous-growing and less hardy. The flowerheads have a few white ray-flowers with four sepals; the fertile flowers are yellow. The plant is endemic in western China, where it was found by George Forrest. It also inhabits Assam, Sikkim, and Nepal. Wilson sent plants to Great Britain with larger flowerheads. Material from Sikkim has evergreen leaves. Wynn-Jones collected seeds in Sikkim. The leaves of these plants are thin-textured and turn purple over the winter. This plant is rarely available. It needs a well-sheltered place.

H. anomala subsp. *glabra*

An isolated colony, maybe an undescribed subspecies, whose taxonomic status is more than doubtful. The name was published without designation of a type. A climbing plant, developing aerial roots, it was collected by Wynn-Jones in Taiwan in 1996. Leaves evergreen, oval. Flowers in lacy terminal panicles, 14 cm (5.5 inches) wide, white or pinkish. Plant reaches 20 m (66 feet) high in its habitat.

H. anomala subsp. *petiolaris* (Siebold & Zuccarini) McClintock 1956

Common name: Climbing hydrangea. This shrub is a well-known climber. The branches form aerial roots and can cover walls and fences. The egg-shaped leaves have serrate margins and are variable in size; they have tufts of white down on the veins. The flowerheads are irregular, white, with up to 10 ray-flowers with four sepals, on long stalks. Flowering time is from June to August. A variegated form of this subspecies has been found in Japan by Y. Hirose. Synonym: *H. scandens* Maximowicz 1867, not *H. scandens* Seringe 1830. Japanese name: 'Tsuru ajisai'. This popular climber does well on a north-facing wall. RHS Award: AGM 1992.

Hydrangea anomala subsp. *petiolaris*, Trelissick Garden.

Hydrangea anomala subsp. *petiolaris* 'Brookside Littleleaf', Rein and Mark Bulk nursery.

Hydrangea anomala subsp. *petiolaris* 'Firefly', courtesy Wout Kromhout.

H. anomala subsp. *petiolaris* 'Brookside Littleleaf'

This slow-growing climber is a miniature form of the subspecies, most probably identical to 'Cordifolia'. A very useful little climber for small walls.

H. anomala subsp. *petiolaris* 'Cordifolia'

A climbing plant with small, rounded leaves, closely related to *H. anomala* subsp. *petiolaris* but with more regular rayflowers. It forms aerial roots on the branches. Siebold described this plant (Haworth-Booth 1984). Despite its "wild" background it is considered to be a cultivar and possibly even identical to 'Brookside Littleleaf'. In the United States it is a really miniature form in cultivation under the name *H. cordifolia* f. *minor*. The name is doubtful. Sometimes misspelled "Conchifolia.

H. anomala subsp. *petiolaris* 'Firefly'

A climbing plant much like the subspecies. The leaves have pale yellow margins. Variegated forms are rare in hydrangea, so this plant might attract the attention of collectors. Note that the name 'Firefly' is also attached to a cultivar of *H. serrata*. Raised and introduced by Spring Meadow Nursery, Grand Haven, Michigan, United States.

Hydrangea anomala subsp. *petiolaris* f. *yakusimana*, Crûg Farm Nursery.

Hydrangea anomala subsp. *petiolaris* 'Tiliifolia', Le Vastérival.

Hydrangea arborescens subsp. *arborescens*, Rein and Mark Bulk nursery.

Hydrangea anomala subsp. *petiolaris* 'Tiliifolia', Trelissick Garden.

H. anomala subsp. *petiolaris* 'Tiliifolia'

This small-leaved climber can easily be confused with *H. anomala* subsp. *petiolaris*. The differences are minor, and according to McClintock it is synonymous, under the name *H. tilaefolium* Léveillé.

H. anomala subsp. *petiolaris* f. *yakusimana*

Wynn-Jones collected this form on Yakushima Island, Japan. The plants are more compact than those of the sub-species, almost creeping. Leaves heavily serrate. It is better to give this plant a cultivar name, 'Yakushima', in spite of the plants being a population. According to McClintock, this taxon might be *H. scandens* subsp. *chinensis* f. *grossiser-rata* Engler 1918, which also has its habitat on Yakushima. We feel she has been misled by the confusion of *H. scandens* Maximowicz as this plant belongs to *H. anomala* and cannot be mistaken for *H. scandens*. The name was published without designation of a type.

Hydrangea arborescens 'Annabelle', Sir Harold Hillier Gardens and Arboretum.

Hydrangea arborescens subsp. *arborescens*, C. Esveld Nurseries.

Hydrangea arborescens 'Annabelle', C. Esveld Nurseries.

H. arborescens Linnaeus subsp. *arborescens* 1753

Common names: Smooth hydrangea, snowhill hydrangea. Type of the genus *Hydrangea*. An untidy shrub with upright but straggling, weak branches, growing up to 1.5 m (5 feet). The leaves are egg shaped, serrate, with acuminate tips; the lower surface is glabrous. The corymbs are up to 15 cm (6 inches) across with a few ray-flowers surrounding the fertile flowers. The flowers are long-stalked and have four sepals each. The true species is rare. It inhabits the eastern United States, from Louisiana to Florida, and north to Iowa. This species was introduced to Great Britain by Peter Collinson about 1736. Most names of varieties and formas are now sunk in synonymy; they deserve cultivar status at most. Only a few are propagated vegetatively. This is true for var. *acarpa* and var. *australis*. The subspecies' areas of distribution barely touch each other.

H. arborescens 'Annabelle'

A somewhat untidy shrub up to 1.25 m (3.5 feet). The flowerheads are extremely large and do not contain fertile flowers. Flowering branches should be staked, as the stems are not strong enough to carry the flowers in bad weather conditions, although it helps to restore the balance between branch and flower by not pruning. This plant was found by J. C. McDaniel in Illinois. It is now a very popular cultivar, produced in quantity. RHS Awards: AM 1978, AGM 1992. Raised by Gulfstream Nursery, United States, before 1975.

Hydrangea arborescens 'Astrid Lindgren', Rutten garden.

Hydrangea arborescens 'Dardom', Darthuizer Nurseries.

Hydrangea arborescens 'Dardom', Darthuizer Nurseries.

Hydrangea arborescens subsp. discolor, Rutten garden.

H. arborescens 'Astrid Lindgren'

This cultivar is very similar to the species itself. It carries small white flowerheads and is surpassed by several more attractive cultivars.

H. arborescens 'Blenheim Lacecap'

An inconspicuous shrub, found in the wild. Flowerheads white, with only a few ray-flowers. Mentioned by Michael Dirr (1997).

H. arborescens 'Bounty'

A fairly compact shrub with small mopheads but otherwise similar to the species itself. It is present in RHS Garden Wisley, United Kingdom.

H. arborescens 'Dardom'

A free-flowering shrub with lacecap flowerheads. Many ray-flowers surround the greenish fertile flowers. It has firm branches, like 'Grandiflora'. Leaves are heart shaped. Trademarked name is WHITE DOME. Raised by Darthuizer Nurseries, Netherlands, before 1992.

H. arborescens subsp. *discolor* (Seringe) McClintock 1956

A well-branched, bushy shrub up to 2 m (6.5 feet). Young branches downy. Leaves egg shaped, gray below, margins serrate. The corymbs are flattened, 10–15 cm (4–6 inches), with a few small white ray-flowers, placed in a ring around the fertile white flowers. The subspecies is endemic in Arkansas, Indiana, Oklahoma, and adjacent regions in the United States. Pilatowski (1982) considers this subspecies to be a valid species, *H. cinerea* Small 1898.

Hydrangea arborescens subsp. *discolor* 'Sterilis', Boering garden.

Hydrangea arborescens 'Grandiflora', Hemelrijk Tuinen.

Hydrangea arborescens subsp. *discolor* 'Sterilis', Spinners Garden.

Hydrangea arborescens 'Grandiflora', Trebah Garden.

H. arborescens subsp. *discolor* 'Sterilis'

A shrub of about 1.5 m (5 feet), with slender stems. The flowerheads are globular, creamy white, similar to those of 'Grandiflora'. This form was known before 1900. Described by Torrey and Gray originally, renamed by H. St. John in 1921. RHS Award: AGM 1984.

H. arborescens 'Eco Pink Puff'

Found by Don Jacobs of Eco Gardens, United States. A strong bushy plant with light pink flowers. Mentioned by Michael Dirr before 1996.

H. arborescens 'Grandiflora'

A much-branched shrub up to 1.25 m (3.5 feet). The stems are weak and the plant makes a somewhat untidy impression. The corymbs are larger than those of the species itself. This well-known cultivar is classified under subsp. *arborescens*. It has been surpassed by 'Annabelle'. Found in the wild in the United States before 1900. RHS Awards: AM 1907, AGM 1992.

H. arborescens 'Green Knight'

A shrub up to 2 m (6.5 feet) high and wide. Flowerheads pure white in clusters, turning to green with age. This form was discovered in the wild in the United States. Mentioned by Michael Dirr (1997).

H. arborescens 'Highland Lace'

This form has been found and collected in the Appalachian Mountains of eastern United States. Flowers are huge mopheads, pure white and almost as large as those of 'Annabelle'. Mentioned by Michael Dirr before 1996.

Hydrangea arborescens 'Hills of Snow', Rutten garden.

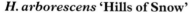

Hydrangea arborescens subsp. *radiata*, Sir Harold Hillier Gardens and Arboretum.

Hydrangea arborescens subsp. *radiata*, Sir Harold Hillier Gardens and Arboretum.

H. arborescens 'Hills of Snow'

A bushy shrub up to 1.5 m (5 feet). The flowerheads carry almost only fertile flowers, with a few ivory white sterile florets. This form is very close to the species, if not identical. Bred by Pieter Zwijnenburg, Boskoop, Netherlands, in 1990.

H. arborescens subsp. *radiata* (Walter) McClintock 1956

A shrubby plant, in habit like the species. The main difference is in the foliage. The leaf underside has a whitish felty pubescence, and the leaf itself is more tapered and egg shaped. The corymbs are flattened and carry numerous white, sterile florets on long stalks. This subspecies is endemic in North and South Carolina in the United States. RHS Awards: AM 1978, AGM 1992.

H. arborescens subsp. *radiata* 'Samantha'

Hardly differs from the subspecies. It is present in the Shamrock collection. Discovered by plantsman Clarence Towe in a garden in South Carolina. and now present in some European collections.

H. aspera D. Don subsp. *aspera* 1825

This very variable species is usually a shrub up to 3 m (10 feet), occasionally more or also less in width. The leaves are also sometimes differently shaped on the same plant, so it is difficult to determine *H. aspera* and its close allies with certainty. The leaves of subsp. *aspera* are broadly lanceolate, 5–15 cm (2–6 inches) long, and with acuminate tips. The flowerheads are saucer shaped with about 10 ray-flowers surrounding the fertile flowers. Remarkably, the flowers of this species do not respond to soil acidity: blue forms stay blue on alkaline soils, red and pink forms keep the same color on acid soils. True *H. aspera* subsp. *aspera* is not

Hydrangea aspera, Royal Botanic Garden, Edinburgh.

Hydrangea aspera 'Bellevue', Jardin Bellevue.

Hydrangea aspera, Rutten garden.

Hydrangea aspera 'Farrall', Maurice Foster garden.

often seen under its proper name; it is sometimes labeled *H. villosa* or *H. aspera* var. *villosa*. The distribution of *H. aspera* and its subspecies is widespread: the eastern Himalayas, central and eastern China, Taiwan, Philippines, and Indonesia. Synonym: *H. oblongifolia* Blume 1824.

H. aspera 'Bellevue'
A huge shrub or almost a multistemmed tree up to 4–5 m (13–16 feet) tall and even wider. The enormous flowerheads consist of lilac ray-flowers surrounding pink fertile flowers. The leaves are equally large. This magnificent plant needs a lot of space. It is difficult to propagate. Bred by Lemonnier of France, in 1996.

H. aspera 'Farrall'
A huge shrub with large broadly oval leaves. The flowerheads consist of purplish fertile flowers surrounded by pure white ray-flowers. The sepals overlap each other and have entire or slightly serrate margins. Young plants are tender and can suffer from a late frost. This plant has been named after the house of Michael Haworth-Booth. Bred by Maurice Foster of Kent, United Kingdom, before 2000.

Hydrangea aspera 'Kawakami', Rutten garden.

Hydrangea aspera f. *kawakamii* × *H. involucrata*, Holehird Gardens.

Hydrangea aspera 'Kawakami', Rutten garden.

H. aspera 'Kawakami'

This shrub grows up to 2 m (6.5 feet) with a spreading habit. The leaves are velvety grayish. Flowers carry serrate white florets with three to four sepals; fertile flowers are lilac. This tender form comes from Taiwan and is now considered a cultivar. It is closely related to *H. villosa*. It flowers a month later than comparable cultivars.

H. aspera f. *kawakamii* × *H. involucrata*

A shrub of about 1.5 m (5 feet). Leaves elongated and acuminate, grayish, slightly velvety. Flowers half open buds, intermediate to the parents. Flowering time is late in the season, the influence of *H. involucrata* is hardly visible. More plants of this hybrid have been developed in Japan and are expected to come into cultivation in the coming years. The plant is present in the Holehird Gardens, United Kingdom. Origin Japanese.

H. aspera 'Macrophylla'

A huge shrub with stout branches up to 2 m (6.5 feet) and about as wide. The branches are more or less hairy. Leaves large, broadly ovate, about 10–12 cm (4–4.75 inches) long. The flowerheads are disc shaped, with violet fertile flowers, surrounded by whitish lilac ray-flowers. Flowering time is from July to August or September. This cultivar is very vigorous and easy to grow, one of the most preferable cultivars of the species. It is a garden form of unknown origin and must not be confused with Hemsley's plant, described in 1887. That plant is probably no longer in cultivation since it is not hardy enough to be cultivated outdoors. Origin unknown. RHS Award: AGM 1992.

Hydrangea aspera 'Macrophylla', Crûg Farm Nursery.

Hydrangea aspera 'Macrophylla', Jardin de Valérianes.

Hydrangea aspera 'Macrophylla', C. Esveld Nurseries.

Hydrangea aspera 'Peter Chappell', Le Thuit Saint-Jean.

H. aspera 'Peter Chappell'

A variant of *H. aspera* subsp. *aspera*, growing into a bush of 1.5 m (5 feet). The leaves are large, up to 25 cm (10 inches). The flowerheads have white sterile flowers and creamy white florets, with four sepals. The cultivar is named after Peter Chappell, a well-known English plantsman and nurseryman. Bred by Maurice Foster of Kent, United Kingdom.

H. aspera 'Pink Cloud'

A shrub found in Sichuan province, China, by Roy Lancaster. This very conspicuous form has soft pink fertile and sterile flowers on large flowerheads. It was named by one of the authors during his visit to Trelissick Garden in the United Kingdom. It promises to be an interesting addition to the range of available cultivars. Introduced by C. J. van Gelderen and B. Champion in 2002.

Hydrangea aspera 'Pink Cloud', Trelissick Garden.

Hydrangea aspera subsp. *robusta*, Maurice Foster garden.

Hydrangea aspera subsp. *robusta*, Maurice Foster garden.

Hydrangea aspera subsp. *robusta* var. *longipes*, Maurice Foster garden.

H. aspera subsp. **robusta** (Hooker f. & Thomson) McClintock 1956

A shrub up to 4 m (13 feet), of spreading habit. Leaves large, ovate-lanceolate, margins serrate, hairy below, on very long reddish pedicels. The flowerheads are large, up to 30 cm (1 foot), ray-flowers white, fertile flowers violet. There is a form in the trade as *H. longipes*. Although it has been known for more than a century, subspecies *robusta* is very rare in cultivation. It lacks hardiness, as it comes from Bhutan and Sikkim. Synonym: *H. aspera* subsp. *robusta* f. *rosthornii* Diels 1901 (larger leaves and longer petioles).

Hydrangea aspera subsp. *robusta* var. *longipes*, Maurice Foster garden.

Hydrangea aspera subsp. *robusta* var. *longipes*, Holehird Gardens.

Hydrangea aspera 'Rocklon', Jardin Bellevue.

H. aspera subsp. *robusta* var. *longipes* (Franchet) Diels 1885

The authors, having seen several plants labeled *H. longipes*, propose to maintain the name of Diels and to restore these plants again as a variety of subsp. *robusta*. A medium-sized shrub, barely over 1.5 m (5 feet). The leaves are densely hairy, 20 cm (8 inches) long and lanceolate, petioles are often red or reddish. Flowerheads large, white sepals surround the fertile flowers. The plant needs some shade for best results. Its habitat is in northwestern China.

H. aspera 'Rocklon'

A shrubby plant, maybe up to 1.5 m (5 feet). The flowerheads are very similar to those of 'Kawakami' and quite large but flower a month earlier. Ray-flowers are white, sterile flowers lilac. Bred by Mark Fillon, United Kingdom.

H. aspera 'Rowallane'

A shrub of about 1.5 m (5 feet), with upright branches. Flowerheads white, sepals serrate, and slightly fragrant. This cultivar is similar to 'Taiwan' and not fully hardy. Raised by Rowallane Garden, Saintfield, Northern Ireland, United Kingdom, before 1985.

Hydrangea aspera subsp. *sargentiana*, Maurice Foster garden.

Hydrangea aspera subsp. *sargentiana*, C. Esveld Nurseries.

Hydrangea aspera subsp. *strigosa*, Crûg Farm Nursery.

Hydrangea aspera subsp. *sargentiana*, Rutten Garden.

H. aspera subsp. *sargentiana* (Rehder) McClintock 1956

A slow-growing shrub, developing to a huge plant in time, up to 2.5 m (8 feet). Stems very stout and clad with bristly hairs. Leaves large, almost round, petioles bristly up to 30 cm (12 inches) long and 20 cm (8 inches) wide. The flowerheads are flat, ray-flowers arranged in a ring, with whitish flowerheads carrying four to five sepals, irregularly shaped, and pale pink-lilac fertile flowers. This subspecies can be propagated by root suckers. It is endemic in western Hubei province, China, and was introduced by Wilson in 1908. It needs some shelter for best results but is otherwise fully hardy unless touched by late spring frosts. RHS Awards: AM 1912, AGM 1992.

Hydrangea aspera subsp. *strigosa*, courtesy Maurice Foster.

Hydrangea glandulosa, Crûg Farm Nursery

Hydrangea aspera subsp. *strigosa*, Le Vastérival.

H. aspera subsp. *strigosa* (Rehder) McClintock 1956

An erect shrub up to 2 m (6.5 feet). Branches and stems are densely bristly. The leaves are large, lanceolate, ending in a long point. The underside is also bristly. The flowerhead is flattened, 15 cm (6 inches) across, with whitish purple ray-flowers and lilac fertile flowers. The true subspecies is rare and often confused with *H. aspera* 'Macrophylla' in the trade. Wynn-Jones introduced this subspecies from Sapa, North Vietnam. His description differs from that of McClintock and states that the habit is spreading instead of erect. Synonym: *H. strigosa* var. *angustifolia* Rehder 1911.

H. aspera 'Taiwan'

A strong-growing plant with large lilac-pink flowerheads. It is related to 'Kawakami' and similar to 'Rowallane'. Bred by M. Mason, United Kingdom, before 1985.

H. diplostemona Standley 1921

A woody climber or shrub with pubescent branchlets and flowerheads. Leaves oval, 15–25 cm (10 inches) long, glabrous above, sometimes pubescent below, margins entire. Flowers pink, sterile flowers usually not present. This species inhabits the mountains of Costa Rica and northerly Andes at 1000–1500 m (3300–4950 feet) elevation.

H. glandulosa Elmer 1908

An evergreen climber from the Philippines. We have no living plant, only this photo of a plant in Wales.

Hydrangea heteromalla, Arboretum de Dreijen.

Hydrangea heteromalla, Maurice Foster garden.

Hydrangea heteromalla, Crûg Farm Nursery.

Hydrangea heteromalla, Crûg Farm Nursery.

Hydrangea heteromalla, a form with pubescent foliage, Holehird Gardens.

Hydrangea heteromalla, Maurice Foster garden.

H. heteromalla D. Don 1825

A large shrub to a medium-sized tree, often with peeling bark. The leaves are variable in size, up to 20 cm (8 inches), ovate-lanceolate with a long point, smooth above, downy below, margins usually serrate. The petioles are usually red. The flowerheads are about 15 cm (6 inches) across, ray-flowers white or pink or reddish, sepals creamy white or pinkish. This variable species inhabits central and western China, also Yunnan province, and Vietnam. Several different formas and cultivars are cultivated in Europe. Synonym: *H. heteromalla* var. *mollis* Rehder 1911 (pubescent foliage). Probable synonym: *H. kamienskii* Léveillé 1903.

H. heteromalla 'Arhetuse'

A selection of wild plants collected in Nepal by T. Schilling about 1980. This shrub has stout branches and a weeping habit. It is very free-flowering with white corymbs, of about 15 cm (6 inches). Leaves large, 15–20 cm (6–8 inches) long, ovate. Raised by Corrine Mallet, France, in 1992.

Hydrangea heteromalla 'Bellevue', Rein and Mark Bulk nursery.

Hydrangea heteromalla "Crûg Farm," Rein and Mark Bulk nursery.

Hydrangea heteromalla 'Bretschneideri', Crûg Farm Nursery.

Hydrangea heteromalla 'Dumicola', Maurice Foster garden.

H. heteromalla 'Bellevue'

A large shrub with pendulous flowerheads. Originated in the Jardin Bellevue in Normandy, France. Bred by Lemonnier of France. Not to be confused with *H. aspera* 'Bellevue'.

H. heteromalla 'Bretschneideri'

Formerly considered a species, then a forma, now reduced to a cultivar. A huge shrub or small tree, very much like *H. heteromalla* itself. It differs mainly in its stronger peeling bark and its hardiness. More than one clone is in the trade. RHS Award: AGM 1992.

H. heteromalla "Crûg Farm"

Possibly a hybrid with *H. paniculata* and not a pure form of *H. heteromalla*. Flowers cream, turning to white, not in panicles. Leaves are light green with red petioles. This plant is present in Dutch nurseries. It was not named by Wynn-Jones of Crûg Farm Nursery.

H. heteromalla 'Dumicola'

The differences between the species and this former variety are so minor and unreliable that it is now treated as a cultivar. Synonym: *H. heteromalla* var. *dumicola* W. W. Smith 1917.

H. heteromalla 'Edouard Avdeew'

A huge shrub up to 3–4 m (10–13 feet), with stout branches. The plant is sparsely branched. Flowerheads large, 16–18 cm (6.25–7 inches), creamy white turning to pink. Very free-flowering, in June and July. Faded flowers are attractive too. Named after Edouard Avdeew, a French plantsman and garden architect. Raised by Robert Mallet, France, in 1992.

Hydrangea heteromalla 'Gidie', Rein and Mark Bulk nursery.

Hydrangea heteromalla 'Jermyn's Lace', Sir Harold Hillier Gardens and Arboretum.

Hydrangea heteromalla 'Gidie', Rein and Mark Bulk nursery.

Hydrangea heteromalla 'June Pink', courtesy R. Houtman.

Hydrangea heteromalla 'Jermyn's Lace', Sir Harold Hillier Gardens and Arboretum.

H. heteromalla **'Gidie'**

A huge shrub up to 3 m (10 feet), selected out of several hundreds of seedlings. The branches are almost black and the bark is peeling. The flowerheads are large, light yellow-green, turning to cream, later changing to red. The flowers are sweetly scented. This cultivar is named after Gidie van Vugt, a Dutch plantsman and nurseryman. Bred by P. Vanlaerhoven, Netherlands, in 1997.

H. heteromalla **'Jermyn's Lace'**

A vigorous-growing shrub, with a peeling bark. Leaves large. The large white flowers turn to pink in summer. Plant habit is much the same as the species itself. Synonym: *H. xanthoneura* var. *wilsonii*. Bred by Sir Harold Hillier Gardens and Arboretum, United Kingdom, in 1981.

Hydrangea heteromalla 'Kalmthout', Arboretum Kalmthout.

Hydrangea heteromalla 'Krista', Rutten garden.

Hydrangea heteromalla 'Long White', PlantenTuin de Oirsprong.

H. heteromalla 'June Pink'

A huge shrub up to 5 m (16 feet). Leaves as in the species itself. The large flowerheads begin appearing in June, first pink than turning to dark red. Sepals entire and rounded. The fertile flowers are light green and turn to purplish red. A valuable cultivar. Bred by Sir Harold Hillier Gardens and Arboretum, United Kingdom, in 1996.

H. heteromalla 'Kalmthout'

A huge shrub with very conspicuous glowing-red petioles. The leaves are green with a reddish hue. The flowerheads are large and turn to a fiery red. This plant is present in the Arboretum Kalmthout in Belgium and is propagated by C. Esveld Nurseries, in Boskoop, Netherlands. Bred by Jelena de Belder of Arboretum Kalmthout, Belgium, in 1999.

H. heteromalla 'Krista'

A large vigorous-growing shrub. The green leaves turn claret-red, becoming very red in the autumn. Named after Krista Bontan. Bred by Pieter Zwijnenburg, Boskoop, Netherlands, in 1990.

H. heteromalla 'Long White'

This cultivar has very long white flowerheads. The habit is like that of all the cultivars of *H. heteromalla*. Bred by Gidie van Vugt, Netherlands, before 1997.

Hydrangea heteromalla 'Morrey's Form', Stourton House Flower Garden.

Hydrangea heteromalla 'Nepal Beauty', C. Esveld Nurseries.

Hydrangea heteromalla 'Morrey's Form', Rein and Mark Bulk nursery.

Hydrangea heteromalla 'Snowcap', Rein and Mark Bulk nursery.

H. heteromalla 'Morrey's Form'

A more or less spreading shrub up to 3 m (10 feet), vigorous-growing. Flowerheads large, up to 20 cm (8 inches) across, florets white, sepals four, elongated, entire. This plant is very free-flowering, in June to July. Synonym: 'Morrey'. Origin unknown.

H. heteromalla 'Moss'

A vigorous-growing shrub, with tomentose branches. The leaves are moss colored and turn to yellow-orange in the autumn. Bred by Pieter Zwijnenburg, Boskoop, Netherlands, in 1990.

H. heteromalla 'Nepal Beauty'

The plant resembles various clones of *H. heteromalla* more than those of *H. aspera,* but it may not belong to *H. heteromalla.* It is difficult to propagate. Flowers are white in loose, open corymbs. The leaves are very large and have conspicuous red margins and red petioles, not unlike some large-leaved clones of *H. aspera.* From C. Esveld Nurseries, Netherlands, in 1994. Possibly a hybrid, it was raised from wild-collected seed, harvested in Nepal. Only one plant survived.

H. heteromalla 'Snowcap'

This hydrangea was cultivated at Sir Harold Hillier Gardens and Arboretum, United Kingdom, under a wrong name (*H. robusta*) for many years. It is a huge shrub, with large and flat corymbs about 25 cm (10 inches) across. The leaves are also large and cordate with red petioles; they turn yellow in autumn. This plant was originally cultivated from seed collected in the Himalayas. It is a distinct form, worthy of cultivation.

H. heteromalla 'Willy'

A huge shrub up to 4–5 m (13–16 feet) as is usual in this species. Leaves grass green, turning golden yellow in autumn. Bred by Pieter Zwijnenburg, Boskoop, Netherlands, in 1990.

Hydrangea heteromalla 'Xanthoneura', Maurice Foster garden.

Hydrangea hirta, Holehird Gardens.

Hydrangea heteromalla 'Yalung Ridge', Holehird Gardens.

Hydrangea hirta, Darthuizer Nurseries.

H. heteromalla 'Xanthoneura'

Formerly considered a species, then a forma, now reduced to a cultivar. A small tree or large shrub up to 6–7 m (20–23 feet). Bark chestnut brown, strongly exfoliating. The leaves are large, green, and acuminate. Flowerheads in corymbs, with numerous ray-flowers, white fading to pink, sepals heart shaped and partly overlapping. The florets have long stalks, longer than the species. The flowers are often hidden by the foliage or too high in the plant to be seen. This plant comes originally from Sichuan province, China. It was imported by Messrs. Veitch about 1904. Although this cultivar is very similar to the species itself, it can be distinguished by its stronger peeling bark. More than one clone of this cultivar is in the trade.

H. heteromalla 'Yalung Ridge'

A large shrub up to 3 m (10 feet). The young leaves are crimson, mature leaves are dark green, large, and elongated. The petioles are red. Flowerheads medium-sized, white to pale pink. Flowering time is from June to July. The original plant grew from seed collected in Nepal. Raised by T. Schilling, United Kingdom.

H. hirta (Thunberg) Siebold 1828

A small shrub up to 1.5 m (5 feet) but usually smaller. Branches are green or purple. The leaves are deeply serrate with dark stems. Flowerheads small, usually without ray-flowers, fertile flowers are pinkish white. At least three different clones are in cultivation. This species is rare in cultivation and has only a modest horticultural value. It is endemic on Honshu, Japan, and on Okinawa, Ryukyu Islands, and can be considered the Asian counterpart of the American *H. arborescens*. The Japanese name for the species is 'Ko ajisai'.

H. hirta 'Amagi'

Discovered on Mount Amagi in Japan, this plant is said to be a natural hybrid between *H. hirta* and *H. scandens* subsp. *chinensis* f. *luteovenosa*. Corinne Mallet found this hybrid in Japan in 2000, but she did not mention a name. It is a shrub of about 75 cm (30 inches). See *H. amagiana*.

Hydrangea integrifolia, Sir Harold Hillier Gardens and Arboretum.

Hydrangea involucrata, Rutten garden.

Hydrangea integrifolia, Sir Harold Hillier Gardens and Arboretum.

Hydrangea involucrata, Rutten garden.

H. hirta 'Midori ko ajisai'

A slow-growing shrub with dentate leaves. It was discovered in Shizuika prefecture, Japan. The flowerheads are green (midori) because of disease. A green-colored plant of *H. serrata* was found next to this cultivar.

H. hirta 'Okutama'

The leaves are less dentate and purplish when unfolding. Small flowerheads without sterile flowers. Origin Japanese.

H. integrifolia Hayata 1906

A woody climber or shrub. The stems and branchlets are covered with red pubescence. The evergreen leaves are oval, 5–18 cm (2–7 inches) long and 3–9 cm (1–3.5 inches) wide. Margins entire to slightly dentate. The upper surface is glabrous, the undersurface with occasional coarse hairs, or glabrous too. Flowerheads small, white; the sterile flowers have one or two sepals. This species inhabits Taiwan in mountainous regions, about 1500 m (4950 feet) in altitude and is reported in the Philippines. It is occasionally found in cultivation. This species is the only member of section *Cornidia* growing outside the Americas.

H. involucrata Siebold & Zuccarini 1839

A small shrub usually not more than 1 m (3 feet) and often shorter. The leaves are lanceolate, ending in a sharp point, about 15 cm (6 inches) long, covered with grayish pubescence above. Leaves, stems, and pedicels are covered with bristly hairs. The flowerheads are remarkable. The flowers are enclosed by rounded bracts, which give the impression of a firm, round closed bud. When opening, the corymbs show almost white flowers, with four or five sepals. The fertile flowers are bluish. Flowering time is from August to September. This very beautiful plant needs a well-sheltered place and a lot of care. Even in moderate winters it can suffer badly. Native to Japan, it was imported by Siebold to Europe. Its Japanese name is 'Tama ajisai'.

Hydrangea involucrata, Rutten garden.

Hydrangea involucrata 'Hortensis', Le Thuit Saint-Jean.

Hydrangea involucrata, C. Esveld Nurseries.

H. *involucrata* 'Gokyodanka'
A small shrub with complex salmon pink double flowers; fertile flowers few. Origin Japanese.

H. *involucrata* 'Green tama'
A small shrub with serrate leaves. The flowerheads are irregularly arranged, fertile flowers are lilac-blue and the few sterile florets are green (but not because of disease). Origin Japanese.

H. *involucrata* 'Han temari tama'
A shrub of the usual size. The white flowerheads are large, sterile and fertile florets are mixed. Origin Japanese.

H. *involucrata* 'Hortensis'
A very slow-growing shrublet with thin, floppy branchlets. The leaves are lanceolate and smaller than in the species. The flowerheads are enclosed by bracts, which open to reveal an irregular corymb with coral-pink florets, partly double, surrounding the pink fertile flowers. This delicate, little shrub is very attractive but demands much care and a well-sheltered place. Imported from Japan to Europe by T. Smith in 1867. Described by Carl J. Maximowicz. RHS Award: AGM 1992.

H. *involucrata* 'Kohfu yōraku tama ajisai'
A plant with small white double flowers and pink fertile flowers. Origin Japanese,

H. *involucrata* f. *leucantha* Sugimoto 1977
A small shrub with white flowers and single sepals. Habit is as for the species itself.

H. *involucrata* 'Mihara kokonoe'
This shrub has interesting flowerheads: the fertile flowers are greenish white, surrounded by white starlike florets. Yamamoto (1998) calls it a heavenly plant.

H. *involucrata* 'Numa ajisai'
This shrubby plant has reddish fertile flowers and a few salmon yellow florets consisting of four sepals. Origin Japanese.

Hydrangea involucrata 'Plena', Crûg Farm Nursery.

Hydrangea involucrata 'Sterilis', Rein and Mark Bulk nursery.

Hydrangea involucrata 'Sterilis', C. Esveld Nurseries.

Hydrangea involucrata 'Takaho hira', courtesy Maurice Foster.

H. involucrata 'Plena'

A small shrub of the same size as the species itself. Leaves bristly, green-gray, narrow with a sharp apex. Fertile flowers purple-pink, surrounded by double cream-colored sepals. This cultivar needs a protected site in part shade. It was imported from Japan.

H. involucrata 'Raseita tama'

This shrub produces large fertile flowerheads with only a few florets consisting of four white sepals. The leaves are thicker than usual and more tomentose. Is this plant possibly hybridized with some *H. aspera*? Origin Japanese.

H. involucrata 'Sterilis'

A fairly strong growing shrub up to 1 m (3 feet). The massive flowerheads are white; many sterile flowers surround lilac to white fertile flowers. Leaves ovate-lanceolate. This plant is in cultivation in Netherlands. Origin Japanese.

H. involucrata 'Takaho hira'

A small shrublet with tomentose leaves. The florets consist of double sepals, pale pink to white. There are almost no fertile flowers. Origin Japanese.

H. involucrata 'Tama kanzashi'

A slow-growing shrublet up to 1 m (3 feet). The flowers are globular bracts, opening blue and white like in the species, and unsymmetrical. The leaves are broadly ovate, instead of more or less lanceolate. Synonym: 'Tama kanzashi ajisai'. Origin Japanese.

H. involucrata 'Tama yae'

A shrub with very elegant flowerheads. The pink fertile flowers are surrounded by snow-white double florets. Origin Japanese.

Hydrangea involucrata 'Viridescens', Maurice Foster garden.

Hydrangea involucrata 'Yokudanka', C. Esveld Nurseries.

Hydrangea involucrata 'Yoraku tama, courtesy Maurice Foster.

H. *involucrata* 'Urakisao yae temari'
A large-leaved shrub with double, white flowers, arranged in a more or less spherical flowerhead. Origin Japanese.

H. *involucrata* 'Viridescens'
Similar to the species in all aspects, the only difference is that the sterile flowers are green and not mauve or white. The ray-flowers display a good show with the violet fertile flowers. This cultivar was found on the island of Yakushima in Japan. It flowers later in the season than the species. Origin Japanese.

H. *involucrata* 'Yae no gyokudanka'
A shrub with strangely built flowerheads: long stalks bear double light green flowers and small dots of fertile flowers, also green. This plant is shown in Siebold's work, *Flora Japonica* (1840). Origin Japanese.

H. *involucrata* 'Yahagi gyokudanka'
A low shrublet with small pinkish flowers. Origin Japanese.

H. *involucrata* 'Yokudanka'
A small shrub up to 1 m (3 feet). The flowers are much like those of 'Viridescens', but the sepals are double and pink. The flowerheads look like begonias. Origin Japanese.

H. *involucrata* 'Yoraku tama'
A small shrub up to 1 m (3 feet). Flowerheads large, sepals double, white to mauve, fertile flowers blue. This cultivar is not clonal, there are small differences. Origin Japanese.

H. *jelskii* Szyszylowicz 1895
A woody climbing plant. Flowerheads pubescent with lax hairs, fertile flowers only, small, white. Leaves evergreen, 8–13 cm (3–5 inches) long, and half as wide, glabrous above, some pubescence below. This species inhabits mountainous regions in southern Ecuador and northern Peru. It is poorly known and has been collected only twice. It is related to *H. matthewsii*.

Hydrangea macrophylla, Boering garden.

H. macrophylla (Thunberg) Seringe subsp. *macrophylla* 1830

Common name: Bigleaf hydrangea. The Japanese name is 'Hime ajisai' or 'Gaku ajisai'. Subsp. *macrophylla* covers the extremely many cultivated forms, usually called "hortensia." It is doubtful that the true wild subspecies still exists. If it does, 'Joseph Banks' is very close to it. There are many synonyms for the true species, due to the fact of ignorance in the earlier years. Old synonyms are *H. hortensia* Siebold 1829 and *H. hortensis* Smith 1792. Originally described as a separate species by Carl Thunberg; described as a subspecies by Seringe in 1830.

Most cultivars of *Hydrangea macrophylla* are bushy shrubs up to 2 m (6.5 feet) high and wide, or occasionally even larger. They form flowerbuds on short two-year-old twigs. The foliage of most cultivars is much the same: broadly ovate, more or less dentate or serrate, and rarely fully entire. The size varies from 8 to 20 cm (3–8 inches) long and 4 to 12 cm (4.75 inches) wide. It is almost impossible to identify cultivars of *H. macrophylla* with any certainty on the basis of their foliage, with a few exceptions.

The flowers of most *Hydrangea macrophylla* cultivars are formed as corymbs, or flowerheads, and are either fertile or sterile. The fertile flowers are usually not described, as they look very much the same. Each corymb has three to five sepals.

Corymbs with no or few fertile flowers are called mophead hortensias, or simply mopheads. The corymb is usually globose shaped. Corymbs with many fertile flowers and surrounded by ray-flowers are called lacecap hortensias, or *Tellerhortensien* in German.

Flower color depends on the soil: pink and red on alkaline soil, blue, purple or mixed colors in acid to very acid soil. Feeding with additional aluminum sulfate is essential for good blue colors.

Many cultivars have been lost to cultivation (see appendix 2) and the parentage of most cultivars is usually unknown. Just because a cultivar name is preceded by the words "*Hydrangea macrophylla*" does not always mean that the plant belongs to the true species.

Hydrangea macrophylla, Trebah Garden.

Hydrangea macrophylla (Hortensia Group) 'Admiration', C. Esveld Nurseries.

Hydrangea macrophylla, Maurice Foster garden.

Hydrangea macrophylla (Hortensia Group) 'Admiration', Pieter Zwijnenburg, courtesy Arborealis.

Hydrangea Hortensia Group

Also known as mopheads, this group of cultivars is characterized by large, rounded heads of mostly sterile flowers.

H. macrophylla (Hortensia Group) 'Aarburg'

A strong-growing shrub up to 1.25 m (3.5 feet). The large leaves are light green. The flattened corymbs are scarlet red. Suitable as a garden plant and only rarely available. Bred by E. Haller, Switzerland, in 1973. The Haller Nursery no longer exists and documents for this plant have been destroyed. Named for a city and a castle in Switzerland. Also spelled Aaberg.

H. macrophylla (Hortensia Group) 'Adelaide'

A shrubby plant to 1 m (3 feet), of moderate growth. Flowers rich pink, in large somewhat spreading corymbs. Probably no longer in cultivation. Bred by H. J. Jones, United Kingdom, in 1927.

H. macrophylla (Hortensia Group) 'Adèle Schauer'

A heavily growing shrub, with fresh pink flowers. Bred by Schauer of Troppau, Germany, before 1930. Offered by two Dutch nurseries (C. Esveld Nurseries, D. A. Koster), but now probably lost to cultivation.

H. macrophylla (Hortensia Group) 'Admiration'

A large-leaved shrub. Flowerheads compact, crimson or blue. According to Krüssmann (1976–1978), this cultivar was introduced by Draps-Dom in 1950, not by Cayeux in 1932. Dussine states that the two are different plants. The plant in the picture has small serrate sepals and large flowerheads and grows at the Research Station in Boskoop, Netherlands. Bred by Henri Cayeux of France, in 1932.

Hydrangea macrophylla (Hortensia Group) 'Adria', Arboretum de Dreijen.

Hydrangea macrophylla (Hortensia Group) 'All Summer Beauty', Holehird Gardens.

Hydrangea macrophylla (Hortensia Group) 'Albrechtsburg', Research Station for Nursery Stock.

H. macrophylla (Hortensia Group) 'Adria'
A shrub of moderate growth. Flowers in flattened corymbs, late, pink or light blue, with remote white stripes. Not often seen in gardens, it is an excellent pot plant. Not suitable for alkaline soils. Bred by August Steiniger, Germany, in 1957.

H. macrophylla (Hortensia Group) 'Agnès Barillet'
Large flowerheads of creamy white florets. In cultivation in the Netherlands before 1940 by Ebbinge-Van Groos nursery. Also called 'Mademoiselle Agnès Barillet'. Bred by Mouillère, France, in 1909.

H. macrophylla (Hortensia Group) 'Agnes Pavell'
A medium-sized shrub up to 1.5 m (5 feet), with large white mopheads. Tolerates sun quite well. The flowers turn to a rich crimson in the fall. Origin French.

H. macrophylla (Hortensia Group) 'Alaska'
Plants under this name were available in the Netherlands, but proved to be very similar or identical to 'Pax', which see.

H. macrophylla (Hortensia Group) 'Albrechtsburg'
A large shrub with large flattened mopheads, sepals serrate, always pink or pinkish creamy white. According to the Shamrock list, it might be 'Dentelle Rose' which is of French origin (Lemoine). Bred by Nieschütz, Germany, in 1993.

H. macrophylla (Hortensia Group) 'All Summer Beauty'
A shrub about 1.5 m (5 feet) high and wide. Flowerheads large, flattened, usually pink or reddish, but becoming blue or light blue easily. Foliage often tinged with purple during the flowering season. Not generally available in Europe, more common in the United States. Origin United States.

Hydrangea macrophylla (Hortensia Group) 'Alpenglühen', Trelissick Garden.

Hydrangea macrophylla (Hortensia Group) 'Altona', Trelissick Garden.

Hydrangea macrophylla (Hortensia Group) 'Altona', Research Station for Nursery Stock.

Hydrangea macrophylla (Hortensia Group) 'America', Trelissick Garden.

H. macrophylla (Hortensia Group) 'Alpenglühen'

A shrubby plant up to 1.25 m (3.5 feet), bushy and healthy. Flowers usually red or dark pink, late in the season. It does not become blue on acid soils, but remains rosy red. A very reliable cultivar with a very bright color. Generally available in both Europe and North America. Also useful as a houseplant. 'Deutschland' is very similar, but has larger leaves. *Alpenglühen* means "alpen glow." Bred by Brügger, Germany, in 1950.

H. macrophylla (Hortensia Group) 'Altona'

A medium-sized shrub up to 1.25 m (3.5 feet), free-flowering, dark pink to blue, with serrate sepals. The corymbs can change to attractive red colors. This common cultivar is generally available. It is also suitable as pot plant. It can easily be confused with 'Hamburg' or 'Europa', but 'Altona' has smaller, serrate leaves. Bred by H. Schadendorff, Germany, in 1931. RHS Awards: AM 1957, AGM 1992. Synonym: 'Althone'.

H. macrophylla (Hortensia Group) 'Amazonas'

A new houseplant, belonging to the RIVER-LINE. Large flowerheads glowing pink with acuminate sepals. Not to be confused with 'Amazone', raised by Lemoine Nursery of France, in 1918, which had pure white, serrate sepals and is probably no longer in cultivation, according to the Shamrock list. Bred by Rampp Nursery, Germany, before 1995.

H. macrophylla (Hortensia Group) 'America'

A strong-growing shrub that flowers late in the season, with large corymbs, pink or blue, depending on soil conditions. Bred by Mouillère, France, in 1928 or 1925. It was in cultivation at D. A. Koster nursery, Boskoop, Netherlands, in 1932. According to the Shamrock list, it is lost to cultivation, but this is not so as a plant is growing at Trelissick Garden. Synonym: 'Sir Henry Dreer'.

Hydrangea macrophylla (Hortensia Group) 'Amethyst', Le Thuit Saint-Jean.

Hydrangea macrophylla (Hortensia Group) 'Ami Pasquier', Research Station for Nursery Stock.

Hydrangea macrophylla (Hortensia Group) 'Amethyst', Trelissick Garden.

Hydrangea macrophylla (Hortensia Group) 'Ami Pasquier', PlantenTuin de Oirsprong.

H. macrophylla (Hortensia Group) 'Amethyst'

A shrub up to 1 m (3 feet) with stout branches. Very free-flowering with small flattened corymbs, pale lilac to pale pink, with serrate sepals. It is a seedling of 'Europa' selected by Michael Haworth-Booth of the United Kingdom, in 1938. This cultivar is not suitable as a pot plant, and it is difficult to get the flowers pure lilac. It flowers frequently until October. Rarely available, but interesting for collectors.

H. macrophylla (Hortensia Group) 'Ami Pasquier'

A slow-growing shrub, about 1 m (3 feet) high. Very free-flowering. The corymbs are flattened and usually dark lilac-red to wine red. The color does not fade. It is very difficult to get this cultivar to produce flowers that are a good blue color. The branches are very dark, resembling the color of eggplant. This seedling of 'Maréchal Foch' can easily be confused with 'Westfalen'. It is drought tolerant. Selected by Emile Mouillère of France, in 1930. RHS Awards: AM 1953, AGM 1992.

H. macrophylla (Hortensia Group) 'Amsterdam'

A compact plant with firm and rounded corymbs. The sepals are entire, dark rosy red with a greenish center. A member of the CITY-LINE series. Bred by Rampp Nursery, Germany, before 1997.

H. macrophylla (Hortensia Group) 'Ao temari'

A small shrub up to 75 cm (30 inches). The flowerheads are real mopheads, light blue. Origin Japanese.

H. macrophylla (Hortensia Group) 'Apotheose'

A medium-sized shrub. The flowerheads are clear rosy red with a white center. Origin unknown, possibly RHS Garden Wisley, United Kingdom.

Hydrangea macrophylla (Hortensia Group) 'Apotheose', Trelissick Garden.

Hydrangea macrophylla (Hortensia Group) 'Atlantic', Research Station for Nursery Stock.

Hydrangea macrophylla (Hortensia Group) 'Armand Draps', Holehird Gardens.

Hydrangea macrophylla (Hortensia Group) 'Atlantic', PlantenTuin de Oirsprong.

H. macrophylla (Hortensia Group) 'Archie Mowbray'

Flowers rosy mauve. Bred by H. J. Jones, United Kingdom, in 1927.

H. macrophylla (Hortensia Group) 'Ardtornish'

A medium-sized shrub up to 1.25 m (3.5 feet). Flowerheads large, 14–15 cm (5.5–6 inches) wide. The sterile flowers are made up of slightly serrate sepals, usually light blue to whitish lilac, later greenish irregularly over the bush. Can be confused with 'Frillibet'. From Ardtornish Gardens, Scotland, United Kingdom.

H. macrophylla (Hortensia Group) 'Armand Draps'

A small shrub up to 1 m (3 feet) and not tolerant of bad weather. Flowers in medium-sized corymbs, rosy red to pale lilac-pink. Bred by Draps of Belgium.

H. macrophylla (Hortensia Group) 'Arthur Billard'

A compact shrubby plant, with large corymbs, easily becoming blue or purple. Once it was an important cultivar, as it is very easy to force. Needs a sheltered site. Bred by Emile Mouillère, France, in 1931.

H. macrophylla (Hortensia Group) 'Athen'

A compact plant with large corymbs, fresh pink. It is a good houseplant. A member of the CITY-LINE series. Bred by Rampp Nursery, Germany, before 1995.

H. macrophylla (Hortensia Group) 'Atlantic'

A large bush up to 1.5 m (5 feet). Flattened corymbs are 15 cm (6 inches) across, pink to red, flowering in August. Can be grown to produce blue flowers. Good foliage color in late autumn. Synonym: 'Atlantica'. Origin before 1931.

Hydrangea macrophylla (Hortensia Group) 'Autumn Joy', Stourton House Flower Garden.

Hydrangea macrophylla (Hortensia Group) 'Ave Maria', Holehird Gardens.

Hydrangea macrophylla (Hortensia Group) 'Ayesha', Rutten garden.

H. macrophylla (Hortensia Group) 'Atmosphere'

A strong, dense shrub up to 1.25 m (3.5 feet), with large spoonlike leaves. Not very floriferous. The red to deep pink flowers open irregularly.

H. macrophylla (Hortensia Group) 'Auckmann'

A dwarf form, with large vivid pink corymbs, easily turning blue in acid soil. It is an esteemed plant in Australia, according to Haworth-Booth. Most probably not present in Europe or America. Also spelled 'Aukamm'. Bred by Fischer of Germany.

H. macrophylla (Hortensia Group) 'Autumn Joy'

A medium-sized shrub up to 1.25 m (3.5 feet). Flowers in large corymbs, pale blue to white, sepals serrate, keeping the color well in the autumn. Also suitable for drying. Raised by Elizabeth Bullivant, United Kingdom, before 2000.

H. macrophylla (Hortensia Group) 'Avalanche'

A slow-growing shrub with weak, sloppy branches. The flowerheads are large, white, free-flowering, June to August. Bred by Lemoine Nursery, Nancy, France, in 1908.

H. macrophylla (Hortensia Group) 'Ave Maria'

A compact, slow-growing shrub up to 1 m (3 feet). Very free-flowering with small rounded corymbs, pure white, first greenish, sometimes flowering twice a year. It needs a sheltered place and acid soil. Tolerates bad weather. A valuable but rare form. Bred by Brügger, Germany, in 1951.

H. macrophylla (Hortensia Group) 'Ayesha'

This famous cultivar grows to a stately bush of about 1.5 m (5 feet). Its flowers are remarkable: they look like small trusses of lilacs. No other cultivar has these spoonlike sepals. The color varies with the soil, from pink through white to light blue. The flowers are slightly scented, unusual for a hortensia. Originating in Japan, this plant has been

Hydrangea macrophylla (Hortensia Group) 'Ayesha', Le Vastérival.

Hydrangea macrophylla (Hortensia Group) 'Ayesha', Royal Horticultural Society Garden Wisley.

Hydrangea macrophylla (Hortensia Group) 'Ayesha', Rein and Mark Bulk nursery.

Hydrangea macrophylla (Hortensia Group) 'Ayesha', Sequoiahof, courtesy Arborealis.

known in Europe since the 1970s. It is a mutant or sport of 'Joseph Banks'. Plants with flowerheads half 'Ayesha' and half 'Joseph Banks' are known from Trebah Garden and the Sir Harold Hillier Gardens and Arboretum, among others. According to the well-known plantsman, the late James Russell, the original plant was probably imported by the Abbotsbury Garden in Dorset, United Kingdom. Synonym: 'Silver Slipper'. Thoby and Mallet deny that var. *concavosepala* (synonym 'Concavosepala') is identical to 'Ayesha', as some have suggested. Another possibility is that the true name is 'Uzu azisai'. RHS Awards: AM 1974, AGM 1992.

H. macrophylla (Hortensia Group) 'Ayesha Blanc'

Probably a degenerated white-flowering 'Ayesha' and also unstable, according to Thoby. Bred by Pépinières Thoby of France.

H. macrophylla (Hortensia Group) 'Azur'

A strong-growing shrub with firm branches. The corymbs are very large, usually light blue. Suitable as a large pot plant. Raised at Friesdorf Research Station, now Landwirtschaftskammer Rheinland (Rhineland Agricultural Chamber), Germany.

H. macrophylla (Hortensia Group) 'Baardse's Favourite'

A medium-sized shrub about 1.25 m (3.5 feet) high. The corymbs are about 20 cm (8 inches) across, the single sepals 4 cm (1.5 inches). This old cultivar bears pink flowers usually, or purple in very acid soils. The color fades to grayish green. Baardse introduced many new hortensias. Bred by D. Baardse, Netherlands, in 1920.

H. macrophylla (Hortensia Group) 'Baccara'

This novelty lacks a description. It was shown at Floriade 2002, an international horticultural exposition. Bred by Pieter Koek BV, Aalsmeer, Netherlands, in 2002.

Hydrangea macrophylla (Hortensia Group) 'Belgica', Trelissick Garden.

Hydrangea macrophylla (Hortensia Group) 'Benelux', Trelissick Garden.

Hydrangea macrophylla (Hortensia Group) 'Benelux', Trelissick Garden.

Hydrangea macrophylla (Hortensia Group) 'Benelux', PlantenTuin de Oirsprong.

H. macrophylla (Hortensia Group) 'Bagatelle'

A shrub of the usual size, with short and stout branches. Flowers usually pink, becoming light blue on very acid soils. Flowering time is from August to September. Bred by D. Baardse, Netherlands, in 1922. In cultivation at two Dutch nurseries (D. A. Koster, C. Esveld) in 1932. Still in cultivation, at Shamrock.

H. macrophylla (Hortensia Group) 'Beauté Rose'

A strong-growing plant up to 1.5 m (5 feet). Flowerheads large and compact, clear rose, becoming light violet on acid soils. Bred by Henri Cayeux, France, in 1930.

H. macrophylla (Hortensia Group) 'Belgica'

A vigorous-growing cultivar with good garden qualities. The branches are short and stout. Flowers deep pink, sometimes bluish.

H. macrophylla (Hortensia Group) 'Benelux'

A medium-sized shrub with flattened corymbs, 18–20 cm (7–8 inches) across, usually light red, easily turning light blue in acid soils. The center of the sterile flowers may be whitish. It has huge leaves, comparable with 'Yola'. Bred by D. Baardse, Netherlands, in 1950.

H. macrophylla (Hortensia Group) 'Berlin'

A pot plant with dentate lilac-pink sepals. It flowers late in the season. A member of the CITY-LINE series. Synonym: 'Berlino'. Bred by Rampp Nursery, Germany, before 1997.

H. macrophylla (Hortensia Group) 'Berliner Spree'

A compact plant, corymbs pink with a yellowish center. Suitable as a houseplant. A member of the RIVER-LINE series. Bred by Rampp Nursery, Germany, before 1996.

Hydrangea macrophylla (Hortensia Group) 'Bichon', Research Station for Nursery Stock.

Hydrangea macrophylla (Hortensia Group) 'Blauer Zwerg', Research Station for Nursery Stock.

Hydrangea macrophylla (Hortensia Group) 'Blauer Prinz', Trelissick Garden.

Hydrangea macrophylla (Hortensia Group) 'Blauer Zwerg', Research Station for Nursery Stock.

H. macrophylla (Hortensia Group) 'Besserstein'

Present in the Shamrock collection. Bred by E. Haller, Switzerland, in 1964. Named for a hill in northern Switzerland.

H. macrophylla (Hortensia Group) 'Bichon'

A medium-sized shrub up to 1.5 m (5 feet). This plant shows magnificent white to greenish flowerheads, sometimes flowering twice in the same season. The corymbs are compact, with irregular sepals, somewhat dentate. Unfortunately, this cultivar is apt to pest damage and may not flower at all. It needs a shady place. Bred by Dublanchet of France.

H. macrophylla (Hortensia Group) 'Blauer Ball'

A blue mophead in cultivation at Shamrock. Bred by H. Dienemann, Germany, in 1975.

H. macrophylla (Hortensia Group) 'Blauer Prinz'

A shrub up to 1.25 m (3.5 feet). The small corymbs are overcrowded with pointed sepals. Flowers do not open at the same time and are usually pink but easily grown as blue, appearing late in the season and thus sometimes hidden by the foliage. This cultivar is susceptible to attacks by insects. *Blauer prinz* means "blue prince." Bred by F. Matthes, Germany, in 1925.

H. macrophylla (Hortensia Group) 'Blauer Zwerg'

Synonyms: 'Clara', 'Lavblaa', 'Lavender Blue', 'Lovbla'. An upright-growing compact plant up to 1.25 m (3.5 feet). It is free-flowering with medium-sized corymbs. One of the finest blue hortensias when grown in very acid soil and fed additional aluminum. The various synonyms are corruptions of the Danish word for *light blue* and should not be used. A probable synonym is 'Blau Haller'. Bred by August Steiniger, Germany, in 1965.

Hydrangea macrophylla (Hortensia Group) 'Blue Bonnet', Boering garden.

Hydrangea macrophylla (Hortensia Group) 'Blue Diamond', Research Station for Nursery Stock.

Hydrangea macrophylla (Hortensia Group) 'Blue Bonnet', Holehird Gardens.

Hydrangea macrophylla (Hortensia Group) 'Bodensee', Trelissick Garden.

H. macrophylla (Hortensia Group) 'Blaulicht'

A compact shrub, no more than 1 m (3 feet) high. The large corymbs are dark blue, with a greenish center. Suitable as a houseplant or for patios. Raised at Friesdorf Research Station, now Landwirtschaftskammer Rheinland (Rhineland Agricultural Chamber), Germany.

H. macrophylla (Hortensia Group) 'Blue Bonnet'

A sparsely growing shrub that flowers for a long time. The corymbs are nicely round and the color can vary from dark pink to a good blue. It is a branch sport of 'Générale Vicomtesse de Vibraye'. Raised by C. Marchant of the United Kingdom.

H. macrophylla (Hortensia Group) 'Blue Buck'

A compact shrub up to 1.25 m (3.5 feet). The corymbs are dark rosy red with a white center. In cultivation at C. Esveld Nurseries, Netherlands.

H. macrophylla (Hortensia Group) 'Blue Danube'

A dense, dwarf shrub with splendid large mopheads. Flowers usually a beautiful blue. Called "Danube Bleu" in French, "Blaue Donau" in German.

H. macrophylla (Hortensia Group) 'Blue Diamond'

A healthy well-growing shrub. The flattened corymbs are a good blue color with some white centers at least on very acid soil, becoming pink on alkaline or slightly acid soil. Origin United Kingdom.

H. macrophylla (Hortensia Group) 'Blue Earth'

A compact plant with dense foliage. Corymbs dark blue-violet with white margins. A very conspicuous color. A member of the STAR-LINE series. Bred by Rampp Nursery, Germany, before 1998.

Hydrangea macrophylla (Hortensia Group) 'Bodensee', Rein and Mark Bulk nursery.

H. *macrophylla* (Hortensia Group) 'Bodensee'

A shrub up to 1.25 m (3.5 feet), well growing with firm branches. Flowerheads almost round, very free-flowering, pink to red in alkaline soil, lilac to violet in acid soil. It is one of the best hortensias available today. Also one of the best pot plants. Bred by Brügger, Germany, about 1950.

H. *macrophylla* (Hortensia Group) 'Bonna'

A compact plant very suitable as a houseplant and easy to force. Corymbs large dark pink or a good blue. Raised at Friesdorf Research Station, now Landwirtschaftskammer Rheinland (Rhineland Agricultural Chamber), Germany.

H. *macrophylla* (Hortensia Group) 'Bordeaux'

Flowers claret colored. Bred by Henri Cayeux, France, in 1938.

Hydrangea macrophylla (Hortensia Group) 'Bosco', Research Station for Nursery Stock.

H. *macrophylla* (Hortensia Group) 'Bosco'

A robust shrub up to 1.5 m (5 feet), with bold pink corymbs. Raised by Holehird Gardens, United Kingdom.

Hydrangea macrophylla (Hortensia Group) 'Bottstein', Research Station for Nursery Stock.

Hydrangea macrophylla (Hortensia Group) 'Bougy', courtesy Arborealis.

Hydrangea macrophylla (Hortensia Group) 'Bouquet Rose', C. Esveld Nurseries.

H. macrophylla (Hortensia Group) 'Bottstein'
A dwarf to semidwarf shrub, with large flowerheads, usually red and not fading. Flowering time is from June to July. Bred by E. Haller, Switzerland, in 1971.

H. macrophylla (Hortensia Group) 'Bougy'
A large shrub, carrying red mopheads, tinged lilac, and firmly packed together. Only rarely seen.

H. macrophylla (Hortensia Group) 'Bouquet Rose'
A shrubby plant up to 1.2 m (3.5 feet), well-branched. The branches are somewhat weak. Corymbs almost round, usually pink, blue on very acid soils. Flowering time is from July to September. It is one of the best-known garden hortensias. Generally available. Bred by E. Lemoine, Nancy, France, in 1907.

H. macrophylla (Hortensia Group) 'Brestenberg'
A low-growing shrub with large, rounded flowerheads, usually blue or lilac, flowering in June and July. Bred by E. Haller, Switzerland, in 1972. Named for a hill in northern Switzerland.

H. macrophylla (Hortensia Group) 'Bridal Bouquet'
A dwarf shrub up to 1 m (3 feet), with a compact habit. The corymbs are rounded, 12–15 cm (4.75–6 inches) across, clear white. Can be confused with 'Immaculata', which is very similar. Suitable as a pot plant, but a bad plant in the garden.

Hydrangea macrophylla (Hortensia Group) 'Bridal Bouquet', Trelissick Garden.

Hydrangea macrophylla (Hortensia Group) 'Brilliant', Trelissick Garden.

Hydrangea macrophylla (Hortensia Group) 'Brilliant', Holehird Gardens.

Hydrangea macrophylla (Hortensia Group) 'Brügg', Research Station for Nursery Stock.

H. macrophylla (Hortensia Group) 'Brilliant'

A slow-growing shrub about 1 m (3 feet) high. Leaves acuminate up to 12 cm (4.75 inches) long. Flowerheads somewhat crowded, sepals entire, usually lilac-pink. Bred by Pépinières Thoby of France.

H. macrophylla (Hortensia Group) 'Brügg'

A dwarf shrub up to 80 cm (32 inches). It is free-flowering, dark pink, easily grown as a blue or violet mophead. Flowering time is from June to August. This cultivar is tender. Suitable as a pot plant. Similar to 'Kristel'. Bred by E. Haller, Switzerland, in 1971. Named for the city in northern Switzerland where the Haller Nursery was situated.

Hydrangea macrophylla (Hortensia Group) 'Brunegg', Research Station for Nursery Stock.

H. macrophylla (Hortensia Group) 'Brunegg'

A compact shrub up to 1.25 m (3.5 feet). It bears large corymbs, ball shaped, about 20 cm (8 inches) across, pink in alkaline and light acid soil, whitish blue in very acid soil. Bred by E. Haller, Switzerland, in 1960.

Hydrangea macrophylla (Hortensia Group) 'Burg Königstein', Research Station for Nursery Stock.

Hydrangea macrophylla (Hortensia Group) 'Cendrillon', Trelissick Garden.

Hydrangea macrophylla (Hortensia Group) 'Cendrillon', Holehird Gardens.

H. macrophylla (Hortensia Group) 'Burg Königstein'

A large shrub with medium to large flowerheads, usually red. Bred by E. Haller, Switzerland, in 1975. Named for Königstein, a Swiss castle near Aarau.

H. macrophylla (Hortensia Group) 'Carl Spitteler'

This shrub of the usual size has large corymbs with deep rose sepals. Flowering time is from July to August. Bred by Moll Brothers, Germany, in 1946.

H. macrophylla (Hortensia Group) 'Cardinal Red'

Description not available. Mentioned in the Shamrock list. May be 'Cardinal'. Not to be confused with 'Kardinal' which is entirely different.

H. macrophylla (Hortensia Group) 'Carmen'

A dwarf upright-growing plant. Leaves very deep green. Flowers red or purple, with serrated sepals, flowering in August. A nice cultivar if in good health. Needs a protected site. Bred by Emile Mouillère, France, in 1936. Another plant with this name has coppery-crimson flowers and was bred by J. Wintergalen of Germany in 1938.

H. macrophylla (Hortensia Group) 'Carrousel'

Corymbs red, flowering in mid-season, according to Haworth-Booth. Bred in Netherlands (?) before 1967. Mentioned in the 1967 nursery catalog of K. Wezelenburg & Sons, Boskoop, Netherlands.

H. macrophylla (Hortensia Group) 'Cendrillon'

A slow-growing shrub, barely exceeding 1 m (3 feet) high. The corymbs are small but numerous, usually bright dark pink to magenta. Flowering occurs twice in favorable summers. *Cendrillon* means "Cinderella." Bred by E. Lemoine, Nancy, France, in 1921.

H. macrophylla (Hortensia Group) 'C. F. Meyer'

A very slow-growing shrub with large individual flowers, pink or blue. Flowering time is from August to September. Bred by Moll Brothers, Germany, in 1946. Named after Conrad Ferdinand Meyer, a famous German botanist and dendrologist.

H. macrophylla (Hortensia Group) 'Challenge'

A houseplant with pink corymbs. Bred by Pieter Koek BV, Aalsmeer, Netherlands, in 2002.

Hydrangea macrophylla (Hortensia Group) 'Constellation', Research Station for Nursery Stock.

H. macrophylla (Hortensia Group) 'Chaperon Rouge'

A slow-growing shrubby plant, bred by the son of the famous Emile Mouillère. The flowerheads are small but numerous, usually dark pink or red. The sepals are heart shaped. The plant is suitable as a pot plant and in the garden. Bred by Louis Mouillère, France, in 1954.

H. macrophylla (Hortensia Group) 'Chaperon Rose'

Probably a mutant of 'Chaperon Rouge'. Bred by Mouillère, France.

H. macrophylla (Hortensia Group) 'Charles Guillon'

Probably present in the Shamrock collection. Origin French.

H. macrophylla (Hortensia Group) 'Claudie'

This plant is mentioned in the Shamrock list and should be in cultivation. Possible synonym: 'Claudia'.

H. macrophylla (Hortensia Group) 'Colonia'

A well-branched low shrub, not exceeding 1 m (3 feet). The corymbs are usually blue. Raised at Friesdorf Research Station, now Landwirtschaftskammer Rheinland (Rhineland Agricultural Chamber), Germany.

H. macrophylla (Hortensia Group) 'Colorado'

A compact plant with large, light pink corymbs. A member of the RIVER-LINE series. Bred by Rampp Nursery, Germany, before 2000.

H. macrophylla (Hortensia Group) 'Compacta'

An invalid name used for more than one clone, such as 'Glowing Embers', 'Parzifal', 'Monink', and the trademark PINK AND PRETTY. The word *compacta* must not be used for names after 1959.

H. macrophylla (Hortensia Group) 'Constellation'

A vigorous-growing shrub up to 2 m (6.5 feet) high and wide, with large leaves. The very large corymbs are beautifully arranged, globular irregular, and up to 30 cm (12 inches) across. The sepals are dentate, dark pink.

H. macrophylla (Hortensia Group) 'Coquelicot'

An upright-growing plant with stout branches. It flowers early, June to July, with bright crimson corymbs. May no longer be available. Bred by Mouillère, France, in 1922.

H. macrophylla (Hortensia Group) 'Corsaire'

Flowers large, crimson. Bred by L. F. Cayeux of France, in 1937.

H. macrophylla (Hortensia Group) 'Côte d'Azur'

A compact shrub with usually violet flowerheads. Free-flowering. A member of the CITY-LINE series. Bred by Rampp Nursery, Germany, before 1999.

H. macrophylla (Hortensia Group) 'Covent Garden'

A shrub about 1.5 m (5 feet) high and wide, with sturdy dark green foliage. Corymbs pink or light blue, sepals serrate, Flowering time is from July to August. Bred by K. Wezelenburg & Sons, Boskoop, Netherlands, in 1937.

H. macrophylla (Hortensia Group) 'Cristel'

A medium-sized shrub, much like 'Brügg' and 'Burg Königstein'. The flowers are also very similar, leaves dark green. It is quite hardy. Bred by E. Haller, Switzerland. Name also spelled 'Christel'.

H. macrophylla (Hortensia Group) 'Daphne'

A compact shrub, with stout, short branches. Flowerheads numerous, red, becoming the color of ruby port in very acid soil. May be lost to cultivation. Bred by J. Wintergalen, Germany, in 1937.

Hydrangea macrophylla (Hortensia Group) 'Deutschland', C. Esveld Nurseries.

Hydrangea macrophylla (Hortensia Group) 'Draps Pink', Trelissick Garden.

Hydrangea macrophylla (Hortensia Group) 'Deutschland', Trelissick Garden.

Hydrangea macrophylla (Hortensia Group) 'Draps Wonder', Stourton House Flower Garden.

H. macrophylla (Hortensia Group) 'Deutschland'

A medium-sized shrub, sometimes up to 1.5 m (5 feet). The flowerheads are very large and firmly shaped, usually dark pink, turning blue when fed aluminum. Widely available. Suitable as a pot plant. Sometimes confused with 'Alpenglühen', but the sepals of 'Deutschland' are less serrate. Bred by D. Baardse, Netherlands, in 1921.

H. macrophylla (Hortensia Group) 'Directeur Vuillermet'

This cultivar has pale pink flowers in large corymbs. Bred by Mouillère, France, in 1913.

H. macrophylla (Hortensia Group) 'Dr. Bernhard Steiniger'

A shrubby plant, growing in the Shamrock collection. 'Green Shadow' is a mutant of this cultivar. Bred by August Steiniger, Germany.

H. macrophylla (Hortensia Group) 'Drachenfels'

A small and compact plant, very suitable as a houseplant. The corymbs are strongly blue. This plant flowers early and is easy to force. Raised at Friesdorf Research Station, now Landwirtschaftskammer Rheinland (Rhineland Agricultural Chamber), Germany.

H. macrophylla (Hortensia Group) 'Draps Pink'

A fast-growing shrub up to 1.5 m (5 feet). The flowerheads are dense and large, flattened, and an unusual mauve color. Sometimes it flowers twice in the season. According to the Shamrock list, it is synonymous with 'Forever Pink', which seems to be unlikely. Bred by L. J. Draps, Belgium, in 1938.

Hydrangea macrophylla (Hortensia Group) 'Elbtal', Trelissick Garden.

Hydrangea macrophylla (Hortensia Group) 'Eldorado', Kruidtuin.

Hydrangea macrophylla (Hortensia Group) 'Eldorado', Holehird Gardens.

H. macrophylla (Hortensia Group) 'Draps Wonder'

A very vigorous-growing shrub. Leaves almost orbicular, coarsely dentate. Flowerheads large, about 20 cm (8 inches) across, usually dark pink. According to the Shamrock list, it is synonymous with 'Forever Pink', which is not the case. Bred by Draps-Dom, Belgium, in 1951.

H. macrophylla (Hortensia Group) 'Duchess of York'

A slow-growing dwarf shrub with rose-pink flowers. Bred by H. J. Jones, United Kingdom, in 1927.

H. macrophylla (Hortensia Group) 'Düsseldorf'

A compact shrub, about 1 m (3 feet). Very free-flowering with small corymbs, large sepals, a rich dark pink. It has also a good autumn color, rose with greenish. In spite of its reputation, it is not widely available.

H. macrophylla (Hortensia Group) 'E. G. Hill'

A moderately growing shrub, very free-flowering, pink or blue, depending on soil acidity. Parentage: 'Otaksa' × 'Rosea'. 'Otaksa' was the first plant described by Thunberg and is now well known in horticulture. 'Rosea' is a descendant of 'Otaksa'. Bred by Lemoine Nursery, Nancy, France, in 1912.

H. macrophylla (Hortensia Group) 'Eclaireur'

A dwarf shrub, probably not exceeding 1 m (3 feet). It is free-flowering with vivid crimson flowerheads. Now quite rare in cultivation. Bred by Lemoine Nursery, Nancy, France, in 1913.

H. macrophylla (Hortensia Group) 'Elbe'

A dwarf plant. Flowerheads pale pink or dirty bluish. Rare in the trade. Bred by H. Schadendorff, Germany, in 1929.

H. macrophylla (Hortensia Group) 'Elbtal'

A sturdy compact plant with very dark green leaves. Flowerheads firm and large, pink, easily turning blue under the right conditions. Introduced by Rampp Nursery of Germany.

H. macrophylla (Hortensia Group) 'Eldorado'

Almost a miniature shrub, rarely exceeding 1 m (3 feet). Flowering occurs late in the season, with flattened corymbs, salmon pink. It is not a good plant on acid soils and is mainly interesting for its unusual color. Bred by Draps-Dom, Belgium, in 1950.

H. macrophylla (Hortensia Group) 'Electra'

An unknown cultivar, reported to have large pink corymbs. Bred by Henri Cayeux of France, in 1932.

Hydrangea macrophylla (Hortensia Group) 'Elmar Steiniger', Stourton House Flower Garden.

Hydrangea macrophylla (Hortensia Group) 'Emile Mouillèe', Maurice Foster garden.

H. *macrophylla* (Hortensia Group) 'Elite'
Corymbs dark pink.

H. *macrophylla* (Hortensia Group) 'Elmar'
A strong-growing plant with sturdy branches. Corymbs large, pink or purplish, not easily becoming blue. Bred by J. Wintergalen, Germany, in 1923. Offered by several Dutch nurseries (D. A. Koster, M. Koster and Sons) before the Second World War. RHS award: AM 1924.

H. *macrophylla* (Hortensia Group) 'Elmar Steiniger'
A compact plant up to 1.25 m (3.5 feet), with sturdy branches. Leaves are crinkled and tough. The flowerheads are about 15 cm (6 inches) across and an impressive glowing red color. This form is susceptible to several diseases and must be watched. Bred by August Steiniger, Germany, in 1955.

H. *macrophylla* (Hortensia Group) 'Emile Mouillère'
A medium-sized shrub. Flowerheads flattened, white with a blue eye. Not to be confused with 'Madame Emile Mouillère', which is very different. Bred by Mouillère, France.

Hydrangea macrophylla (Hortensia Group) 'Enziandom', Stourton House Flower Garden.

Hydrangea macrophylla (Hortensia Group) 'Enziandom', Stourton House Flower Garden.

Hydrangea macrophylla (Hortensia Group) 'Enziandom', Boering garden.

Hydrangea macrophylla (Hortensia Group) 'Essen', Research Station for Nursery Stock.

H. macrophylla (Hortensia Group) 'Emotion'

A firm shrub with tough branches. The corymbs are large and flattened, deep pink and free-flowering. Very rare in cultivation. Bred by L. F. Cayeux of France, in 1937.

H. macrophylla (Hortensia Group) 'Endless Summer'

A strong shrub with well-shaped large corymbs, pink or blue, flowering late from August to October. Found in Bailey's Nursery in Minnesota, United States. Mentioned by Michael Dirr (1998).

H. macrophylla (Hortensia Group) 'Enziandom'

A shrub up to 1.25 m (3.5 feet) with dark green foliage. The corymbs are relatively small, as are the sepals. The best blue hortensia we know. Also very suitable as a pot plant. It can be confused with 'Mathilde Gütges'. *Enziandom* means "Gentian dome." Bred by August Steiniger, Germany, in 1950.

H. macrophylla (Hortensia Group) 'Essen'

A medium-sized shrub. The flowerheads are usually fresh pink. Sepals are somewhat serrate. Bred by August Steiniger, Germany, in 1966.

H. macrophylla (Hortensia Group) 'Etanin'

A large well-branched shrub. Flowerheads flattened, easily becoming blue on acid soils. Sensitive to late frosts. Similar to 'Ayesha', which also has concave sepals. Origin French.

Hydrangea macrophylla (Hortensia Group) 'Eugen Hahn', Research Station for Nursery Stock.

Hydrangea macrophylla (Hortensia Group) 'Europa', Trelissick Garden.

Hydrangea macrophylla (Hortensia Group) 'Europa', C. Esveld Nurseries.

Hydrangea macrophylla (Hortensia Group) 'Europa', Arboretum de Dreijen.

H. macrophylla (Hortensia Group) 'Eugen Hahn'

Synonym: 'Steina 102'. A dense and compact plant. The leaves are conspicuously wrinkled. Flowers in corymbs, small, grayish wine red. Attractive and very free-flowering for a long time. Autumn colors are appealing. Not suitable as a pot plant. Bred by August Steiniger, Germany, in 1980.

H. macrophylla (Hortensia Group) 'Europa'

A strong-growing shrub up to 2 m (6.5 feet) or more. Its flowerheads are flattened and usually lilac-pink or dull purple. On alkaline soils it may be purplish red. Flowering occurs late in the summer. The sepals are heavily serrate. Not suitable as a pot plant. It can even be used as a hedging plant, due to its strong growth. This cultivar can be confused with the similar 'Hamburg' or 'Altona'. Also well-known for the quality of dried flowers. Autumn color can be very conspicuous. Bred by H. Schadendorff, Germany, in 1931. RHS Award: AGM 1992.

H. macrophylla (Hortensia Group) 'Excelsior'

According to Haworth-Booth, the corymbs are large, deep pink. Said to be a hybrid between *H. macrophylla* and *H. paniculata*, which is highly doubtful. Bred by Chaubert of France, in 1922.

H. macrophylla (Hortensia Group) 'Favorite'

A huge, well-growing shrub, probably up to 2 m (6.5 feet). Leaves large. Flowerheads also large, blue or pink. Needs a climate without extreme conditions. Bred by W. Binz, Rastatt, Germany, in 1934.

H. macrophylla (Hortensia Group) 'Felix'

A sturdy shrub with large, glossy foliage. The corymbs are large, creamy white. This cultivar is quite free-flowering. Bred by Moll Brothers, Germany, in 1934.

Hydrangea macrophylla (Hortensia Group) 'Fiancailles', Trelissick Garden.

Hydrangea macrophylla (Hortensia Group) 'Fisher's Silberblau', Trelissick Garden.

Hydrangea macrophylla (Hortensia Group) 'Fisher's Silberblau', Maurice Foster garden.

Hydrangea macrophylla (Hortensia Group) 'Flamboyant', Holehird Gardens.

H. macrophylla (Hortensia Group) 'Fiancailles'
A medium-sized shrub with stout, stiff branches and leaves. The corymbs are flattened and irregularly shaped and often lilac-pink. Name sometimes misspelled 'Franchailles'. Origin French.

H. macrophylla (Hortensia Group) 'Fireflame'
No description so far. Offered by Pépinières Thoby, France, and present in the Shamrock collection as 'Rosewarne'.

H. macrophylla (Hortensia Group) 'Fischer's Silberblau'
A conspicuous and curious cultivar, small, about 1 m (3 feet) high. Flowerheads globular, about 20 cm (8 inches) across, sepals rounded, a shiny silvery blue in acid soil, pink in alkaline soil. *Silberblau* means "silver blue." Bred by Fischer of Germany, in 1930, not by Moll Brothers of Germany.

H. macrophylla (Hortensia Group) 'Flambard'
A dwarf shrub, with compact corymbs, pink turning red in full sun. Bred by Henri Cayeux of France, in 1932.

H. macrophylla (Hortensia Group) 'Flambeau'
Flowers are vivid red. Bred by Cayeux of France, in 1931.

H. macrophylla (Hortensia Group) 'Flamboyant'
A medium-sized shrub about 1.5 m (5 feet) high. The flowerheads are rounded with vivid red sepals, which turn to a warm violet when fed with aluminum sulfate. Suitable for drying. Bred by Louis Mouillère, France, in 1946.

H. macrophylla (Hortensia Group) 'Flandria'
This cultivar is grown in the Shamrock collection. It may not be available.

Hydrangea macrophylla (Hortensia Group) 'Floralia', Research Station for Nursery Stock.

Hydrangea macrophylla (Hortensia Group) 'Floralia', Trelissick Garden.

Hydrangea macrophylla (Hortensia Group) 'Forever Pink', C. Esveld Nurseries.

H. macrophylla (Hortensia Group) 'Floralia'

A strong-growing impressive shrub, sometimes over 2 m (6.5 feet). The flowerheads are large, 18–20 cm (7–8 inches) across, a lovely pink, and curiously shaped, folded into a point. Flowering time is early in the season, often in June. Bred by Gijseling of Belgium, before 1958.

H. macrophylla (Hortensia Group) 'Florence Bolt'

A medium-sized shrub. The corymbs are large and soft pink or pale blue, depending on soil conditions. Bred by H. J. Jones, United Kingdom, in 1927.

H. macrophylla (Hortensia Group) 'Forever Pink'

A shrubby plant up to 1.2 m (3.5 feet). The flowerheads are almost perfectly rounded, rich pink. May be identical to 'Glowing Embers' or 'Draps Wonder'. The flowers turn blue easily despite the plant's name. Very useful as a pot plant and for dried flowers.

H. macrophylla (Hortensia Group) 'Fortschritt'

A medium-sized shrub up to 1.25 m (3.5 feet). Flowering time is early in the season, with cherry pink or purple corymbs. According to Haworth-Booth this cultivar should be popular in Australia. In Europe it is out of cultivation. Bred by F. Matthes, Germany, in 1931.

H. macrophylla (Hortensia Group) Frau series

The cultivars in this series have names starting with "Frau" and were developed by Hiroshi Ebihara of Tochigi, Japan, in 1994. They are distinguished from other cultivars by the strongly bicolored florets with sepals edged in white. Unfortunately, the plants in this beautiful series need much protection against cold and bad weather as the flowerbuds are easily destroyed by frost.

Hydrangea macrophylla (Hortensia Group) 'Frau Fujiyo', Trelissick Garden.

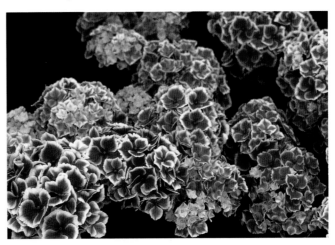

Hydrangea macrophylla (Hortensia Group) 'Frau Mariko', Floriade 2002.

Hydrangea macrophylla (Hortensia Group) 'Frau Fujiyo', Boering garden.

Hydrangea macrophylla (Hortensia Group) 'Frau Mikako', Floriade 2002.

Hydrangea macrophylla (Hortensia Group) 'Frau Fujiyo', C. Esveld Nurseries.

Hydrangea macrophylla (Hortensia Group) 'Frau Nobuko', Sir Harold Hillier Gardens and Arboretum.

Hydrangea macrophylla (Hortensia Group) 'Frau Taiko', Sir Harold Hillier Gardens and Arboretum.

Hydrangea macrophylla (Hortensia Group) 'Frau Yoshimi', Floriade 2002.

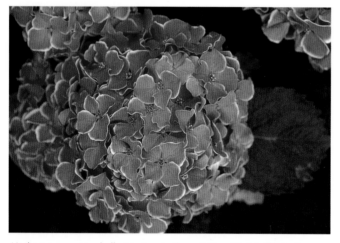

Hydrangea macrophylla (Hortensia Group) 'Frau Toshi', Floriade 2002.

Hydrangea macrophylla (Hortensia Group) 'Freudenstein', C. Esveld Nurseries.

Five or six cultivars are available in Europe under trademarked names: **'Frau Fujiyo'** (trademarked name LADY FUJIYO) and **'Frau Katsuko'** (trademarked name LADY KATSUKO), red or blue flowers edged white; **'Frau Mariko'** (trademarked name LADY MARIKO), lilac-violet flowers edged white; **'Frau Mikako'** (trademarked name LADY MIKAKO), pink flowers edged white; **'Frau Nobuko'** (trademarked name LADY NOBUKO), dark purple flowers edged white; and **'Frau Taiko'** (trademarked name LADY TAIKO), blue or pink flowers edged white. **'Frau Toshi'** and **'Frau Yoshimi'** have dark red flowers edged white but the sepals of 'Frau Yoshimi' are heavily serrate. Many of the other cultivars lack a description: 'Frau Haruko', 'Frau Iseko', 'Frau Kinue', 'Frau Megumi', 'Frau Ocho', 'Frau Ome', 'Frau Otaki', 'Frau Satshiko', 'Frau Sayoko', 'Frau Sumiko', and 'Frau Yoshiko'.

H. macrophylla (Hortensia Group) 'Freudenstein'

A large shrub up to 1.5 m (5 feet) high and wide. Free-flowering, with rounded corymbs. The sepals are evenly pink, sometimes with a hint of purple. An attractive, conspicuous cultivar. Bred by E. Haller, Switzerland, in 1960.

H. macrophylla (Hortensia Group) 'Friesdorf'

A medium-sized shrub with strong branches. The flower-heads are a shiny light red. Flowering time is August. Raised at Friesdorf Research Station, now Landwirtschaft-skammer Rheinland (Rhineland Agricultural Chamber), Germany.

H. macrophylla (Hortensia Group) 'Frillibet'

A large and robust shrub up to 1.5 m (5 feet). The corymbs are globular and frilly looking. The sepals open unevenly, from cream through pale blue to blue. Of course, this is not the case on alkaline soil. This cultivar is a branch sport of

Hydrangea macrophylla (Hortensia Group) 'Freudenstein', PlantenTuin de Oirsprong.

Hydrangea macrophylla (Hortensia Group) 'Frillibet', Maurice Foster garden.

Hydrangea macrophylla (Hortensia Group) 'Frillibet', Stourton House Flower Garden.

Hydrangea macrophylla (Hortensia Group) 'Frillibet', Sir Harold Hillier Gardens and Arboretum.

the well-known 'Madame Emile Mouillère', but despite its beauty is rarely available in the trade. According to an anecdote, the late Princess Margaret of England called her sister, Queen Elizabeth, Frillibet in her childhood. Selected by Michael Haworth-Booth in the 1950s (United Kingdom).

H. macrophylla (Hortensia Group) 'Fulgurant'

A strong-growing shrub with sturdy branches. The flowers are held in compact corymbs, deep pink or purple. Bred by L. F. Cayeux of France, in 1937.

H. macrophylla (Hortensia Group) 'Gartenbaudirektor Kühnert'

A medium-sized shrub up to 1.5 m (5 feet). The large, flattened corymbs have good blue sepals. On alkaline soil, however, they become muddy purplish. Flowering time is from August to September. Rare in the trade. The name is almost always wrongly spelled. Bred by F. Matthes, Germany, in 1926.

Hydrangea macrophylla (Hortensia Group) 'Gartenbaudirektor Kühnert', Trelissick Garden.

Hydrangea macrophylla (Hortensia Group) 'Générale Vicomtesse de Vibraye', Le Vastérival.

Hydrangea macrophylla (Hortensia Group) 'General Patton', Stourton House Flower Garden.

Hydrangea macrophylla (Hortensia Group) 'Générale Vicomtesse de Vibraye', Stourton House Flower Garden.

Hydrangea macrophylla (Hortensia Group) 'Gerda Steiniger', Arboretum de Dreijen.

H. macrophylla (Hortensia Group) 'Gärtnerbörse'

A compact plant suitable as a houseplant. The corymbs are large and light pink. With a lot of aluminum sulfate, it turns blue very easily. Raised at Friesdorf Research Station, now Landwirtschaftskammer Rheinland (Rhineland Agricultural Chamber), Germany, in 1991.

H. macrophylla (Hortensia Group) 'Générale Vicomtesse de Vibraye'

A large shrub with long and slender branches, up to 2 m (6.5 feet) or more, which makes the plant often untidy. The flowers are borne in rounded corymbs of 15–20 cm (6–8 inches). In harsh weather, such as wind and rain, branches bearing flowers bend to the ground and should be staked. The flowers easily turn light blue on acid soil, but are pink in more alkaline soils, despite the plant's "blue" reputation. It is a hybrid between 'Otaksa' and 'Rosea'. Long forgotten, this cultivar is back in cultivation. Bred by Emile Mouillère, France, in 1909. RHS Awards: AM 1947, AGM 1992.

H. macrophylla (Hortensia Group) 'General Geke'

According to Haworth-Booth, it is tall growing and has pink flowers.

H. macrophylla (Hortensia Group) 'General Patton'

A compact and dense shrub up to 1 m (3 feet). The flowers are borne in firm corymbs, rosy red or purple. Easy to grow and very healthy.

H. macrophylla (Hortensia Group) 'Gerda Steiniger'

A very tidy shrub up to 1.5 m (5 feet), with beautiful glossy green leaves. The corymbs are almost globular, up to 20 cm (8 inches) across, sepals large, crimson pink. This plant needs much space and tolerates full sun. The dried flowers can be used for decoration. Bred by August Steiniger, Germany, in 1946.

Hydrangea macrophylla (Hortensia Group) 'Gerda Steiniger', Trelissick Garden.

Hydrangea macrophylla (Hortensia Group) 'Gertrud Glahn', Maurice Foster garden.

Hydrangea macrophylla (Hortensia Group) 'Gertrud Glahn', H. J. van Paddenburgh garden.

Hydrangea macrophylla (Hortensia Group) 'Glärnisch', Trelissick Garden.

H. macrophylla (Hortensia Group) 'Germaine Mouillère'

A medium-sized shrub up to 1.25 m (3.5 feet). The flowers are greenish white, turning to pink. The sepals are serrate. Flowering time is in August. Bred by Mouillère, France, in 1920.

H. macrophylla (Hortensia Group) 'Gertrud Glahn'

A shrubby plant up to 1.5 m (5 feet). The flowerheads are relatively small, with clear pink sepals; they can easily turn blue if fed with aluminum sulfate. Very suitable as a pot plant. This older cultivar is still common in cultivation. Sometimes wrongly spelled as 'Gertrude Glahn'. Bred by F. Matthes, Germany, in 1923.

H. macrophylla (Hortensia Group) 'Gilles Goujon'

A large shrub up to 1.5 m (5 feet). The flowers are white, and set in small corymbs. It is free-flowering. Similar to 'Madame Gilles Goujon' but, according to Dussine, not identical. Origin French.

H. macrophylla (Hortensia Group) 'Glärnisch'

A medium-sized shrub up to 1.25 m (3.5 feet). The flowerheads are small, rosy red, packed in tight corymbs. The florets consist of four or five sepals, rounded and entire. It is a hybrid with 'Madame Henri Cayeux'. Named for a mountain in central Switzerland. Introduced by Federal Research Institute for Horticulture, Wädenswil, Switzerland, in 1964.

Hydrangea macrophylla (Hortensia Group) 'Glenfuren', Trelissick Garden.

Hydrangea macrophylla (Hortensia Group) 'Glowing Embers', Arboretum de Dreijen.

Hydrangea macrophylla (Hortensia Group) 'Gloria', Stourton House Flower Garden.

Hydrangea macrophylla (Hortensia Group) 'Goffersberg', courtesy Arborealis.

H. macrophylla (Hortensia Group) 'Glenfuren'

A large shrub, with large leaves and rosy red flowerheads. The sepals are acuminate. This plant can be found in Trelissick Garden. Origin United Kingdom.

H. macrophylla (Hortensia Group) 'Gloire de Vendôme'

Synonym: 'Brightness'. A dwarf shrub with stout, short branches. Flowers usually deep crimson, late in the season. Not free-flowering, but the flowers last very long. Bred by Louis Mouillère, France, in 1935. In cultivation before 1940 in some Dutch nurseries, such as M. Koster and Sons.

H. macrophylla (Hortensia Group) 'Gloria'

Synonym: 'Glory'. A dwarf shrub with pink or mauve sepals somewhat pointed on medium-sized corymbs. Bred by Henri Cayeux of France, in 1932.

H. macrophylla (Hortensia Group) 'Glory Blue' Anthony Bullivant, United Kingdom. Probably a blue expression of 'Gloria'.

H. macrophylla (Hortensia Group) 'Glowing Embers'

A medium-sized shrub up to 1.2 m (3.5 feet). Flowerheads very compact and rounded, a glowing deep pink, sepals 3 cm (1 inch). Free-flowering. Flowers held for a long time. Almost no fertile flowers. Bred in the United States or Canada before 1987. Introduced in Europe by D'n Oerts nurseries, Netherlands. It can easily be confused with the very similar 'Forever Pink'.

H. macrophylla (Hortensia Group) 'Godesberg'

Flowerheads large, sepals serrate, florets white with some green, becoming blue when fed with aluminum sulfate. This shrub is a challenge for amateurs to grow. Raised at Friesdorf Research Station, now Landwirtschaftskammer

Hydrangea macrophylla (Hortensia Group) 'Golacha', Trelissick Garden.

Hydrangea macrophylla (Hortensia Group) 'Goliath', Stourton House Flower Garden.

Hydrangea macrophylla (Hortensia Group) 'Goliath', Trelissick Garden.

Hydrangea macrophylla (Hortensia Group) 'Gonda', Holehird Gardens.

Rheinland (Rhineland Agricultural Chamber), Germany. Named for the village where the Research Station is located.

H. macrophylla (Hortensia Group) 'Goffersberg'

Up to 1.2 m (3.5 feet). Flowers in medium-sized corymbs, light pink or lilac with a yellowish hint, very free-flowering. Bred by E. Haller, Switzerland, in 1978. Named for a hill in northern Switzerland.

H. macrophylla (Hortensia Group) 'Golacha'

A neat shrub up to 1.25 m (3.5 feet). The flowerheads are bright red, in small corymbs, sepals acuminate. This plant grows in Trelissick Garden. Bred by Burncoose Nurseries, United Kingdom.

H. macrophylla (Hortensia Group) 'Goliath'

A vigorous-growing shrub up to 1.5 m (5 feet). Corymbs large, 20–22 cm (8–9 inches) across, sepals equally large, heart shaped, soft pink or pale blue. The plant needs some

protection in a harsh winter. According to Haworth-Booth, it is suitable for seaside plantings. Bred by F. Matthes, Germany, in 1923. It is available from several Dutch nurseries.

H. macrophylla (Hortensia Group) 'Gonda'

A large free-flowering shrub. Flowerheads large, white with a light blue hue, sepals tightly packed, greenish when opening. Bred by Holehird Gardens, United Kingdom.

H. macrophylla (Hortensia Group) 'Gottfried Keller'

A dwarf shrub. Very free-flowering. Corymbs large, bright rosy red. Flowering time is from August to September. Bred by Moll Brothers, Germany, in 1946. Named for a famous Swiss writer.

H. macrophylla (Hortensia Group) 'Graf Zeppelin'

A compact and sturdy plant. The flowerheads are deep pink, with serrate sepals. Bred by F. Matthes, Germany, in 1929. It was cultivated at several Dutch nurseries before 1935.

Hydrangea macrophylla (Hortensia Group) 'Grand Chef', Research Station for Nursery Stock.

Hydrangea macrophylla (Hortensia Group) 'Habsburg', Research Station for Nursery Stock.

Hydrangea macrophylla (Hortensia Group) 'Green Shadow', C. Esveld Nurseries.

Hydrangea macrophylla (Hortensia Group) 'Hamburg', Holehird Gardens.

H. macrophylla (Hortensia Group) 'Grand Chef'

A large shrub, with corymbs of the usual size, sepals tightly packed, usually pink. Bred by Dublanchet, France, in 1966.

H. macrophylla (Hortensia Group) 'Green Shadow'

A low-growing shrub with a compact habit. Free-flowering. Corymbs small, dark red. Less useful as a garden plant, but very nice for patios and as houseplant. It is a mutant of 'Dr. Bernhard Steiniger'. Raised by van Bergen/Hofstede of Netherlands.

H. macrophylla (Hortensia Group) 'Grünherz'

A medium-sized shrub, usually not exceeding 1 m (3 feet). Flowerheads rosy red, with a greenish center when opening. Raised at Friesdorf Research Station, now Landwirtschaftskammer Rheinland (Rhineland Agricultural Chamber), Germany, in 1991.

H. macrophylla (Hortensia Group) 'Gudrun'

A strong-growing shrub with stout branches. Flowerheads bright pink or blue, depending on soil conditions. Bred by J. Wintergalen, Germany, in 1923.

H. macrophylla (Hortensia Group) 'Gypsy'

According to Haworth-Booth, it is early flowering, with red flowers.

H. macrophylla (Hortensia Group) 'H. J. Jones'

A dwarf shrub less than 1 m (3 feet) high. Flowerheads flat, with rounded edges, usually deep pink. Bred by H. J. Jones, United Kingdom, in 1927. RHS Award: AM 1928.

H. macrophylla (Hortensia Group) 'Habsburg'

A shrub up to 1.5 m (5 feet). The flattened compact, rosy red corymbs consist of four or five sepals. Bred by E. Haller, Switzerland, in 1960.

Hydrangea macrophylla (Hortensia Group) 'Harlequin', C. Esveld Nurseries.

Hydrangea macrophylla (Hortensia Group) 'Harry's Pink Topper', C. Esveld Nurseries.

Hydrangea macrophylla (Hortensia Group) 'Harlequin', Maurice Foster garden.

Hydrangea macrophylla (Hortensia Group) 'Harry's Red', Maurice Foster garden.

H. macrophylla (Hortensia Group) 'Hamburg'

A strong-growing shrub with massive foliage. Flowers deep pink or purple, or blue, in huge corymbs, sepals serrate. Flowering time is from August to September. This cultivar is easily confused with its sister seedlings 'Europa' and 'Altona'. The differences are minor. Still in cultivation. Bred by H. Schadendorff, Germany, in 1931. RHS Award: AGM 1992. Rampp Nursery introduced a different plant (light pink flowers in a tight corymb) with same name in the CITY-LINE. This practice is against the ICNCP rules of nomenclature.

H. macrophylla (Hortensia Group) 'Harlequin'

A strong-growing shrub with many thin, but firm branches. The flowers are remarkably bicolored, the sepals are red with white margins. The whole plant looks somewhat untidy, but is interesting for its unique flowers. Synonyms: 'Bicolor', 'Sensation 75'. Sometimes misspelled as 'Harlekijn'. Bred by August Steiniger, Germany, in 1957.

H. macrophylla (Hortensia Group) 'Harry's Pink Topper'

A weak grower but suitable as a pot plant. The flowers are salmon pink and form a firm mophead.

H. macrophylla (Hortensia Group) 'Harry's Red'

A medium-sized shrub, with unusual flowerheads, unevenly shaped, sepals also equally uneven, bright red, with green center if still immature, not turning to blue.

Hydrangea macrophylla (Hortensia Group) 'Hatfield Rose', Trelissick Garden.

Hydrangea macrophylla (Hortensia Group) 'Heinrich Seidel', Trelissick Garden.

Hydrangea macrophylla (Hortensia Group) 'Heinrich Seidel', C. Esveld Nurseries.

Hydrangea macrophylla (Hortensia Group) 'Heinrichsburg', Trelissick Garden.

H. macrophylla (Hortensia Group) 'Hatfield Rose'

A moderate-growing shrub up to 1.25 m (3.5 feet). The corymbs are rounded and bright pink to red. The sepals are slightly cordate and serrate. Free-flowering. Usually flowering from August to September. Bred by Stuart Low of the United Kingdom. Named after Hatfield House, the home of the Marquess of Salisbury.

H. macrophylla (Hortensia Group) 'H. B. May'

A semidwarf shrub with a compact habit. The flowerheads are large, usually pink, turning blue easily under the right conditions. Bred by H. J. Jones, United Kingdom, in 1927. RHS Award: AM 1928.

H. macrophylla (Hortensia Group) 'Heidelberg'

A compact plant with large flowerheads, fresh pink with lighter center. Suitable as a houseplant and on patios. A member of the CITY-LINE series. Bred by Rampp Nursery, Germany, before 2000.

H. macrophylla (Hortensia Group) 'Heinrich Lambert'

A dwarf form with sturdy, short branches. The flowerheads are a vivid pink. Bred by A. Rosenkrantzer, Germany, in 1913.

H. macrophylla (Hortensia Group) 'Heinrich Seidel'

A large shrub up to 2 m (6.5 feet). The corymbs are flattened and the sepals are large. In its pink or cherry red form, it is a very nice cultivar. In acid soil, it becomes mauve, or brick red. Synonyms: 'Glory of Aalsmeer' (bred by D. Baardse, Netherlands, in 1930), 'Aalsmeer's Glory'. Very similar to 'Hobergine', which was introduced by Hofstede. Introduced by F. Matthes, Germany, in 1929 and probably renamed by Baardse in 1930.

Hydrangea macrophylla (Hortensia Group) 'Hobergine', Royal Horticultural Society Garden Wisley.

Hydrangea macrophylla (Hortensia Group) 'Holehird Purple', Holehird Gardens.

Hydrangea macrophylla (Hortensia Group) 'Holehird Purple', Holehird Gardens.

H. macrophylla (Hortensia Group) 'Heinrichsburg'

A compact shrub with large flattened corymbs, pale lilac or pink, sepals strongly serrate. Suitable as a pot plant. Bred by VEB of Germany, in 1983.

H. macrophylla (Hortensia Group) 'Helsinki'

A compact shrub with large corymbs, pink or dark pink. A good pot plant. A member of the CITY-LINE series. Bred by Rampp Nursery, Germany, before 1999.

H. macrophylla (Hortensia Group) 'Highland Glory'

According to Haworth-Booth, this plant is "tall, crimson." Bred by H. J. Jones, United Kingdom, in 1927.

H. macrophylla (Hortensia Group) 'Hobergine'

A medium-sized shrub up to 1 m (3 feet). The corymbs are purplish black, but can be dark lilac or bluish violet. Trade-marked name is HOVARIA. Bred by K. and W. Hofstede, Netherlands, in 1996.

H. macrophylla (Hortensia Group) 'Holehird Purple'

A small plant with small, deep violet flowers. The color is very stable. Found 20 years ago but not named until 2002 by Toni Lawson-Hall, United Kingdom. 'Hobergine' is very similar but a bit lighter shade of purple

Hydrangea macrophylla (Hortensia Group) 'Holstein', Trelissick Garden.

Hydrangea macrophylla (Hortensia Group) 'Homigo', C. Esveld Nurseries.

Hydrangea macrophylla (Hortensia Group) 'Holstein', Stourton House Flower Garden.

Hydrangea macrophylla (Hortensia Group) 'Homigo', Royal Horticultural Society Garden Wisley.

H. *macrophylla* (Hortensia Group) 'Holstein'

A medium-sized shrub up to 1.5 m (5 feet). The flower-heads are not very large, but single sepals are extremely large, up to 7 cm (2.75 inches), serrate. Color usually pink or sky blue. Flowering time is in August. Very free-flowering. Needs some shade for good results. Bred by H. Schadendorff, Germany, in 1928.

H. *macrophylla* (Hortensia Group) 'Homigo'

A tidy, compact shrub. The flowers change color twice, just like in 'Hobella' and 'Hopaline'. They start usually light blue and turn through green to cherry red. This cultivar is trademarked under the name HOVARIA. Bred by K. and W. Hofstede, Netherlands, in 1997.

H. *macrophylla* (Hortensia Group) 'Honnef'

A very low growing plant, suitable for house and patio. Flowerheads firm and tight, bright red without a trace of blue. A good cultivar for forcing. Raised at Friesdorf Research Station, now Landwirtschaftskammer Rheinland (Rhineland Agricultural Chamber), Germany.

Hydrangea macrophylla (Hortensia Group) 'Hopaline', C. Esveld Nurseries.

Hydrangea macrophylla (Hortensia Group) 'Hörnli', Arboretum de Dreijen.

Hydrangea macrophylla (Hortensia Group) 'Horben', Research Station for Nursery Stock.

Hydrangea macrophylla (Hortensia Group) 'Hörnli', Trelissick Garden.

H. macrophylla (Hortensia Group) 'Hopaline'

A compact shrub about 1 m (3 feet) high. The flowers change color twice, just like in 'Homingo' and 'Hobella'. They start green and turn pink to cherry red, eventually starting light blue. Trademarked name is HOVARIA. Bred by K. and W. Hofstede, Netherlands, in 1996.

H. macrophylla (Hortensia Group) 'Horben'

A dwarf shrub up to 1 m (3 feet). Foliage tight, dark green. The flowerheads are rounded, about 15 cm (6 inches) across, sepals entire, usually mauve-pink. Bred by E. Haller, Switzerland, in 1973.

H. macrophylla (Hortensia Group) 'Hörnli'

A dwarf form developed in Switzerland, rarely over 50 cm (20 inches) high. The flowerheads are pink, with elongated sepals, separated from each other. Free-flowering. Demands good care and hates excessive water. The name is often misspelled 'Hornli', 'Hornly', or even 'Mini-Hornli'. Introduced by Federal Research Institute for Horticulture, Wädenswil, Switzerland, in 1952.

Hydrangea macrophylla (Hortensia Group) 'Hortulanus H. Witte', courtesy Arborealis.

Hydrangea macrophylla (Hortensia Group) 'Hortulanus H. Witte', Research Station for Nursery Stock.

Hydrangea macrophylla (Hortensia Group) 'Immaculata', Holehird Gardens.

H. macrophylla (Hortensia Group) 'Hortulanus H. Witte'

A medium-sized shrub up to 1.25 m (3.5 feet). The small corymbs are flattened, pale pink to blue. Flowering time is early in the season. Bred by D. Baardse, Netherlands, in 1915. Named for a curator of the Botanic Gardens of Leiden University, Netherlands. This cultivar is now rare in the trade.

H. macrophylla (Hortensia Group) 'Hortus'

A compact shrub, probably not exceeding 1.25 m (3.5 feet). The flowerheads are deep pink or purple. Flowering time is from August to September. Bred by F. Matthes, Germany, before 1935.

H. macrophylla (Hortensia Group) 'Hoso hime azisai'

A cultivar with blue flattened corymbs. Origin Japanese.

H. macrophylla (Hortensia Group) 'Ice Blue'

A medium-sized shrub, unique in its production of well-formed corymbs of a very light blue to white, all through the season. Bred by Louisiana Nurseries, United States.

H. macrophylla (Hortensia Group) 'Immaculata'

A moderate-growing shrub, hardly more than 1 m (3 feet). When heavily pruned, the flowerheads can be very large, of the purest white. When not pruned, the corymbs are much smaller, but abundantly produced. In bad weather this plant is easily spoiled. It can be confused with 'Madame Emile Mouillère', a taller, less tidy plant. Bred by August Steiniger, Germany, in 1951.

H. macrophylla (Hortensia Group) 'Indigo'

A low, compact shrub. Flowerheads are very dark blue, when given heavy feedings of aluminum sulfate. Sepals are slightly serrate. Raised at Friesdorf Research Station, now Landwirtschaftskammer Rheinland (Rhineland Agricultural Chamber), Germany.

Hydrangea macrophylla (Hortensia Group) 'Intermezzo', Holehird Gardens.

Hydrangea macrophylla (Hortensia Group) 'Iris', courtesy Arborealis.

Hydrangea macrophylla (Hortensia Group) 'Intermezzo', Trelissick Garden.

Hydrangea macrophylla (Hortensia Group) 'Jeanne Pencher', Research Station for Nursery Stock.

H. macrophylla (Hortensia Group) 'Intermezzo'

A shrub of the usual size. Corymbs dark pink and flattened. Sepals are slightly dentate. In cultivation at Holehird Gardens, United Kingdom.

H. macrophylla (Hortensia Group) 'Iris'

A medium-sized shrub with weak branches. It flowers exceptionally long, from June to September. The sepals are large, saucer shaped and usually blue. Bred by August Steiniger, Germany, in 1960.

H. macrophylla (Hortensia Group) 'J. F. McCleod'

A shrub of moderate vigor, probably not exceeding 1.5 m (5 feet). The flowerheads are compact and vary from pink to blue. Bred by H. J. Jones, United Kingdom, in 1927.

H. macrophylla (Hortensia Group) 'Jeanne d'Arc'

A strong-growing shrub with slender branches. The stems are almost black. The flowerheads have pointed sepals. This sport of 'Thomas Hogg' was raised by Jacket of France, in 1896.

H. macrophylla (Hortensia Group) 'Jeanne Pencher'

A shrubby plant up to 1.2 m (3.5 feet). The flowerheads are not spectacular, the sepals are spade shaped. Flowers uneven in shape, usually purple. The name is also written as 'Jeannepencher'. Bred by Dublanchet of France.

Hydrangea macrophylla (Hortensia Group) 'Joseph Banks', Le Thuit Saint-Jean.

Hydrangea macrophylla (Hortensia Group) 'King George V', Royal Horticultural Society Garden Wisley.

Hydrangea macrophylla (Hortensia Group) 'Joseph Banks', Stourton House Flower Garden.

Hydrangea macrophylla (Hortensia Group) 'King George V', Research Station for Nursery Stock.

H. macrophylla (Hortensia Group) 'Joseph Banks'

A tall shrub with stout, sturdy branches. Foliage shiny green, elliptic. The flowerheads are very large, bun shaped, and white with very pale pink or blue. The sepals are slightly serrate. Suitable for seaside plantings. Tolerates lime. It only flowers from terminal buds. Sometimes mistaken for 'Otaksa' and also named 'Sir Joseph Banks'. Haworth-Booth classifies this cultivar in his Maritima Group. Origin Chinese; introduced in 1789.

H. macrophylla (Hortensia Group) 'Jupiter'

No description is available, although according to the Shamrock list, it is still in cultivation. Bred by K. Wezelenburg & Sons, Boskoop, Netherlands, in 1936.

H. macrophylla (Hortensia Group) 'Kasteln'

A large shrub, very free-flowering with large deep pink corymbs. In cultivation in the United States. Bred by E. Haller, Switzerland, in 1967.

H. macrophylla (Hortensia Group) 'King George'

A medium-sized shrub up to 1.25 m (3.5 feet). Corymbs well shaped, cherry pink or blue, depending on soil conditions. Flowering time is late in the season, usually from August to September. Bred by E. Draps, Belgium, in 1938. Not to be confused with 'King George V'.

Hydrangea macrophylla (Hortensia Group) 'Kluis Superba', Trelissick Garden.

H. macrophylla (Hortensia Group) 'Kluis Superba'

A very large bushy shrub, over 2 m (6.5 feet) high. The flowerheads are large, up to 18 cm (7 inches) across, tightly packed, pink, purple, or purplish pink, fading soon. Parentage: 'Maréchal Foch' × 'La Marne'. Still in cultivation but superseded by several newer forms. Bred by E. M. Kluis of Kluis & Koning, Boskoop, Netherlands, in 1932.

H. macrophylla (Hortensia Group) 'Kölner'

A compact shrub, not exceeding 1 m (3 feet). Flowerheads small, sepals serrate and usually royal blue. Raised at Friesdorf Research Station, now Landwirtschaftskammer Rheinland (Rhineland Agricultural Chamber), Germany, in 1965.

H. macrophylla (Hortensia Group) 'Koningin Emma'

A dwarf form with salmon pink flowers. Named for Queen Emma (d. 1934), wife of King William III of the Netherlands. Bred by D. A. Koster nursery (?), Netherlands, before 1940.

Hydrangea macrophylla (Hortensia Group) 'Kluis Sensation', courtesy Arborealis.

H. macrophylla (Hortensia Group) 'King George V'

Flowers rosy pink to dark lilac, sepals large and serrate. Very free-flowering. Suitable as a pot plant. RHS Award: AM 1927. Not to be confused with 'King George'. Sometimes sold as 'King George VII', though there never was a historical King George VII. Bred by H. J. Jones, United Kingdom, in 1927.

H. macrophylla (Hortensia Group) 'Kluis Sensation'

A medium-sized shrub up to 1.25 m (3.5 feet). The flowerheads are relatively small, but abundant, on every branch, light blue or more often pink. Flowering time is very early in the season, from June to mid-July. Bred by Kluis & Koning, Boskoop, Netherlands, before 1939.

Hydrangea macrophylla (Hortensia Group) 'Koningin Wilhelmina', Maurice Foster garden.

Hydrangea macrophylla (Hortensia Group) 'Koningin Wilhelmina', Holehird Gardens.

Hydrangea macrophylla (Hortensia Group) 'Koningin Wilhelmina', Trelissick Garden.

H. macrophylla (Hortensia Group) 'Koningin Wilhelmina'

A medium-sized shrub, not higher than 1.5 m (5 feet), with sturdy branches. Flowerheads of the usual size, an unusual color—salmon pink—turning violet when fed aluminum sulfate. Flowering time is from July to August. Named for Queen Wilhelmina of Netherlands, who reigned from 1898 until 1948. Bred by D. Baardse, Netherlands, in 1922.

H. macrophylla (Hortensia Group) 'Königswinter'

A small compact plant. Flowerheads flattened and large, sepals serrate, pure light red. Suitable for patios and balconies. Raised at Friesdorf Research Station, now Landwirtschaftskammer Rheinland (Rhineland Agricultural Chamber), Germany.

H. macrophylla (Hortensia Group) 'Kopenhagen'

A compact plant with red flowers. Suitable as a pot plant or in tubs. Bred by Rampp Nursery, Germany, before 1997.

H. macrophylla (Hortensia Group) 'Kristel'

Hydrangea macrophylla (Hortensia Group) 'La France', Research Station for Nursery Stock.

Hydrangea macrophylla (Hortensia Group) 'La France', C. Esveld Nurseries.

Hydrangea macrophylla (Hortensia Group) 'La France', Rinus Zwijnenburg, courtesy Arborealis.

H. macrophylla (Hortensia Group) 'Kristel'
A large shrub with firm corymbs dark pink to red depending on soil conditions. Differs from 'Brügg'. Bred in Germany (?).

H. macrophylla (Hortensia Group) 'Lafayette'
A slow-growing shrub with cherry pink flowers. Flowering time is from July to August. Free-flowering. Bred by Emile Mouillère, France, in 1932.

H. macrophylla (Hortensia Group) 'La France'
A medium-sized shrub up to 1.5 m (5 feet). It is a very free-flowering plant with masses of flowerheads, soft pink or more often light blue. The sepals are slightly serrate. Flowering time is from July to the end of August. The plant withstands harsh conditions in the garden. Bred by D. Baardse, Netherlands, in 1915. A second cultivar with the same name was bred by Emile Mouillère in France in 1913. It has disappeared from cultivation. It had white flowers with a colored eye and serrate sepals.

Hydrangea macrophylla (Hortensia Group) 'La Lande', Research Station for Nursery Stock.

Hydrangea macrophylla (Hortensia Group) 'La Marne', Holehird Gardens.

Hydrangea macrophylla (Hortensia Group) 'La Marne', Hydrangeum.

Hydrangea macrophylla (Hortensia Group) 'Lancelot', Trelissick Garden.

H. macrophylla (Hortensia Group) 'Lakmé'
Flowers creamy white turning to pink. Sepals serrate. Bred by Lemoine Nursery, Nancy, France, in 1920.

H. macrophylla (Hortensia Group) 'La Lande'
A small shrub up to 1 m (3 feet). Flowers large, up to 20 cm (8 inches) across, blue or pink. Foliage very nice. Synonym: 'Land Express'. Bred by Draps-Dom of Belgium.

H. macrophylla (Hortensia Group) 'La Lorraine'
Flowerheads very large, pink, sepals crimped. Origin French, before 1915. This plant was offered in 1936 by the old Dutch nursery of Ebbinge-Van Groos, in Boskoop.

H. macrophylla (Hortensia Group) 'La Marne'
A strong-growing plant up to 1.5 m (5 feet), with masses of large leaves. Its flowerheads are pale pink or light blue, flowering late in the season with very large corymbs composed of serrate sepals (we saw entire sepals, except in plants growing in the Hydrangeum collection in Belgium). Withstands harsh conditions and sea breezes. One of the best French introductions. Bred by Mouillère, France, in 1920 or 1917.

H. macrophylla (Hortensia Group) 'Lancelot'
A compact plant, probably not more than 1.25 m (3.5 feet). Conspicuous dark green leaves in abundance. Corymbs pink or blue, sepals heavily serrated, with a small central apex, overlapping, of irregular width. A good plant but difficult to obtain. Bred by J. Wintergalen, Germany, in 1920.

H. macrophylla (Hortensia Group) 'La Perle'
Flowers white with serrate sepals. Bred by Mouillère, France, in 1910.

Hydrangea macrophylla (Hortensia Group) 'Lausanne', Trelissick Garden.

H. macrophylla (Hortensia Group) 'Late Summer Magic'

A medium-sized shrub, with very large dark pink corymbs. Mentioned in Lancaster's book *What Plant Where*. Introduced by Roy Lancaster of the United Kingdom.

H. macrophylla (Hortensia Group) 'La Tosca'

A large stately plant with huge corymbs of light pink florets. Some florets have more sepals and appear to be doubled. Bred by Louisiana Nurseries, United States.

H. macrophylla (Hortensia Group) 'Lausanne'

A tall shrub up to 2 m (6.5 feet), with stout branches. Corymbs round, purple or purplish pink. Free-flowering. Flowering time is from August to September. Possibly identical to 'Blue Danube'.

H. macrophylla (Hortensia Group) 'Le Cygne'

A large shrub up to 2 m (6.5 feet), vigorous-growing. The flowerheads are small, white with a hint of pink. The sepals are serrate. Parentage: 'Madame Emile Mouillère' × 'Caprice'. Although it has been neglected, this plant is a worthwhile one for the garden. *Le Cygne* means "swan." 'Alberta' may be a synonym. Bred by Henri Cayeux of France, in 1919 or 1923.

Hydrangea macrophylla (Hortensia Group) 'Le Cygne', Boering garden.

Hydrangea macrophylla (Hortensia Group) 'Lemmenhof', Arboretum de Dreijen.

Hydrangea macrophylla (Hortensia Group) 'Leopold III', Trelissick Garden.

Hydrangea macrophylla (Hortensia Group) 'Lemmenhof', Trelissick Garden.

Hydrangea macrophylla (Hortensia Group) 'Le Reich', Maurice Foster garden.

H. *macrophylla* (Hortensia Group) 'Lemmenhof'

A strong-growing shrub about 150 high and wide. The round corymbs have four or five sepals. The main color is soft lilac, also pink in alkaline soil. A good plant but uncommon in the trade. Bred by August Steiniger, Germany, in 1947.

H. *macrophylla* (Hortensia Group) 'Leopold III'

A dwarf plant, barely exceeding 1 m (3 feet), with short and stout branches. The flowerheads open in July to August, are carmine red, and last quite a long time. Parentage: 'Merveille' × 'Rosabella'. Bred by D. Draps, Belgium, in 1936.

H. *macrophylla* (Hortensia Group) 'Le Reich'

A shrub with white flowerheads. The sepals are rounded, firmly packed, and slightly serrate. Bred by R. Michel Kerneur of France.

H. *macrophylla* (Hortensia Group) 'Le Vendômoise'

A vigorous-growing shrub, with stout branches. Flowerheads rose-pink. Bred by Emile Mouillère, France, in 1932.

H. *macrophylla* (Hortensia Group) 'Leuchtfeuer'

A very shapely, compact plant up to 1.5 m (5 feet). The flowerheads are medium sized, not too tight, dark crimson to red, sepals green when not yet open. Flowering time continues until October. The plant tolerates bad weather. It is suitable for forcing. *Leuchtfeuer* means "lighthouse." Bred by H. Dienemann, Germany, in 1962.

Hydrangea macrophylla (Hortensia Group) 'Leuchtfeuer', Research Station for Nursery Stock.

Hydrangea macrophylla (Hortensia Group) 'Liebegg', Research Station for Nursery Stock.

Hydrangea macrophylla (Hortensia Group) 'Leuchtfeuer', Floriade 2002.

Hydrangea macrophylla (Hortensia Group) 'Louis Mouillère', Stourton House Flower Garden.

H. macrophylla (Hortensia Group) 'Liebegg'

A low-growing shrub up to 1 m (3 feet). The flowerheads are beautifully deep pink, in rounded corymbs. Suitable as a pot plant. Bred by E. Haller, Switzerland, in 1967.

H. macrophylla (Hortensia Group) 'London'

A compact plant with firm light red corymbs. Suitable as a houseplant. Bred by Rampp Nursery, Germany, before 1999.

H. macrophylla (Hortensia Group) 'Lord Lambourne'

Flowers deep pink. Bred by H. J. Jones, United Kingdom, in 1927. RHS Award: AM 1927.

H. macrophylla (Hortensia Group) 'Louis Mouillère'

A medium-sized shrub. Flowerheads pure white, creamy greenish when opening. The sepals are serrate, the corymbs are about 15 cm (6 inches). Almost lost to cultivation, but worthy of a revival. Bred by Mouillère, France, in 1920.

H. macrophylla (Hortensia Group) 'Louis Pasteur'

A dwarf plant with large corymbs, deep pink. In cultivation at some Dutch nurseries such as M. Koster and Sons, Boskoop, before 1935.

H. macrophylla (Hortensia Group) 'Louis de Sauvage'

A compact, medium-sized shrub. Flowerheads cherry red, rarely blue, sepals irregularly shaped. Flowering time is from August to September. A very good cultivar for forcing as a pot plant. Bred by Mouillère, France, in 1928.

Hydrangea macrophylla (Hortensia Group) 'Madame A. Riverain', Holehird Gardens.

Hydrangea macrophylla (Hortensia Group) 'Madame Emile Mouillère', Trelissick Garden.

Hydrangea macrophylla (Hortensia Group) 'Madame A. Riverain', Stourton House Flower Garden.

Hydrangea macrophylla (Hortensia Group) 'Madame Emile Mouillère', Maurice Foster garden.

H. macrophylla (Hortensia Group) 'Madame A. Riverain'

A vigorous-growing shrub up to 2 m (6.5 feet). Flowerheads unshapely, usually pink or light blue. Similar to the well-known 'Générale Vicomtesse de Vibraye' and distinguished from it by the colored sepals. Bred by Mouillère, France, in 1909. Offered by several Dutch nurseries about 1932.

H. macrophylla (Hortensia Group) 'Madame Aimee Gijseling'

A medium-sized shrub up to 1.5 m (5 feet). The foliage is not of superior quality, but the flowers are attractive, with small but numerous corymbs. Sepals are fringed or serrate, reddish pink, tinged white. Bred by Gijseling of Belgium, about 1954.

H. macrophylla (Hortensia Group) 'Madame Emile Mouillère'

A vigorous-growing shrub up to 2 m (6.5 feet) high and wide. The branches are weak, so plants are often untidy. The flowerheads are numerous, of medium size, with sepals packed together, pure white, serrate, fading to light pink, long lasting. Flowering occurs in June. This hortensia is the best-known white cultivar. It is also suitable as a pot plant. Parentage: 'Mariesii Grandiflora' × 'Rosea'. Bred by Emile Mouillère, France, in 1909. RHS Awards: AM 1910, AM 1963, AGM 1992.

Hydrangea macrophylla (Hortensia Group) 'Madame Faustin Travouillon', Stourton House Flower Garden.

Hydrangea macrophylla (Hortensia Group) 'Madame Faustin Travouillon', Holehird Gardens.

Hydrangea macrophylla (Hortensia Group) 'Madame Faustin Travouillon', Trelissick Garden.

H. macrophylla (Hortensia Group) 'Madame Faustin Travouillon'

A vigorous-growing shrub up to 1.5 m (5 feet). The flowers are globular corymbs, fresh pink or light blue. Flowering time is from July to August. Easily confused with 'Générale Vicomtesse de Vibraye' but differing by its smaller flowers and foliage. Synonym: 'Peacock'. Bred by Travouillon-Buret of France, in 1930.

Hydrangea macrophylla (Hortensia Group) 'Madame G. F. Bier', Stourton House Flower Garden.

Hydrangea macrophylla (Hortensia Group) 'Madame Gilles Goujon', Research Station for Nursery Stock.

Hydrangea macrophylla (Hortensia Group) 'Madame G. F. Bier', courtesy Arborealis.

Hydrangea macrophylla (Hortensia Group) 'Madame J. de Smedt', Stourton House Flower Garden.

H. *macrophylla* (Hortensia Group) 'Madame Foucard'

A strong-growing tall shrub. The flowerheads are crimson pink or blue. Bred by Foucard of France, in 1912.

H. *macrophylla* (Hortensia Group) 'Madame G. Allery'

A free-flowering shrub, with bright pink or blue flowers. Bred by Mouillère, France, in 1910.

H. *macrophylla* (Hortensia Group) 'Madame G. F. Bier'

A dwarf shrub up to 1 m (3 feet). The flowerheads are small, usually deep pink or red, sometimes light blue, with serrate sepals. Flowering time is from July to August. An attractive cultivar. Suitable as a pot plant. Bred by E. Draps, Belgium, in 1938.

H. *macrophylla* (Hortensia Group) 'Madame G. Mornay'

A tall vigorous-growing shrub with stout branches The foliage is conspicuously dark green. Flowerheads large, pink, with serrate sepals. Bred by Louis Mouillère, France, in 1936.

H. *macrophylla* (Hortensia Group) 'Madame Gilles Goujon'

A medium-sized shrub. The large flowerheads have white sepals, which are pointed and wrinkled. Very free-flowering. Flowering time is August to September. Bred by Mouillère, France, in 1912.

H. *macrophylla* (Hortensia Group) 'Madame Henri Cayeux'

A medium-sized shrub with strong, sturdy branches. The corymbs are crimson or even darker red. Bred by Henri Cayeux of France, in 1932.

Hydrangea macrophylla (Hortensia Group) 'Madame J. de Smedt', Stourton House Flower Garden.

Hydrangea macrophylla (Hortensia Group) 'Madame Marie Bossard', Research Station for Nursery Stock.

H. macrophylla (Hortensia Group) 'Madame J. de Smedt'

A well-growing medium-sized shrub. Free-flowering with overcrowded bun-shaped flowerheads. Flowering occurs relatively late in the season, in August or September. Flowers usually pink, becoming gentian blue if fed with aluminum sulfate. Needs some shade for good results. Bred by E. Draps, Belgium, in 1938.

H. macrophylla (Hortensia Group) 'Madame Jobert'

A medium-sized shrub up to 1.25 m (3.5 feet). Foliage rounded, flowers in small corymbs, florets usually light blue or pink. It is a nice compact plant. Origin French, before 1956.

H. macrophylla (Hortensia Group) 'Madame Legoux'

A tall vigorous-growing shrub. The flowerheads are white with a hint of blue. This plant is not very free-flowering. Flowering time is September. Bred by Mouillère, France, in 1912.

H. macrophylla (Hortensia Group) 'Madame Lucienne Chaurée'

Sepals pink, serrate. Synonym: 'Mademoiselle Lucienne Chaurée'. Bred by Mouillère, France, in 1923.

H. macrophylla (Hortensia Group) 'Madame Maurice Hamard'

Stems strong, flowerheads pink. Easy to force. Changes color well. Mentioned in old Dutch nursery catalogs. Probable synonym: 'Madame H. Hamar'. Bred by Mouillère, France, in 1909.

H. macrophylla (Hortensia Group) 'Madame Marie Bossard'

A medium-sized shrub with large flattened corymbs, pink or purplish pink. Bred by Dublanchet of France.

H. macrophylla (Hortensia Group) 'Madame Nicolaus Lambert'

Corymbs large, pink. Bred by J. Lambert and Sons, Germany.

H. macrophylla (Hortensia Group) 'Madame Paul Gianoli'

A medium-sized shrub. The corymbs have serrate sepals, of a warm pink, which last for a long time. Bred by Louis Mouillère, France, in 1938.

H. macrophylla (Hortensia Group) 'Madame Philippe de Vilmorin'

A moderate-growing shrub up to 1.5 m (5 feet). The flowerheads are large, deep pink, with serrate sepals. Flowering time is from August to September. Bred by Mouillère, France, in 1926. Offered by some Dutch nurseries before the Second World War.

Hydrangea macrophylla (Hortensia Group) 'Madame Plumecoq', Research Station for Nursery Stock.

Hydrangea macrophylla (Hortensia Group) 'Magicien', Research Station for Nursery Stock.

Hydrangea macrophylla (Hortensia Group) 'Madame Renée Bossard', Research Station for Nursery Stock.

Hydrangea macrophylla (Hortensia Group) 'Maman', Hydrangeum.

H. macrophylla (Hortensia Group) 'Madame Plumecoq'

A medium-sized shrub up to 1.25 m (3.5 feet) at the most. The flowerheads are light pink, sepals entire, rounded. Flowering time is in August. Bred by Draps-Dom of Belgium.

H. macrophylla (Hortensia Group) 'Madame Rabot'

Offered by Dutch nurseries ca. 1932. Its special virtue was that it became blue very easily. Synonym: 'Maman Rabot'. Origin French.

H. macrophylla (Hortensia Group) 'Madame Renée Bossard'

A compact rounded shrub up to 1.5 m (5 feet). The flowerheads are small, about 15 cm (6 inches) across, pinkish purple, and susceptible to late frost. Bred by Dublanchet, France, in 1964.

H. macrophylla (Hortensia Group) 'Madame Truffaut'

A slow-growing shrub up to 1.5 m (5 feet). The flowerheads are medium-sized, the sepals are frilly-edged, pink or light blue. Immature flowers have an attractive white center. Bred by Henri Cayeux of France.

H. macrophylla (Hortensia Group) 'Madame de Vries'

A huge shrub up to 2 m (6.5 feet). Flowers greenish yellow at first, becoming pale pink or exceptionally light blue on very acid soils. This cultivar resembles 'Joseph Banks' but is smaller. Bred by D. Baardse, Netherlands, in 1915 and cultivated before World War II.

Hydrangea macrophylla (Hortensia Group) 'Marathon', C. Esveld Nurseries.

H. macrophylla (Hortensia Group) 'Mademoiselle Renée Gaillard'

Flowers milky-white, sepals frilly. Bred by Chaubert of France, in 1919. In cultivation at Ebbinge-Van Groos nursery and G. W. van Gelderen, both in Boskoop, Netherlands, before 1940.

H. macrophylla (Hortensia Group) 'Mademoiselle Renée Jacquet'

Flowers pink. Bred by Mouillère, France, in 1920.

H. macrophylla (Hortensia Group) 'Madrid'

A compact plant with clear pink, large corymbs. Suitable as a houseplant. Synonym: 'Rama'. Bred by Rampp Nursery, Germany, before 1995.

H. macrophylla (Hortensia Group) 'Magicien'

A medium-sized shrub with flattened corymbs, sepals large, margins entire, rosy red. Bred by Cayeux, France, in 1967.

H. macrophylla (Hortensia Group) 'Maman'

A shrub up to 1.5 m (5 feet) or slightly more. The flowerheads are about 15 cm (6 inches) across, uniformly colored a very good red on alkaline soils. The sepals are even in size and look velvety. This cultivar is one of the best reds. It is suitable for forcing and as a pot plant. Bred by Dublanchet of France.

H. macrophylla (Hortensia Group) 'Mamembara'

A plant about 1 m (3 feet) high and wide. The flowerheads are large mopheads, usually light blue. Origin Japanese.

H. macrophylla (Hortensia Group) 'Marathon'

A compact plant with clear red flowerheads. It flowers poorly as a young plant but shows good autumn colors. Bred in Netherlands before 1967. Offered by the nursery of K. Wezelenburg & Sons, Boskoop, Netherlands.

Hydrangea macrophylla (Hortensia Group) 'Maréchal Foch', H. J. van Paddenburgh garden.

Hydrangea macrophylla (Hortensia Group) 'Maréchal Foch', Research Station for Nursery Stock.

Hydrangea macrophylla (Hortensia Group) 'Marie-Claire', Holehird Gardens.

H. macrophylla (Hortensia Group) 'Maréchal Foch'

A medium-sized shrub up to 1.25 m (3.5 feet). Free-flowering. The flowerheads are real mopheads, borne on terminal and lateral branches. The sepals do not overlap. One of the best cultivars for blue flowers, though the pink form is also attractive. Suitable as a pot plant. Bred by Mouillère, France, in 1924. RHS Award: AM 1922.

H. macrophylla (Hortensia Group) 'Marie-Claire'

A medium-sized shrub, usually wider than high. Flowerheads small, light blue or light pink with darker center. The sepals have narrow edges and are slightly serrate with an acuminate apex. Leaves rounded. Origin French.

H. macrophylla (Hortensia Group) 'Marie Louise Dussine'

A large shrub up to 2 m (6.5 feet). The flowerheads are also large, up to 30 cm (12 inches) across, pink or light blue. They are especially suitable for drying. A sport of 'Rosita'. Bred by Dublanchet of France.

Hydrangea macrophylla (Hortensia Group) 'Marquise', Research Station for Nursery Stock.

Hydrangea macrophylla (Hortensia Group) 'Masja', Boering garden.

Hydrangea macrophylla (Hortensia Group) 'Mascotte', Research Station for Nursery Stock.

H. macrophylla (Hortensia Group) 'Marquise'

A moderately strong-growing shrub up to 1.5 m (5 feet). The untidy flowerheads are light pink, with only a few sepals per corymb, on long stalks or petioles. Bred by Henri Cayeux of France, before 1964.

H. macrophylla (Hortensia Group) 'Mars'

A huge plant exceeding 1.5 m (5 feet). Depending on soil conditions, the flowers are deep pink or purple. Bred by K. Wezelenburg & Sons, Netherlands, in 1936. A second cultivar with the same name has salmon red florets and small sepals with narrow white edges; it comes from Rampp Nursery, Germany, and is suitable as a pot plant. Of course, it is against the rules of the ICNCP for two cultivars to have the same name.

H. macrophylla (Hortensia Group) 'Mascotte'

A well-growing shrub up to 1.5 m (5 feet). The flowerheads are small, 10–15 cm (4–6 inches) across, pinkish lilac. Very hardy. Needs maintenance to keep it tidy. Bred by Emile Mouillère, France, in 1952.

H. macrophylla (Hortensia Group) 'Masja'

A low, compact shrub up to 1 m (3 feet). Flowerheads perfectly rounded, a very uniform warm red color. Frequently flowers twice a year. Very suitable as a pot plant. A sport of the well-known 'Alpenglühen', it is extremely similar to, if not identical to, 'Sibylla'. Origin Netherlands (?), before 1977. Gold Medal, 1976, at Flora Nova Show of the Royal Boskoop Horticultural Society and named the best new plant.

H. macrophylla (Hortensia Group) 'Matador'

A sturdy shrub, with stout branches, up to 1.5 m (5 feet). It is free-flowering, usually crimson. Bred by Henri Cayeux of France, in 1928.

Hydrangea macrophylla (Hortensia Group) 'Mathilde Gütges', Spinners Garden.

Hydrangea macrophylla (Hortensia Group) 'Mathilde Gütges', Trelissick Garden.

Hydrangea macrophylla (Hortensia Group) 'Mathilde Gütges', Holehird Gardens.

Hydrangea macrophylla (Hortensia Group) 'Max Loebner', Trelissick Garden.

H. macrophylla (Hortensia Group) 'Mathilde Gütges'

A dwarf plant hardly reaching 1 m (3 feet). It forms flattened flowerheads, with slightly serrate sepals, pink or blue. This cultivar seems to change color very easily. It is not easily obtainable in the trade. Bred by August Steiniger, Germany, in 1946.

H. macrophylla (Hortensia Group) 'Mavis'

A shrub of moderate growth. The flowers are pink or eventually deep blue.

H. macrophylla (Hortensia Group) 'Max Loebner'

A strong-growing shrub. Florets light red to pink, sepals acuminate and overlapping. Bred by August Steiniger, Germany, in 1952.

H. macrophylla (Hortensia Group) 'Mein Ideal'

A tall vigorous-growing shrub, easily more than 1.5 m (5 feet) high. Flowerheads bright pink to mauve. Bred by F. Matthes, Germany, in 1924. In cultivation in Netherlands before 1935.

Hydrangea macrophylla (Hortensia Group) 'Mein Liebling', Maurice Foster garden.

Hydrangea macrophylla (Hortensia Group) 'Merveille', Trelissick Garden.

Hydrangea macrophylla (Hortensia Group) 'Merritt's Supreme', Holehird Gardens.

H. *macrophylla* (Hortensia Group) 'Mein Liebling'

A dwarf shrub, with short branches. Flowers a good pale pink, similar to those of 'Otaksa', sepals strongly serrate. Flowering time is in June. It is difficult to get this plant to bear blue flowers. *Mein liebling* means "my darling." Bred by F. Matthes, Germany, in 1926.

H. *macrophylla* (Hortensia Group) 'Mephisto'

A medium-sized shrub. The corymbs are brilliant red. This cultivar is very suitable for forcing and is a good house-plant. Bred by Draps-Dom, Belgium, about 1960.

H. *macrophylla* (Hortensia Group) 'Merritt's Beauty'

A low-growing compact shrub. The leaves are glossy green. Flowers are large mopheads, dark pink to red. Bred by Louisiana Nurseries, United States.

H. *macrophylla* (Hortensia Group) 'Merritt's Supreme'

A compact shrub, not exceeding 1.5 m (5 feet) high. Branches are thick and sturdy. The flowerheads have five or six sepals, making the flower look double, though the sepals are in fact overlapping. Color purplish rose. Bred by Louisiana Nurseries, United States.

H. *macrophylla* (Hortensia Group) 'Merkur'

A semidwarf shrub, rarely over 1 m (3 feet) high. The flow-erheads are large, sepals heart shaped, and pointed, dark red. This cultivar sometimes flowers twice a year. Bred by Brügger, Germany, in 1978.

H. *macrophylla* (Hortensia Group) 'Merveille'

A well-growing shrub up to 1.25 m (3.5 feet). It has many desirable characters, such as stout and short branches, very beautiful dark reddish green foliage, and shapely flower-heads of an attractive pink. Flowering time is from July to August, but the flowers are not long lasting. This cultivar is considered the most important novelty between the two World Wars. It gave birth to several sports. Bred by Henri Cayeux of France, in 1927.

Hydrangea macrophylla (Hortensia Group) 'Merveille Sanguine', Maurice Foster garden.

Hydrangea macrophylla (Hortensia Group) 'Merveille Sanguine', courtesy Arborealis.

Hydrangea macrophylla (Hortensia Group) 'Merveille Sanguine', C. Esveld Nurseries.

H. macrophylla (Hortensia Group) 'Merveille Sanguine'

A sport from 'Merveille', obtained 10 years later. The branches are also stout, the foliage even darker, and really maroon, turning to a glowing crimson red in early autumn. The flowers are blood red in medium-sized corymbs. This very conspicuous plant is well worth a place in the garden. Trademarked name is BRUNETTE. Bred by Henri Cayeux of France, in 1939.

H. macrophylla (Hortensia Group) 'Mesdag'

A medium-sized shrub up to 1.25 m (3.5 feet). Flowers pink. Bred by K. Wezelenburg & Sons, Boskoop, Netherlands, in 1927. Named for a famous Dutch painter.

H. macrophylla (Hortensia Group) 'Mevrouw Baardse'

A small plant with stiff, short branches. Flowerheads usually bright pink or blue. An attractive cultivar. Bred by D. Baardse, Netherlands, in 1918. RHS Award: AM 1927.

H. macrophylla (Hortensia Group) 'Mignon'

A dwarf shrub, about 1 m (3 feet) high. Flowerheads pink. Bred by D. Baardse, Netherlands, in 1915.

H. macrophylla (Hortensia Group) 'Mike's Red'

A free-flowering dwarf plant with large red corymbs, somewhat flattened. Bred by Louisiana Nurseries, United States.

H. macrophylla (Hortensia Group) 'Mirai'

A low shrub up to about 1 m (3 feet). The new leaves are bronze-green. The sepals are white with conspicuous red margins, firmly packed to a round flowerhead. This plant needs protection in harsh weather. Among the group of cultivars influenced by 'Kiyosumi', 'Mirai' is one of the few mopheads; the majority are lacecaps. Bred by Yatabe Mototeru of Japan.

Hydrangea macrophylla (Hortensia Group) 'Mignon', Trelissick Garden.

Hydrangea macrophylla (Hortensia Group) 'Miss Belgium', Holehird Gardens.

Hydrangea macrophylla (Hortensia Group) 'Mirai', C. Esveld Nurseries.

Hydrangea macrophylla (Hortensia Group) 'Miss Belgium', Trelissick Garden.

H. macrophylla (Hortensia Group) 'Miss Belgium'

A medium-sized shrub about 1.25 m (3.5 feet) high. It is early flowering, with purplish carmine flowerheads. In acid soils, flower color is a dirty purplish blue. Suitable as a pot plant. Bred by E. Draps, Belgium, in 1935.

H. macrophylla (Hortensia Group) 'Miss Hepburn'

A shrub up to 1.25 m (3.5 feet) The flowers are large, pink to dark pink with a purplish hue. Flowering time is from June to July or somewhat later. Susceptible to aphids. Synonym: 'Mrs. W. J. Hepburn'. Bred by H. J. Jones, United Kingdom, in 1927.

Hydrangea macrophylla (Hortensia Group) 'Miss Hepburn', Trelissick Garden.

H. macrophylla (Hortensia Group) 'Miss Phyllis Cato'

A compact plant, maybe up to 1 m (3 feet). Flowering occurs early in the season, from the end of June to July. The large flowerheads are warm pink or eventually blue. Bred by H. J. Jones, United Kingdom, in 1927.

Hydrangea macrophylla (Hortensia Group) 'Monink', Research Station for Nursery Stock.

Hydrangea macrophylla (Hortensia Group) 'Montfort Perle', courtesy Arborealis.

Hydrangea macrophylla (Hortensia Group) 'Montfort Perle', Research Station for Nursery Stock.

Hydrangea macrophylla (Hortensia Group) 'Morgenrot', Trelissick Garden.

H. macrophylla (Hortensia Group) 'Monink'
A compact, free-flowering plant with pink flowerheads. Trademarked name is PINK AND PRETTY. Bred by Monrovia Nurseries, California, United States, in 1986.

H. macrophylla (Hortensia Group) 'Monred'
A compact, free-flowering plant with red flowerheads. Trademarked named is RED AND PRETTY. Bred by Monrovia Nurseries, California, United States, in 1986.

H. macrophylla (Hortensia Group) 'Monrey'
A compact, free-flowering plant with tight trusses. Trademarked name is BUTTONS 'N RED. Bred by Monrovia Nurseries, California, United States, in 1986.

H. macrophylla (Hortensia Group) 'Monsieur Ghys'
Flowers large, pink. Bred by Mouillère, France, in 1912.

H. macrophylla (Hortensia Group) 'Montfort Perle'
A shrub up to 1.25 m (3.5 feet) high. The flowers are rosy red, in tight round corymbs. The single florets are 5 cm (2 inches), sepals serrate. Also spelled 'Monfort Pearl'. Bred by Brügger, Germany, in 1946.

H. macrophylla (Hortensia Group) 'Montgomery'
A medium-sized shrub up to 1.5 m (5 feet). The flowerheads are small but of unusual colors. In alkaline soil they are ruby red to beet red, in acid soil, magenta purple with a blue center. Probable synonym: *H. macrophylla* (Hortensia Group) 'Monty'. Bred by Draps-Dom, Belgium, in 1945.

H. macrophylla (Hortensia Group) 'Morgenrot'
A shrub up to 1.25 m (3.5 feet). The flowerheads are large, glowing rosy red with entire sepals, some sepals partly and slightly serrate. *Morgenrot* means "morning red." Bred by August Steiniger, Germany, in 1950.

Hydrangea macrophylla (Hortensia Group) 'Mousseline', Holehird Gardens.

Hydrangea macrophylla (Hortensia Group) 'Mousseline', H. J. van Paddenburgh garden.

H. macrophylla (Hortensia Group) 'Moskau'

A compact plant with large flowerheads, dark red. A member of the CITY-LINE series. Bred by Rampp Nursery, Germany, before 1995.

H. macrophylla (Hortensia Group) 'Mousseline'

A large shrub exceeding 1.5 m (5 feet). It flowers for a long time, from June to August. Flowerheads are pale blue or pink, with a lighter center, lasting well. This seedling from 'Rosea', one of the first introductions to Europe, is a valuable cultivar but not widespread. Selected by E. Lemoine of Nancy, France, in 1909.

H. macrophylla (Hortensia Group) 'Mrs. Alice Blandy'

Flowers pink. Bred by H. J. Jones, United Kingdom, in 1927.

H. macrophylla (Hortensia Group) 'Mrs. A. Simmonds'

Sepals pink, serrate. Bred by H. J. Jones, United Kingdom, in 1927. RHS Award: AM 1928.

H. macrophylla (Hortensia Group) 'Mrs. Charles Davis'

A strong-growing shrub. The flowerheads are deep pink, sepals serrate. Bred by H. J. Jones, United Kingdom, in 1927.

H. macrophylla (Hortensia Group) 'Mrs. H. J. Jones'

A small but vigorous-growing shrub. The flowerheads are pink, sepals serrate. RHS Award: AM 1926. This cultivar is proof that Jones and Mouillère knew each other! Bred by Mouillère, France, in 1923.

H. macrophylla (Hortensia Group) 'Mrs. Kumiko'

A compact plant up to 1.25 m (3.5 feet). Corymbs large, flattened, tightly held, single sepals are serrate. Flower color is lilac-pink to purple with hints of yellow in the center. Trademarked name is ASKA. Origin Japanese. Not included in LADIES series.

H. macrophylla (Hortensia Group) 'Mrs. L. J. Endtz'

A medium-sized shrub with pink flowers. Mr. Endtz was a well-known nurseryman in Boskoop, but the nursery no longer exists. Bred by H. J. Jones, United Kingdom, in 1927.

H. macrophylla (Hortensia Group) 'Münster'

A slow- and low-growing cultivar. Flowering time is from July to August. Large corymbs with violet velvety crimson or deep blue flowers. Requires attention in the garden. Bred by J. Wintergalen, Germany, in 1937.

H. macrophylla (Hortensia Group) 'Myosotis'

A strong-growing bush. The flowerheads are small, the florets are pink. This is the counterpart of 'Azur'. Raised at Friesdorf Research Station, now Landwirtschaftskammer Rheinland (Rhineland Agricultural Chamber), Germany, before 1965.

Hydrangea macrophylla (Hortensia Group) 'Niedersachsen', Trelissick Garden.

Hydrangea macrophylla (Hortensia Group) 'Nigra', Royal Horticultural Society Garden Wisley.

Hydrangea macrophylla (Hortensia Group) 'Nigra', Holehird Gardens.

Hydrangea macrophylla (Hortensia Group) 'Nigra', Stourton House Flower Garden.

H. macrophylla (Hortensia Group) 'Niedersachsen'

A tall vigorous-growing shrub exceeding 1.5 m (5 feet). Its corymbs are packed with entire sepals, pale pink, or blue if fed with aluminum sulfate. Flowering time is from August to September. Needs some shade for good results. Bred by J. Wintergalen, Germany, in 1914. RHS Award: AM 1968.

H. macrophylla (Hortensia Group) 'Nigra'

A huge shrub with slender purplish black branches (a distinguishing characteristic), sometimes up to 2 m (6.5 feet). The flowerheads are untidy, pale pink or lightest blue, sepals entire. Flowering time is from August to September. This interesting plant was forgotten for many years but is again available. Synonyms: 'Cyanoclada', 'Kuro jaku', 'Mandshurica'. Imported from China to the United States by E. H. Wilson in 1853. RHS Award: FCC 1895.

Hydrangea macrophylla (Hortensia Group) 'Nikko Blue', Holehird
Gardens.

Hydrangea macrophylla (Hortensia Group) 'Nikko Blue', Arboretum
de Dreijen.

Hydrangea macrophylla (Hortensia Group) 'Nymphe', Holehird
Gardens.

H. macrophylla (Hortensia Group) 'Nikko Blue'
A medium-sized shrub up to 1.5 m (5 feet). The branches
are thin. Flowerheads very numerous, rounded, 15 cm (6
inches) across, usually light blue, pink on alkaline soils,
sepals entire. It needs a year or so to become established in
the garden. Also requires some shade. In these conditions it
is very free-flowering. Origin Japanese, before 1970.

H. macrophylla (Hortensia Group) 'Nymphe'
A dwarf shrub not more than 1.25 m (3.5 feet) high. It
flowers abundantly with pure white florets, sepals heavily
serrate. The flowerheads become mottled with red dots.
Flowering time is from June to July. The plant does not tol-
erate bad weather, especially heavy rain. Suitable as a pot
plant. Probable synonym: 'Pax'. Bred by H. Dienemann,
Germany, in 1965.

H. macrophylla (Hortensia Group) 'Odense'
A compact plant very suitable as a pot plant. Flowerheads
large, rosy purple. A member of the CITY-LINE series.
Bred by Rampp Nursery, Germany, before 1995.

Hydrangea macrophylla (Hortensia Group) 'Oregon Pride', Sir Harold Hillier Gardens and Arboretum.

Hydrangea macrophylla (Hortensia Group) 'Oregon Pride', Holehird Gardens.

Hydrangea macrophylla (Hortensia Group) 'Otaksa', Research Station for Nursery Stock.

H. macrophylla (Hortensia Group) 'Oregon Pride'

A huge shrub with very dark violet branches, much like the well-known 'Nigra'. Flowers borne in flat corymbs, lilac purple. The leaves are dark green with a purple hint. Origin United States. Possibly introduced by Greer Gardens, Eugene, Oregon.

H. macrophylla (Hortensia Group) 'Oriental'

A firm and strong shrub. Not very free-flowering. Bears large pink or bluish corymbs in August. Suitable for seaside plantings. Bred by Chaubert, France, in 1922. A second cultivar with the same name was bred by Henri Cayeux of France, in 1935. It has strong branches with large cherry pink to crimson corymbs.

H. macrophylla (Hortensia Group) 'Orion'

A large plant, wider than high. Flowers bicolor, dark red with wide white edges. A member of the STAR-LINE series. Bred by Rampp Nursery, Germany, before 2000.

H. macrophylla (Hortensia Group) 'Ornement'

Large corymbs with serrate sepals, purplish pink. Bred by Lemoine Nursery, Nancy, France, in 1909. RHS Award: AM 1910.

H. macrophylla (Hortensia Group) 'Oslo'

A compact plant with large light pink corymbs, sepals serrate. Very suitable as a house-plant. A member of the CITY-LINE series. Bred by Rampp Nursery, Germany, before 1995.

H. macrophylla (Hortensia Group) 'Otaksa'

A large shrub up to 2 m (6.5 feet) or eventually more. The foliage is almost orbicular. The flowerheads are large, about 20 cm (8 inches) across, light pink or light blue, sepals entire. Flowering time is from July to August. Very free-flowering. The autumn color of the sepals is white with red dots. This form is most interesting for its history. It is iden-

Hydrangea macrophylla (Hortensia Group) 'Otaksa', Trelissick Garden.

Hydrangea macrophylla (Hortensia Group) 'Otaksa', PlantenTuin de Oirsprong.

Hydrangea macrophylla (Hortensia Group) 'Paris', Trelissick Garden.

tical to Thunberg's specimen, forming the type of the "mophead" hortensias. According to Mallet (*New Plantsman* 1994/3), the cultivar was named after a beautiful young Japanese girl, whom Siebold met. At one time the girl's name was Taki Kusomoto, changed to O taki san, meaning "Honorable Miss Taki." Philipp Franz von Siebold, who introduced the plant in 1862, heard the name as Otaksa and it was thus that the plant became known worldwide. Origin Japanese.

H. macrophylla (Hortensia Group) 'Otaksa Monstrosa'

A branch sport of 'Otaksa', with larger flowers. Otherwise the same. Propagated by Lemoine Nursery, Nancy, France, in 1894.

H. macrophylla (Hortensia Group) 'Otaksa Monstrosa Nana'

Probably a mutant of 'Otaksa Monstrosa'. Bred by Brunnemann in 1909.

H. macrophylla (Hortensia Group) 'Paradiso'

Flowers salmon pink. Bred by Decault of France.

H. macrophylla (Hortensia Group) 'Paris'

A fast-growing shrub, with thick branches. Its flowerheads are also large, deep pink to crimson, almost never blue. Flowering time is from July to early August. The single flowers are 4 cm (1.5 inches), sepals heavily serrate. As it is very free-flowering, this is one of the best cultivars from Mouillère. Bred in France in 1926. In cultivation at Koster's nurseries, before 1940, and still available in the trade. A second cultivar with the same name was bred by Rampp Nursery, Germany, before 1999. This compact plant has large rosy red corymbs and is suitable as a pot plant. It is a member of the CITY-LINE series.

Hydrangea macrophylla (Hortensia Group) 'Parzifal', Holehird Gardens.

Hydrangea macrophylla (Hortensia Group) 'Parzifal', Trelissick Garden.

H. macrophylla (Hortensia Group) 'Parzifal'
A sturdy plant of moderate growth, usually not more than 1.25 m (3.5 feet) high. The corymbs are numerous but not large, the sepals are serrate. Flower color usually crimson pink to red, but varying enormously, also in less appealing tints, becoming dark blue-purple in very acid soil. Suitable as a pot plant. Bred by J. Wintergalen, Germany, in 1922. RHS Awards: AM 1922, AGM 1992. The name is often wrongly spelled "Parzival," "Parsival," or "Parsifal."

H. macrophylla (Hortensia Group) 'Pasteur'
Corymbs deep pink, large. Bred by J. Wintergalen, Germany, before 1924. RHS Award: AM 1925.

H. macrophylla (Hortensia Group) 'Patio White'
A small to medium-sized shrub, quite free-flowering, with medium-sized corymbs, pure white. Bred by Louisiana Nurseries, United States.

H. macrophylla (Hortensia Group) 'Paw Paw Pink'
A vigorous-growing medium-sized shrub up to 1.5 m (5 feet). The corymbs are large, fresh pink. Bred by Louisiana Nurseries, United States.

H. macrophylla (Hortensia Group) 'Pax'
A medium-sized shrub up to 1.5 m (5 feet). The flower-heads are large, pure white. Flowering time is from July to August. Probable synonym: 'Nymphe'.

H. macrophylla (Hortensia Group) 'Penny Mac'
A small shrub, continuously flowering until the first frost. Bred by Penny McHenry and introduced by Louisiana Nurseries, United States.

H. macrophylla (Hortensia Group) 'Pensee'
A small shrub up to 1.25 m (3.5 feet). The flowerheads are small, pale pink, fading to white, florets 3 cm (about 1 inch), sepals entire. Some authors consider this cultivar synonymous with 'Marie Claire'. Origin French, in 1931.

Hydrangea macrophylla (Hortensia Group) 'Pia', Research Station for Nursery Stock.

Hydrangea macrophylla (Hortensia Group) 'Pink Dream', Stourton House Flower Garden.

Hydrangea macrophylla (Hortensia Group) 'Pia', Holehird Gardens.

Hydrangea macrophylla (Hortensia Group) 'Pink Princess', Research Station for Nursery Stock.

H. macrophylla (Hortensia Group) 'Perfecta'

A dwarf shrub, not exceeding 1 m (3 feet). Flowerheads spherical, pink. A seedling of 'Merveille'. Bred by L. F. Cayeux of France, in 1936. Not to be confused with 'Mariesii Perfecta'.

H. macrophylla (Hortensia Group) 'Phoebus'

A tall shrub with pink flowers.

H. macrophylla (Hortensia Group) 'Pia'

Possibly the smallest hortensia cultivar. It grows quite slowly. The flowerheads are equally small, the sepals pointed and tightly set. The color is usually crimson. Named after Pia di Tolomei, one of Dante's heroines in *Divina Commedia*. Synonyms: 'Comet', 'Piamina', 'Pink Elf', 'Winning Edge'. Origin Japanese.

H. macrophylla (Hortensia Group) 'Pieta'

A splendid dwarf and compact shrublet up to 50 cm (20 inches). It flowers freely with dense pink flowerheads. Bred by Louisiana Nurseries, United States.

H. macrophylla (Hortensia Group) 'Pink Dream'

A modest shrub up to 1.25 m (3.5 feet). The flowerheads are small, fresh pink. Raised by Elizabeth Bullivant, United Kingdom.

H. macrophylla (Hortensia Group) 'Pink Princess'

According to Haworth-Booth, this cultivar is tall growing with pink flowers.

H. macrophylla (Hortensia Group) 'Pirate'

A large shrub up to 1.5 m (5 feet). The leaves are very dark green. The flowerheads are flattened corymbs, dark pink. The plant is tender. Origin French.

Hydrangea macrophylla (Hortensia Group) 'Pompadour', courtesy Arborealis.

H. macrophylla (Hortensia Group) 'Pompadour'

A medium-sized shrub up to 1.5 m (5 feet). The flowerheads are very large, up to 25 cm (10 inches) across, pink to salmon pink, the sepals are serrate with green mottling when opening. Suitable as a pot plant. Generally available. Parentage: 'Soeur Thérèse' × 'Val de Loir'. Bred by J. Neilz, France, in 1962.

H. macrophylla (Hortensia Group) 'Porta Nigra'

A strong-growing shrub. Flowerheads dark pink. Bred by J. Lambert and Sons, Germany. Named for a gate in the 9th-century town of Trier.

H. macrophylla (Hortensia Group) 'Porzellan'

A compact low-growing shrub. Flowerheads are light blue, carried by firm and stout branches. Flowering occurs very early in the season. A good cultivar for forcing. Raised at Friesdorf Research Station, now Landwirtschaftskammer Rheinland (Rhineland Agricultural Chamber), Germany.

H. macrophylla (Hortensia Group) 'Prag'

A compact plant, flowers dark red. Suitable as a houseplant. A member of the CITY-LINE series. Bred by Rampp Nursery, Germany, before 1995.

H. macrophylla (Hortensia Group) 'Président Fallières'

A vigorous-growing shrub with bright pink flowers. Bred by Émile Mouillère, France, in 1910.

H. macrophylla (Hortensia Group) 'Président R. Touchard'

A slow-growing shrub. The flowerheads are not tightly packed, purple to crimson, with green dots, sepals elongated to round. Bred by E. Draps, Belgium, in 1938.

Hydrangea macrophylla (Hortensia Group) 'Président R. Touchard', Maurice Foster garden.

Hydrangea macrophylla (Hortensia Group) 'Prima', Trelissick Garden.

Hydrangea macrophylla (Hortensia Group) 'Président R. Touchard', Holehird Gardens.

Hydrangea macrophylla (Hortensia Group) 'Princess Beatrix', C. Esveld Nurseries.

H. macrophylla (Hortensia Group) 'Président Viger'

A strong-growing shrub. Flowerheads pink or light blue. Parentage: 'Otaksa' × 'Générale Vicomtesse de Vibraye'. Bred by Mouillère, France, in 1909.

H. macrophylla (Hortensia Group) 'Prestige'

A strong cultivar with light red flowerheads. Easily forced. Bred by Draps-Dom, Belgium, about 1960.

H. macrophylla (Hortensia Group) 'Prima'

A medium-sized shrub. Flowerheads deep pink or light red. Flowering time is from July to August. Bred by E. Draps-Dom, Belgium, in 1938.

H. macrophylla (Hortensia Group) 'Prince Henry'

A dwarf shrub. The corymbs are crimson pink. It should be a sport of 'Parzifal'.

H. macrophylla (Hortensia Group) 'Prince Rouge'

A small slow-growing shrub. Flowerheads about 15 cm (6 inches), clear dark pink to red. Early leaves conspicuously longer than usual. According to the Shamrock list, this cultivar is synonymous with 'Blauer Prinz'.

H. macrophylla (Hortensia Group) 'Princess Beatrix'

A dwarf shrub, neat and compact, up to 1 m (3 feet). Flowerheads large, crimson to purplish, not turning blue on acid soil. The sepals are pointed, heart shaped. Flowering time is from the end of June to July. Very free-flowering. The name is also spelled "Prinses Beatrix." Bred by E. Draps, Belgium, in 1946.

H. macrophylla (Hortensia Group) 'Princess Elizabeth'

A tall shrub up to 2 m (6.5 feet). Flowerheads pink or blue. Bred by H. J. Jones, United Kingdom, in 1927.

Hydrangea macrophylla (Hortensia Group) 'Queen Elizabeth', Sir Harold Hillier Gardens and Arboretum.

Hydrangea macrophylla (Hortensia Group) 'R. F. Felton', PlantenTuin de Oirsprong.

Hydrangea macrophylla (Hortensia Group) 'Queen Elizabeth', Trelissick Garden.

H. macrophylla (Hortensia Group) 'Princess Juliana'

A slow-growing, medium-sized shrub. Flowerheads at first creamy white, blush pink when mature. Sepals entire, round. Flowering time is from August to September. Tolerates sun. Synonym: 'Juliana. Named after Princess Juliana of Netherlands. Bred by D. Baardse, Netherlands, in 1920, and introduced by D. A. Koster nursery, Boskoop, Netherlands.

H. macrophylla (Hortensia Group) 'Professeur D. Bois'

A medium-sized shrub. Flowerheads large, warm pink, flowers and sepals rounded. Bred by Emile Mouillère, France, in 1909. RHS Award: AM 1922.

H. macrophylla (Hortensia Group) 'Professeur De Vries'

Corymbs large, light pink. Bred by D. A. Koster nursery, Netherlands, in 1932.

H. macrophylla (Hortensia Group) 'Progrès'

A shrub, probably not exceeding 1.5 m (5 feet). Flowering period very long. Flowerheads cherry pink, eventually deep blue. Bred by Lemoine Nursery, Nancy, France, in 1915.

H. macrophylla (Hortensia Group) 'Queen Elizabeth'

A large shrub, up to almost 2 m (6.5 feet). Leaves strongly dentate. According to Sir Harold Hillier Gardens and Arboretum, United Kingdom, this plant has rose-pink flowers, becoming blue easily. According to the Shamrock list, this cultivar is identical to 'Princess Elizabeth'. Origin United Kingdom.

H. macrophylla (Hortensia Group) 'Queen Emma'

A vigorous-growing shrub up to 1.5 m (5 feet). Flowerheads crimson, large. Flowering time is in August. Bred by D. Baardse, Netherlands, in 1920. Possibly the same as 'Koningin Emma'.

H. macrophylla (Hortensia Group) 'Queen Wilhelmina'

A huge shrub. Flowers pink, readily turning blue. Flowering time is from July to August. Reportedly a seedling from 'Rosea'. Raised by Lemoine Nursery, Nancy, France, in 1910.

H. macrophylla (Hortensia Group) 'R. F. Felton'

A huge shrub up to 1.5 m (5 feet) or even more. The large corymbs are whitish pink or grayish blue, not very attractive, sepals rounded. It can easily be confused with 'Miss Hepburn'. Synonym: 'Mrs. R. F. Felton'. Bred by H. J. Jones, United Kingdom, in 1927.

Hydrangea macrophylla (Hortensia Group) 'Raymond Draps', PlantenTuin de Oirsprong.

Hydrangea macrophylla (Hortensia Group) 'Red Star', Holehird Gardens.

Hydrangea macrophylla (Hortensia Group) 'Raymond Draps', PlantenTuin de Oirsprong.

Hydrangea macrophylla (Hortensia Group) 'Regula', Trelissick Garden.

H. macrophylla (Hortensia Group) 'Radiant'

A dwarf shrub up to 1 m (3 feet). The modest flowerheads are flattened, and attractively crimson pink. Flowering occurs at a very young age and very early in the season. Bred by Lemoine Nursery, Nancy, France, in 1908. One of the best cultivars at M. Koster and Sons nurseries in Boskoop before 1940. RHS Award: AM 1915.

H. macrophylla (Hortensia Group) 'Raymond Draps'

A medium-sized shrub. The flowerheads are pink, sepals rounded. Flower color easily turns blue. Leaves turn bright red in the autumn. Bred by Draps-Dom, Belgium, in 1951.

H. macrophylla (Hortensia Group) 'Red Emperor'

A medium-sized shrub up to 1.5 m (5 feet). Flowerheads flattened, round, medium sized, 12–15 cm (4.75–6 inches) across, rich crimson and ruby red on acid soils, never blue. Flowering time is late in the season. Bred by E. Draps, Belgium, in 1938.

H. macrophylla (Hortensia Group) 'Red Star'

A medium-sized shrub with well-formed red flowerheads, freely produced. In spite of the name, the flowers easily become blue. Bred by Louisiana Nurseries, United States.

H. macrophylla (Hortensia Group) 'Regula'

A strong-growing plant up to 1.25 m (3.5 feet), with large white corymbs. Flowering time is from the end of July to September. Suitable as a pot plant. Possible synonyms: 'White Bouquet' or 'Bouquet Blanc'. Bred by Moll Brothers, Germany, in 1934.

Hydrangea macrophylla (Hortensia Group) 'Renate Steiniger', Boering garden.

Hydrangea macrophylla (Hortensia Group) 'Rex', Stourton House Flower Garden.

Hydrangea macrophylla (Hortensia Group) 'Renate Steiniger', C. Esveld Nurseries.

Hydrangea macrophylla (Hortensia Group) 'Rheinland', Royal Horticultural Society Garden Wisley.

H. macrophylla (Hortensia Group) 'Renate Steiniger'

A medium-sized, compact shrub up to 1.25 m (3.5 feet). The flowerheads are rounded, 15 cm (6 inches) across, sepals denticulate. This may be the best blue hortensia. In alkaline soils the color changes to purplish blue. This cultivar is not very free-flowering, but otherwise nothing but virtues. Very good as a pot plant. According to the Shamrock list, it should be synonymous with 'San Marcos'. Bred by August Steiniger, Germany, in 1964.

H. macrophylla (Hortensia Group) 'Rénovation'

A tall shrub. The corymbs are large and rich pink. Flowering time is from June to August. Bred by Henri Cayeux of France, in 1930.

H. macrophylla (Hortensia Group) 'Revelation'

A compact plant about 1.25 m (3.5 feet). The flowerheads are brick red, sometimes mixed with purple. Origin French.

H. macrophylla (Hortensia Group) 'Rex'

A medium-sized shrub. The flowerheads are crimson, large. Now quite rare in collections. Bred by Henri Cayeux of France, in 1935.

H. macrophylla (Hortensia Group) 'Rheinland'

A small shrub with claret-red or even purple flowers. Flowering occurs in midseason. Bred by August Steiniger, Germany, in 1952.

Hydrangea macrophylla (Hortensia Group) 'Rigi', Research Station for Nursery Stock.

H. *macrophylla* (Hortensia Group) 'Rigi'

A slow-growing shrub up to 1.25 m (3.5 feet). The flower-heads are enormous, with sharply serrate sepals, salmon pink. The branches are often not strong enough to carry the inflorescences. The plant needs a sheltered place. Named for a mountain in central Switzerland. Introduced by Federal Research Institute for Horticulture, Wädenswil, Switzerland, in 1960.

H. *macrophylla* (Hortensia Group) 'Rio Grande'

A compact shrub, with large flowerheads, usually blue. Foliage quite coarse. Suitable as a pot plant. A member of the RIVER-LINE series. Bred by Rampp Nursery, Germany, before 1995.

H. *macrophylla* (Hortensia Group) 'Ripple'

A compact shrublet with bicolored flowerheads. The sepals are white with red edges, much like 'Mirai', but smaller. Bred by Yatabe Mototeru of Japan.

Hydrangea macrophylla (Hortensia Group) 'Ripple', Floriade 2002.

Hydrangea macrophylla (Hortensia Group) 'Robur', Holehird Gardens.

H. macrophylla (Hortensia Group) 'Robur'

A dwarf, spreading shrub. Leaves irregularly ovate and acuminate. The margins are coarsely serrate. Flowerheads rosy pink, quickly spoiled by bad weather. Rare in cultivation.

H. macrophylla (Hortensia Group) 'Roma'

A shrub about 1 m (3 feet) high and wide. Flowers reddish purple. The flowerbuds are damaged in a harsh winter. Suitable as a pot plant. Synonym: 'Raro'. A member of the CITY-LINE series. Bred by Rampp Nursery, Germany, 1992.

H. macrophylla (Hortensia Group) 'Romance'

A large shrub up to 1.5 m (5 feet). Flowerheads firm, dark red. Not to be confused with 'Darts Romance', a cultivar of the lacecap group

H. macrophylla (Hortensia Group) 'Rosabella'

A large shrub with flattened corymbs, clear dark violet-red. Very free-flowering. Present at the Boskoop Research Station.

H. macrophylla (Hortensia Group) 'Rosalia'

A compact plant. Flowerheads relatively large, light pink, sepals broadly ovate, not serrate. Bred by Nieschütz, Germany, in 1983.

H. macrophylla (Hortensia Group) 'Rosalinde'

Flowerheads pink, sepals serrate. Probably still in cultivation. Bred by August Steiniger, Germany, in 1952.

H. macrophylla (Hortensia Group) 'Rosa Zwerg'

A very compact and neat plant up to 1 m (3 feet). The round inflorescences are bright pink borne on sturdy stems. Sepals are entire. Also suitable as a pot plant.

Hydrangea macrophylla (Hortensia Group) 'Rosabella', Research Station for Nursery Stock.

H. macrophylla (Hortensia Group) 'Rosdohan Pink'

A medium-sized shrub with large flowerheads. Sepals broadly acuminate, fresh pink in firm trusses. Some fertile flowers are scattered through the corymb. According to the Shamrock list, this cultivar should be synonymous with 'Lausanne', which seems doubtful.

H. macrophylla (Hortensia Group) 'Rosea'

One of the four principal cultivars from which were developed the wealth of hortensias. It was brought to England by Charles Maries for J. H. Veitch nurseries in 1880 and possibly again in 1899. It is a tall shrub with slender branches, up to 2 m (6.5 feet). The flowerheads are pink, fading to greenish, with three or four entire sepals. On acid soil flower color is light blue, fading to greenish. Not cultivated often. Mainly of interest to collectors. Synonyms: *H. opuloides* var. *rosea*, *H. hortensis* var. *rosea*. It is clearly not a variety, but a cultivar. Japanese name is 'Hime azisai' (sometimes spelled 'Hime ajisai'). Origin Japanese.

Hydrangea macrophylla (Hortensia Group) 'Rosdohan Pink', Trelissick Garden.

Hydrangea macrophylla (Hortensia Group) 'Rosea', Holehird Gardens.

Hydrangea macrophylla (Hortensia Group) 'Rosea', Maurice Foster garden.

Hydrangea macrophylla (Hortensia Group) 'Rosita', Boering garden.

H. *macrophylla* (Hortensia Group) 'Rosebelle'

A moderately strong shrub, with more or less upright, clustered branches. Flowerheads pink or mauve, or eventually blue. Flowering time is from July to August. Very hardy. Only present in Australia, where it does well. In earlier years, also cultivated in Netherlands. Bred by Henri Cayeux of France, in 1923.

H. *macrophylla* (Hortensia Group) 'Rose de Tours'

Corymbs rounded, pink. Bred by Barillet of France, in 1913. According to the Shamrock list, this cultivar is probably still in cultivation.

H. *macrophylla* (Hortensia Group) 'Rosenberg'

A shrub up to 1.25 m (3.5 feet), with rounded flowerheads and pointed sepals. Flowers light lilac-pink, abundant. Flowering time is late in the season. Synonym: 'Burg Rosenberg'. Bred by E. Haller, Switzerland, in 1975.

H. *macrophylla* (Hortensia Group) 'Roshidori'

Possibly this plant from Milim Botanical Garden, Korea, is identical to 'Nigra'.

H. *macrophylla* (Hortensia Group) 'Rosita'

A vigorous-growing shrub. Flowerheads rounded, dark pink. Flowering time is very early in the season. Very good as a houseplant. Also spelled "Rosarita." Bred by Draps-Dom, Belgium, in 1964.

H. *macrophylla* (Hortensia Group) 'Rotbart'

This plant is still in cultivation, according to the Shamrock list, but it lacks a description. Bred by H. Dienemann, Germany, in 1965.

H. *macrophylla* (Hortensia Group) 'Rotkäppchen'

This cultivar seems to be in cultivation but lacks an adequate description. Bred by H. Dienemann, Germany, in 1965.

Hydrangea macrophylla (Hortensia Group) 'Sabrina', Plantarium.

Hydrangea macrophylla (Hortensia Group) 'Saint Claire', Research Station for Nursery Stock.

H. macrophylla (Hortensia Group) 'Rotspon'

A medium-sized shrub. Flowerheads dark red without any traces of blue, a good plant for patios and balconies. Rare in the trade. Named for a special wine, traded in the 18th century in Lübeck, Germany; this wine is still available. Raised at Friesdorf Research Station, now Landwirtschaftskammer Rheinland (Rhineland Agricultural Chamber), Germany, before 1960.

H. macrophylla (Hortensia Group) 'Rouget de l'Isle'

A compact shrub. Flowerheads overcrowded, dark pink to crimson, eventually deep blue, depending on soil conditions. Sepals large. Very free-flowering. Bred by Lemoine Nursery, Nancy, France, in 1926.

H. macrophylla (Hortensia Group) 'Royal'

A large shrub up to 1.5 m (5 feet). The flowers are equally large, about 20 cm (8 inches) across, in tight flattened corymbs, usually purplish red. One of the best of its color. Needs a sheltered place.

H. macrophylla (Hortensia Group) 'Rutilant'

A strong-growing shrub up to 1.5 m (5 feet), with sturdy branches. Flowerheads are crimson. Parentage: 'Flambard' × 'Vésuve'. Bred by L. F. Cayeux of France, in 1936.

H. macrophylla (Hortensia Group) 'Sabrina'

A compact shrub up to 1 m (3 feet). Flowerheads medium sized, sepals white with a red edge, much like 'Mirai'. Bred by D. van der Spek, Netherlands, in 2002.

H. macrophylla (Hortensia Group) 'Sachsenkind'

A medium-sized shrub, probably up to 1.5 m (5 feet). Flowers are pink. In cultivation in the Netherlands before 1939. *Sachsenkind* means "infant of Saxe." Bred by F. Matthes, Germany, in 1927.

H. macrophylla (Hortensia Group) 'Saint Bonifaz'

A vigorous-growing shrub. The corymbs are large and white, and the sepals serrate. Bred by F. Matthes of Germany.

H. macrophylla (Hortensia Group) 'Saint Claire'

A medium-sized shrub. Corymbs pale blue or pink, sepals rounded. Flowering time is from July to August. Suitable as a pot plant. Origin French, before 1956.

H. macrophylla (Hortensia Group) 'Samba'

Flowers dark red, and small. Flowering time is midseason. Flowerheads tend to be aborted. Bred by Draps-Dom of Belgium.

H. macrophylla (Hortensia Group) 'Säntis'

A bold shrub up to 1.5 m (5 feet). Flowerheads pink. Named for a mountain in the Toggenburg district of northeastern Switzerland. Introduced by Federal Research Institute for Horticulture, Wädenswil, Switzerland, in 1949.

H. macrophylla (Hortensia Group) 'Sanguinea'

A strong-growing shrub with sturdy branches. The flowers are blood red, the foliage is very dark. According to Haworth-Booth, it is a branch sport of 'Merveille'. Probable synonym: 'Merveille Sanguine'. Raised by A. Truffaut, France, in 1938.

H. macrophylla (Hortensia Group) 'San Vito'

A compact plant with large corymbs, pink-lavender with white. Bred by Louisiana Nurseries, United States.

Hydrangea macrophylla (Hortensia Group) 'Satinette', Maurice Foster garden.

Hydrangea macrophylla (Hortensia Group) 'Schneeball', PlantenTuin de Oirsprong.

Hydrangea macrophylla (Hortensia Group) 'Schadendorff's Perle', Trelissick Garden.

H. macrophylla (Hortensia Group) 'Satellite'

A compact, tidy plant up to 1.5 m (5 feet). The flowerheads are usually crimson, nicely rounded, small, but very decorative. Flowering time is very long, from July to October. Synonym: 'Taspo'. Only rarely cultivated, it deserves better. Raised at Friesdorf Research Station, now Landwirtschaftskammer Rheinland (Rhineland Agricultural Chamber), Germany, before 1967.

H. macrophylla (Hortensia Group) 'Satinette'

A sturdy shrub up to 1.5 m (5 feet). The flowerheads are rounded, usually rosy red, or dark pink, forming a loose mophead. Sepals entire, round. Very free-flowering. Flowering time is from July to August. Bred by Lemoine Nursery, Nancy, France, in 1916.

H. macrophylla (Hortensia Group) 'Saxonia'

Flowers bright rose. Free-flowering. Offered in Netherlands in 1917 by Koloos Nurseries.

H. macrophylla (Hortensia Group) 'Schadendorff's Perle'

A large shrub, corymbs loosely arranged, lilac to rosy lilac. Sepals rounded, with a broad apex. Synonym: 'Schadendorff's Pearl'. Bred by H. Schadendorff, Germany, before 1930.

H. macrophylla (Hortensia Group) 'Schenkenberg'

A dwarf shrub, about 1 m (3 feet). Flowerheads bright red, small. Flowering time is from July to October. Not suitable for acid soil, as it will loose its color, becoming muddy purple. Bred by E. Haller, Switzerland, in 1960.

H. macrophylla (Hortensia Group) 'Schneeball'

A huge shrub, probably up to 2 m (6.5 feet), with huge leaves, dark green and dentate. Corymbs very large, 25 cm (10 inches) or more, pure white. The sepals are serrate. Flowering time is late in the season. Flowers easily damaged by bad weather. Bred by Nieschütz, Germany, and reintroduced (?) in 1987, or by Brügger, Germany, in 1952.

H. macrophylla (Hortensia Group) 'Schneekristall'

Available in the trade. Bred by H. Dienemann, Germany, in 1965.

H. macrophylla (Hortensia Group) 'Schneewittchen'

Available in the trade. Bred by H. Dienemann, Germany, in 1965.

Hydrangea macrophylla (Hortensia Group) 'Schöne Bautznerin', Research Station for Nursery Stock.

Hydrangea macrophylla (Hortensia Group) 'Schwan', Research Station for Nursery Stock.

Hydrangea macrophylla (Hortensia Group) 'Schöne Bautznerin', Trelissick Garden.

Hydrangea macrophylla (Hortensia Group) 'Schwan', PlantenTuin de Oirsprong.

H. macrophylla (Hortensia Group) 'Schöne Bautznerin'

A large sturdy shrub up to 1.5 m (5 feet) or more. Flowerheads flattened, round, usually pink, also blue. Sepals round or triangular. Very suitable as a pot plant. Synonym: 'Red Baron'. 'Bautzen' may be a synonym as well. Bred by H. Dienemann, Germany, in 1975.

H. macrophylla (Hortensia Group) 'Schöne Dresdnerin'

A slow-growing shrub. The flowerheads are dark wine red. Bred by F. Matthes, Germany, in 1926. Offered by some Dutch nurseries before 1939. *Schöne Dresdnerin* means "beauty of Dresden."

H. macrophylla (Hortensia Group) 'Schwan'

A medium-sized shrub up to about 1 m (3 feet). The flowerheads are relatively small and tight, sepals pure white, changing color with age to white with red dots, but easily damaged by bad weather. Bred by E. Haller, Switzerland, in 1966.

H. macrophylla (Hortensia Group) 'Schwester Alba'

A low shrub, usually not exceeding 1 m (3 feet). The flowerheads are about 15 cm (6 inches) across, somewhat untidy, sepals rounded, white. Suitable as a pot plant. Synonym: 'Alba'. Bred by August Steiniger, Germany, in 1981.

H. macrophylla (Hortensia Group) 'Seascape'

A large vigorous-growing bush. Leaves ovate with serrate margins. The flowerheads are convex, palest pink with a rose center, or light blue. Flowering time is from August to September. This cultivar is comparable to 'Sea Foam' and others in that class. Haworth-Booth classified such forms under his Maritima Group. Origin United Kingdom.

H. macrophylla (Hortensia Group) 'Seestadt Wismar'

A sturdy shrub. Flowerheads warm pink. Bred by P. Kipke of Germany.

Hydrangea macrophylla (Hortensia Group) 'Schwester Alba', Research Station for Nursery Stock.

Hydrangea macrophylla (Hortensia Group) 'Seascape', Trelissick Garden.

Hydrangea macrophylla (Hortensia Group) 'Seascape', Holehird Gardens.

Hydrangea macrophylla (Hortensia Group) 'Semperflorens', C. Esveld Nurseries.

H. macrophylla (Hortensia Group) 'Semperflorens'

A shrub up to 1.25 m (3.5 feet). Corymbs medium sized, usually pink but can be a good blue. Flowering time is very long, from June to October. This plant needs a place in light shade.

H. macrophylla (Hortensia Group) 'Sénateur Henri David'

Flowerheads pale pink. Bred by Lemoine Nursery, Nancy, France, in 1910.

H. macrophylla (Hortensia Group) 'Sensation'

A slow-growing plant up to 1.25 m (3.5 feet). Flowerheads are small but numerous and dark pink. On acid soil the flowers are of no value, becoming dull. This rare cultivar deserves more attention in gardens. Not to be confused with 'Harlequin' (synonym 'Sensation 75') or with 'Sensation' (introduced by Gyselinck about 1966). Bred by Henri Cayeux of France, in 1938.

Hydrangea macrophylla (Hortensia Group) 'Shin ozaki', Rein and Mark Bulk nursery.

H. macrophylla (Hortensia Group) 'Shikizaki'

A small shrub, about 1 m (3 feet), with irregular flowerheads and light green foliage. Flowers turn easily to blue. Origin Japanese.

Hydrangea macrophylla (Hortensia Group) 'Sibylla', Trelissick Garden.

Hydrangea macrophylla (Hortensia Group) 'Soeur Thérèse'.

Hydrangea macrophylla (Hortensia Group) 'Soeur Thérèse', courtesy Arborealis.

H. macrophylla (Hortensia Group) 'Shin ozaki'

This cultivar has remarkably large flowerheads, usually blue. The sepals are entire. Origin Japanese.

H. macrophylla (Hortensia Group) 'Shizaki'

A shrub of unknown size. The flowerheads are large and white, and the sepals are aborted. Origin Japanese.

H. macrophylla (Hortensia Group) 'Sibylla'

An average-sized shrub, about 1.25 m (3.5 feet) high. The flowerheads are large, firm, deep pink or almost rosy red. Flowering time is in August or later. Also spelled "Sybille" or "Sybilla." According to De Bree, 'Sibylla' is synonymous with 'Masja' and a trademarked name; we could not confirm this. Bred by August Steiniger, Germany, before 1956.

H. macrophylla (Hortensia Group) 'Sieger'

A tall vigorous-growing shrub. Corymbs large bright pink, sepals serrate. Bred by J. Wintergalen, Germany, in 1943.

H. macrophylla (Hortensia Group) "Sigyn Hartmann'

A shrub up to 1.5 m (5 feet). Flowerheads firm, rounded, bright pink or blue. Bred by J. P. Hartmann of Ghent, Belgium, in 1935.

H. macrophylla (Hortensia Group) 'Sirocco'

Flowers deep pink. Flowering time is in midseason.

H. macrophylla (Hortensia Group) 'Snowcap'

An unusual small plant with nearly pure white foliage edged green and with irregular splashes of white. Bred by Louisiana Nurseries, United States. Not to be confused with *H. heteromalla* 'Snowcap'.

H. macrophylla (Hortensia Group) 'Soeur Thérèse'

A medium-sized shrub 1.25–1.5 m (3.5–5 feet) high. The flowerheads are large and pure white. The sepals are sharply serrate. The single florets have a small blue eye. The plant needs some shade for good results. It is sometimes recommended as a substitute for 'Madame Emile Mouillère', but it is very different from that form, especially in the sepals. Synonym: 'Petite Soeur Thérèse de l'Enfant Jésus', no longer in use. Bred by Gaigne of France, in 1947.

Hydrangea macrophylla (Hortensia Group) 'Sonja', Plantarium.

Hydrangea macrophylla (Hortensia Group) 'Sonja', Plantarium.

H. macrophylla (Hortensia Group) 'Sonja'

A low shrub, very tight with short stout branches. Very free-flowering with flattened corymbs, mixed with a few fertile flowers. Sepals are bright pink and become blue-purple easily. One of the trademarked series DUTCH LADIES. Bred by D. van der Spek, Netherlands, in 2002.

H. macrophylla (Hortensia Group) 'Sonja Steiniger'

A shrub up to 1.25 m (3.5 feet), with tight flowerheads, red to dark pink. A sibling of 'Renate Steiniger'. Bred by August Steiniger, Germany.

H. macrophylla (Hortensia Group) 'Sonnengruss'

A shrub of moderate growth. The flowerheads are compact and usually dark pink, eventually bluish purple. Flowering time is from July to August. *Sonnengruss* means "sun greetings." Bred by F. Matthes, Germany, in 1936.

Hydrangea macrophylla (Hortensia Group) 'Sonja Steiniger', Research Station for Nursery Stock.

Hydrangea macrophylla (Hortensia Group) 'Souvenir du Président Doumer', Holehird Gardens.

Hydrangea macrophylla (Hortensia Group) 'Souvenir de Madame E. Chautard, Research Station for Nursery Stock.

Hydrangea macrophylla (Hortensia Group) 'Souvenir du Président Doumer', Trelissick Garden.

H. macrophylla (Hortensia Group) 'Sonntagskind'

A medium-sized shrub up to 1.25 m (3.5 feet). Flowerheads tight and round, florets dark red, with rounded sepals. It is a very promising cultivar. Bred by August Steiniger, Germany, in 1979.

H. macrophylla (Hortensia Group) 'Souvenir de Claire'

A weak and untidy shrub up to 1.5 m (5 feet). The flowerheads are pink. Flowers are also produced on side shoots. A sport of 'Rosea'. Raised by Mouillère, France, in 1908.

H. macrophylla (Hortensia Group) 'Souvenir de Madame Béranger'

A slow-growing low shrub, quite bushy. Flowerheads pink with a paler center. Bred by Barillet of France, in 1913.

H. macrophylla (Hortensia Group) 'Souvenir de Madame E. Chautard'

A shrub of moderate vigor up to 1.5 m (5 feet). The flowerheads are sparse but a peculiar color that is often impossible to predict. They may be purple with lighter margins, or clear pink, mauve or even blue. Often flowering with different colors on the same plant. It recalls the old-fashioned Japanese picture of hortensias. Parentage: 'Sainte Claire' × 'Rosea'. Bred by Mouillère, France, in 1909.

H. macrophylla (Hortensia Group) 'Souvenir du Président Doumer'

A shrub up to 1.25 m (3.5 feet). The flowerheads are warm velvety red, eventually purple or blue. Flowering time is from July to August. The plant requires some care in the garden. Synonym: 'Souvenir du Président Paul Doumer'. Bred by Henri Cayeux of France, in 1932.

Hydrangea macrophylla (Hortensia Group) 'Splendeur', Trelissick Garden.

Hydrangea macrophylla (Hortensia Group) 'Stephuria', Trelissick Garden.

Hydrangea macrophylla (Hortensia Group) 'Starlet', Holehird Gardens.

Hydrangea macrophylla (Hortensia Group) 'Stratford', Trelissick Garden.

H. *macrophylla* (Hortensia Group) 'Splendeur'
A medium-sized shrub. Flattened flowerheads are tight mopheads very dark pink to red, sepals entire. Bred by Draps-Dom of Belgium.

H. *macrophylla* (Hortensia Group) 'Starlet'
A medium-sized shrub up to 1.25 m (3.5 feet). Branches slender, slow growing. Flowerheads deep salmon pink to bright pink, later turning to wine red. Sepals irregularly serrate. Origin before 1950.

H. *macrophylla* (Hortensia Group) 'Stella'
A shrub up to 1.25 m (3.5 feet), with very large flowerheads, consisting of large deep pink florets. One of the trademarked series DUTCH LADIES. Bred by D. van der Spek of Netherlands.

H. *macrophylla* (Hortensia Group) 'Stephuria'
A large shrub with dark salmon pink corymbs, sepals entire. Foliage bold, dark green. Uncertain whether the name is correctly spelled. This cultivar is present in Trelissick Garden. Introduced by Burncoose Nurseries, United Kingdom.

H. *macrophylla* (Hortensia Group) 'Stockholm'
A compact plant with large dark pink trusses. Suitable as a pot plant. A member of the CITY-LINE series. Bred by Rampp Nursery, Germany, before 1995.

H. *macrophylla* (Hortensia Group) 'Stratford'
A slow-growing shrub, up to 1.25 m (3.5 feet). Flowerheads usually pink, florets 4 cm (1.5 inches), sepals serrate.

Hydrangea macrophylla (Hortensia Group) 'Superba', Trelissick Garden.

Hydrangea macrophylla (Hortensia Group) 'Tödi', Trelissick Garden.

Hydrangea macrophylla (Hortensia Group) 'Thomas Hogg', Maurice Foster garden.

H. macrophylla (Hortensia Group) 'Superba'
A huge shrub up to 1.5 m (5 feet) or more. Very floriferous. Flowerheads are bright pink. Flowering time is from August to September. Bred by Henri Cayeux of France, in 1924.

H. macrophylla (Hortensia Group) 'Superstar'
Flowers red. Flowering time is in July.

H. macrophylla (Hortensia Group) 'Supreme'
A large shrub up to 2 m (6.5 feet). Leaves oval, 15 cm (6 inches), serrate. Inflorescences very large, deep pink. Flowering time is from mid- to late season. Bred by Pépinières Thoby of France.

H. macrophylla (Hortensia Group) 'Surprise'
Flowerheads greenish white. Bred by Lemoine Nursery, Nancy, France, in 1911.

H. macrophylla (Hortensia Group) 'Swanhild'
A moderate-growing shrub. Flowerheads white flushed with pink. Flowering time is in July. Bred by J. Wintergalen, Germany, in 1929.

H. macrophylla (Hortensia Group) 'Tegerfelden'
A sturdy, healthy shrub up to 1.25 m (3.5 feet). The flowerheads are rounded and well shaped, florets about 4 cm (1.5 inches), light pink, sepals rounded and entire. Flowering time is long, as not all flowers open at once. Bred by E. Haller, Switzerland, in 1971. Still available in the trade.

H. macrophylla (Hortensia Group) 'Terre de Feu'
Flowers cherry pink, shaped as in 'Ayesha', easily turning dark pink in alkaline soil. Bred by Lemoine Nursery, Nancy, France, in 1919.

H. macrophylla (Hortensia Group) 'Thomas Hogg'
A weak and inconspicuous shrub. The flowerheads are numerous, pure white sterile florets, of irregular shape, sepals elongated or pointed. This is one of the first hortensias imported from Japan, in 1876.

H. macrophylla (Hortensia Group) 'Ticino'
A dwarf but vigorous-growing cultivar, up to 1.2 m (3.5 feet). The corymbs are rounded and dark pink, the sepals are whitish in the center. Suitable as a pot plant. Raised at Friesdorf Research Station, now Landwirtschaftskammer Rheinland (Rhineland Agricultural Chamber), Germany, in 1969.

H. macrophylla (Hortensia Group) 'Tödi'
A slow-growing shrub up to 1 m (3 feet). Flowerheads perfectly separated, strong pink, sepals entire and round. Autumn colors are interesting: violet with green. This hor-

Hydrangea macrophylla (Hortensia Group) 'Tovelit', Boering garden.

Hydrangea macrophylla (Hortensia Group) 'Trebah Silver', Trebah Garden.

Hydrangea macrophylla (Hortensia Group) 'Tovelit', Holehird Gardens.

Hydrangea macrophylla (Hortensia Group) 'Trebah Silver', Trebah Garden.

tensia is exceptionally hardy. Introduced by Federal Research Institute for Horticulture, Wädenswil, Switzerland, in 1952.

H. macrophylla (Hortensia Group) 'Tosca'

A vigorous-growing shrub. The flowerheads have some double florets, which is unusual. Flower color is dark pink with whitish edges or purplish with lighter margins. Synonym: 'Toska'. Bred by J. Wintergalen, Germany, in 1930.

H. macrophylla (Hortensia Group) 'Touraine'

A strong-growing plant. Flowerheads large, pale pink or pale blue. Sepals are waved. Flowering time is long lasting, from July to August. A sport of 'Merveille'. Bred by Belenfant of France, in 1938.

H. macrophylla (Hortensia Group) 'Tovelit'

A dwarf plant, barely more than 60 cm (2 feet). Its inflorescences are relatively large, in flattened pink or light blue corymbs. Sepals elongated and pointed. It is about the smallest hortensia, but it needs good care. A bit susceptible to diseases. Also wrongly spelled "Tofelil." Origin before 1956.

H. macrophylla (Hortensia Group) 'Trebah Silver'

A huge shrub, probably a hybrid between 'Joseph Banks' and 'Ayesha', found in a large group of mainly 'Joseph Banks'. The flowers are a bit less packed and have a very nice silvery glow over the flowerhead. Raised at Trebah Garden, United Kingdom, and named in 2002 by one of the authors, in accordance with T. Hibbert, owner of the garden.

Hydrangea macrophylla (Hortensia Group) 'Triumphant', Trelissick Garden.

Hydrangea macrophylla (Hortensia Group) 'Universal', Trelissick Garden.

Hydrangea macrophylla (Hortensia Group) 'Trophée', Holehird Gardens.

Hydrangea macrophylla (Hortensia Group) 'Universal', courtesy Arborealis.

Hydrangea macrophylla (Hortensia Group) 'Trophée', Trelissick Garden.

H. *macrophylla* (Hortensia Group) 'Triumphant'

A medium-sized shrub with huge corymbs, dark claret-red, sepals slightly serrate. Origin French.

H. *macrophylla* (Hortensia Group) 'Triomphe'

A compact shrub, up to 1.25 m (3.5 feet). The flowerheads are bright pink or light blue. Free-flowering. Bred by Henri Cayeux of France, in 1920. Offered by some Dutch nurseries before 1939.

H. *macrophylla* (Hortensia Group) 'Trophée'

A dwarf plant probably up to 1 m (3 feet). The corymbs are large rich pink or eventually blue. Bred by Lemoine Nursery, Nancy, France, in 1915.

H. *macrophylla* (Hortensia Group) 'Trostburg'

A medium-sized shrub up to 1.5 m (5 feet). Flowerheads small, 10–15 cm (4–6 inches) across, purple to dark pink. Bred by E. Haller, Switzerland, in 1970. Named for a castle in northeastern Switzerland.

H. *macrophylla* (Hortensia Group) 'United Nations'

Flowers clear pink. Bred by K. Wezelenburg & Sons, Boskoop, Netherlands, in 1967.

Hydrangea macrophylla (Hortensia Group) 'Ursula', Maurice Foster garden.

Hydrangea macrophylla (Hortensia Group) 'Vespa', Maurice Foster garden.

Hydrangea macrophylla (Hortensia Group) 'Val du Loir', Research Station for Nursery Stock.

Hydrangea macrophylla (Hortensia Group) 'Vespa', Trelissick Garden.

H. macrophylla (Hortensia Group) 'Universal'

A medium-sized shrub up to 1.25 m (3.5 feet). It is very conspicuous for the regularity of the flowerheads: the inflorescences are all equal to each other. Flowers turn blue easily. Very free-flowering.

H. macrophylla (Hortensia Group) 'Ursula'

A strong-growing plant up to 1.5 m (5 feet). The flowerheads are made of many florets, with wavy or serrate sepals. Color bright pink or blue. Flowering time is from June to August. Raised at Friesdorf Research Station, now Landwirtschaftskammer Rheinland (Rhineland Agricultural Chamber), Germany.

H. macrophylla (Hortensia Group) 'Val du Loir'

A shrub up to 1 m (3 feet) or sometimes more. The flowerheads are remarkable for being flattened with florets like *Oxalis*, sepals entire but wavy. Main color midpink. Flowering time is from July to August. Bred by Mouillère, France, in 1962.

H. macrophylla (Hortensia Group) 'Vaseyi'

A medium-sized shrub with elliptic leaves. Corymbs large but not overcrowding, sepals heart shaped, usually pinkish lilac with a cream center.

H. macrophylla (Hortensia Group) 'Venus'

A vigorous-growing shrub, probably more than 1.5 m (5 feet) high. Flowerheads clear pink to mauve or blue. Bred by K. Wezelenburg & Sons, Boskoop, Netherlands, in 1936.

H. macrophylla (Hortensia Group) 'Venedig'

A compact plant, with large dark pink flowerheads. Suitable as a houseplant. A member of the CITY-LINE series. Bred by Rampp Nursery, Germany, before 1997.

H. macrophylla (Hortensia Group) 'Vespa'

A low and spreading shrub. Leaves small and ovate. Flowerheads deep rose to salmon, in untidy trusses, sepals entire. Flowering time is from July to August. Bred by Pépinières Thoby of France.

Hydrangea macrophylla (Hortensia Group) 'Vörster Frührot', Trelissick Garden.

Hydrangea macrophylla (Hortensia Group) 'Violetta', Maurice Foster garden.

Hydrangea macrophylla (Hortensia Group) 'Vörster Frührot', Arboretum de Dreijen.

H. macrophylla (Hortensia Group) 'Vésuve'

A tall vigorous-growing shrub, with sturdy branches. Flowerheads dark pink or deep blue, sepals serrate. Another hybrid of 'Merveille'. Bred by Henri Cayeux of France, in 1932.

H. macrophylla (Hortensia Group) 'Vice-président Truffaut'

Flowers dark mauve-pink, sepals frilled. Bred by Mouillère, France, in 1914. Offered by a few Dutch nurseries at that time.

H. macrophylla (Hortensia Group) 'Vieux Château'

Flowers pink. Bred by Mouillère, France, in 1909.

H. macrophylla (Hortensia Group) 'Ville de Vendôme'

A large vigorous-growing shrub. The large corymbs are creamy white with a colored eye. Bred by Mouillère, France, in 1910.

H. macrophylla (Hortensia Group) 'Vindool'

A large shrub with very firm blue or pink corymbs. This American acquisition is very hardy. It was found and introduced by V. J. Dooley. Trademarked name is DOOLEY. Mentioned by Michael Dirr before 1998.

H. macrophylla (Hortensia Group) 'Violetta'

A modest shrub. Very floriferous. The corymbs are small and tightly rounded, wine red to cherry red to purple, never turning blue, not even on very acid soil. Flowers last for a long time. Bred by Michael Haworth-Booth of the United Kingdom.

H. macrophylla (Hortensia Group) 'Vörster Frührot'

A dwarf shrub up to 1.25 m (3.5 feet). The small flowerheads are pink or cherry red and do not develop all at the same time, which gives the plant a bicolored effect. Not a good blue on acid soil. In English-speaking circles the name "Forest Foster" is incorrectly used for the cultivar name. Another synonym is 'Foster Furest'. Bred by August Steiniger, Germany, in 1951.

Hydrangea macrophylla (Hortensia Group) 'Weisse Königin', Research Station for Nursery Stock.

Hydrangea macrophylla (Hortensia Group) 'Wildenstein', Research Station for Nursery Stock.

Hydrangea macrophylla (Hortensia Group) 'Westfalen', Stourton House Flower Garden.

H. macrophylla (Hortensia Group) 'Vulcain'

A dwarf plant, up to 50 cm (20 inches) but sometimes reverting to faster growth. Flowerheads are large crimson or purple, even orange with green. Flowering during a long period. Tolerates sun. Bred by Henri Cayeux of France.

H. macrophylla (Hortensia Group) 'Weisse Königin'

A medium-sized shrub, up to 1.5 m (5 feet). The flowerheads are remarkable for the equally white sterile and fertile flowers. The corymbs are more or less oval. Suitable as a pot plant and also suitable in the garden. *Weisse königin* means "white queen." Bred by August Steiniger, Germany, in 1980.

H. macrophylla (Hortensia Group) 'Westfalen'

A medium-sized bushy shrub, rarely more than 1.5 m (5 feet) high, with thick and sturdy stems. The corymbs are large and strong, usually red to vermilion, turning to purple, and lasting very long, sometimes until the first frost.

Bred by J. Wintergalen, Germany, in 1940. RHS Award: AM 1958. Not be to confused with the similar 'Ami Pasquier', which has dark branches.

H. macrophylla (Hortensia Group) 'Westfalenkind'

This shrub does not fade in full sun; in fact, it grows poorly in shade. Flowers pink or blue. Bred by J. Wintergalen, Germany, in 1913. Offered by Dutch nurseries before 1936.

H. macrophylla (Hortensia Group) 'Wien'

A compact plant. Florets large dark pink with very small double sepals, bluish. A member of the CITY-LINE series. Bred by Rampp Nursery, Germany, before 1998.

H. macrophylla (Hortensia Group) 'Wiesbaden'

A dwarf shrub. The corymbs are deep pink, purple or blue depending on the soil. Bred by Moll Brothers of Germany.

H. macrophylla (Hortensia Group) 'Wiking'

A compact, moderate-growing plant. The corymbs are large, sepals are serrate, color is usually pink. Flowering time is early in the season. Synonym: 'Viking'. Bred by J. Wintergalen, Germany, in 1932.

H. macrophylla (Hortensia Group) 'Wildenstein'

A large well-growing shrub up to 2 m (6.5 feet) with long-lasting flowerheads, usually pink. The plant is very hardy, but the flowerbuds may suffer in harsh conditions. Bred by E. Haller, Switzerland, in 1970.

H. macrophylla (Hortensia Group) 'William Pfitzer'

A medium-sized shrub. Flowers pink or blue. Bred by A. Rosenkrantzer, Germany, in 1913.

Hydrangea macrophylla (Hortensia Group) 'Yola', Research Station for Nursery Stock.

Hydrangea macrophylla (Hortensia Group) 'Yvonne Cayeux', Stourton House Flower Garden.

H. macrophylla (Hortensia Group) 'Willkommen'

Flowers bright pink. Offered by Dutch nurseries before 1940.

H. macrophylla (Hortensia Group) 'Woodworth White'

A dwarf compact plant, very free-flowering with medium-sized corymbs, pure white. Bred by Louisiana Nurseries, United States.

H. macrophylla (Hortensia Group) 'Wryneck'

A weak shrub. The stems twist, so the flowerhead does not hold firmly. Flowers blue or pink. Similar to 'Otaksa'. Origin Japanese.

H. macrophylla (Hortensia Group) 'Yola'

A medium-sized shrub, with irregular corymbs, sepals entire, a conspicuous lilac purple. Origin Japanese.

H. macrophylla (Hortensia Group) 'Yvonne Cayeux'

A medium-sized shrub up to 1.5 m (5 feet). The flowerheads are perfectly regular. The flowers do not open all together, which makes a strange combination of colors. Bred by Henri Cayeux of France, in 1920.

H. macrophylla (Hortensia Group) 'Zukunft'

A moderate-growing shrub with pink flowers. Bred by F. Matthes, Germany, in 1928.

H. macrophylla (Hortensia Group) 'Zürich'

A strong-growing plant with clear pink flowers. Can substitute for 'La Marne' as a pot plant. Bred by Moll Brothers, Germany, in 1947.

H. macrophylla (Hortensia Group) 'Zürich'

A compact shrub with very dark purple flowerheads. A member of the CITY-LINE series. Synonym: 'Razue'. Bred by Rampp Nursery, Germany, before 1995.

Hydrangea macrophylla var. *normalis*, Trelissick Garden.

H. macrophylla subsp. *macrophylla* var. *normalis*
Wilson 1923

This name covers a second group of hortensias, the lacecaps. The flowerheads of this group are flat, and colored or white ray-flowers surround the fertile flowers, which are usually bluish or pinkish. The ray-flowers are arranged in a ring and have four to eight florets with four to six sepals. The foliage of the plants in this group is similar to that of the so-called mophead group.

Synonym: *H. macrophylla* (Lacecap Group) 'Maritima'. According to Wilson (1923) this is the wild type, endemic in southern Japan. It has saucer-shaped flowers with sterile florets in variable numbers. This plant came to the Arnold Arboretum as herbarium material. 'Sea Foam' is quite similar. Haworth-Booth's name *H. maritima* is not accepted by other authorities. Wilson's name, which can be shortened to *H. macrophylla* var. *normalis*, now covers all lacecaps cultivars of *H. macrophylla*.

Hydrangea macrophylla subsp. *macrophylla* var. *normalis*, Le Thuit Saint-Jean.

Hydrangea Lacecap Group

The lacecaps share the general characteristics of the mopheads (see *H. macrophylla* subsp. *macrophylla*), differing in the shape and composition of the flowerheads. While the mopheads have rounded heads of mostly sterile flowers, the lacecaps have flattened heads of tiny fertile flowers surrounded by a ring of larger sterile ray-flowers. The sepals can also be scattered throughout the fertile flowers or form a double or irregular ring.

Hydrangea macrophylla (Lacecap Group) 'Aduarda', Arboretum de Dreijen.

Hydrangea macrophylla (Lacecap Group) 'Angel Light', H. J. van Paddenburgh garden.

Hydrangea macrophylla (Lacecap Group) 'Aduarda', Rutten garden.

Hydrangea macrophylla (Lacecap Group) 'Aureovariegata', courtesy Arborealis.

H. macrophylla (Lacecap Group) 'Aduarda'

This previously nameless clone was many years later identified at the Research Station for Nurseries in Boskoop, Netherlands, as being 'Mousmée'. Bred by G. A. van Klaveren, Netherlands, in 1975. *Aduarda* is the Latinized name of the village Hazerswoude.

H. macrophylla (Lacecap Group) 'Angel Light'

A sturdy shrub up to 1.5 m (5 feet). White ray-flowers are surrounded by lilac-green fertile flowers. Similar to 'Veitchii'. Recently introduced to the trade by Pépinières Cote Sud des Landes, France.

H. macrophylla (Lacecap Group) 'Ao gashima gaku'

A slender, untidy shrub. White ray-flowers surround cream-colored fertile flowers. Origin Japanese.

H. macrophylla (Lacecap Group) 'Aureovariegata'

Several slightly different forms are in cultivation, all with more or less strong yellow-variegated leaves. The flower-heads are usually light pink or dirty white.

Hydrangea macrophylla (Lacecap Group) 'Bachstelze', C. Esveld Nurseries.

Hydrangea macrophylla (Lacecap Group) 'Beauté Vendômoise', Trelissick Garden.

Hydrangea macrophylla (Lacecap Group) 'Bachstelze', Research Station for Nursery Stock.

Hydrangea macrophylla (Lacecap Group) 'Beauté Vendômoise', Trelissick Garden.

H. macrophylla (Lacecap Group) 'Azisai'

According to Haworth-Booth, this cultivar is related to his *H. maritima,* a species not recognized by other authorities. This old Japanese garden plant has been known in Europe for a long time. It was listed in the catalog of Messrs. V. H. Gauntlett, imported by a sea captain as a gift to his wife. Superficially, 'Azisai' looks like 'Mariesii Perfecta'. The ray-flowers have three or four sepals and are pink, purplish, or light blue. The sepals are entire and waved. Pedicels of the ray-flowers are exceptionally long. *Azisai* (alternatively spelled "ajisai") means "hortensia." Synonym: 'Yodogawa'. Renamed by Haworth-Booth to "blue wave."

H. macrophylla (Lacecap Group) 'Bachstelze'

A compact, vigorous-growing shrub up to about 1.5 m (5 feet). White ray-flowers surround greenish pink fertile flowers. The four sepals are cup shaped and entire or slightly dentate. Suitable as a pot plant, also very good for gardens. The lateral branches produce a second flowering period in late summer. *Bachstelze* means "wagtail." This cultivar is related to 'Libelle'. Introduced by Federal Research Institute for Horticulture, Wädenswil, Switzerland, in 1987.

H. macrophylla (Lacecap Group) 'Beauté Vendômoise'

A medium-sized shrub up to 1.5 m (5 feet) or more. The ray-flowers are exceptionally large, up to 10 cm (4 inches), and white flushed light pink. The flowerhead may measure 30 cm (1 foot) across. This hydrangea was almost lost to cultivation but has been revived. Parentage: 'Mariesii Grandiflora' × 'Rosea'. Bred by Emile Mouillère, France, in 1908 or 1909 or 1910.

Hydrangea macrophylla (Lacecap Group) 'Bergfink', Boering garden.

Hydrangea macrophylla (Lacecap Group) 'Blaukehlchen', Research Station for Nursery Stock.

Hydrangea macrophylla (Lacecap Group) 'Blanc Bleu Vastérival', Le Vastérival.

Hydrangea macrophylla (Lacecap Group) 'Bläuling', Trelissick Garden.

H. macrophylla (Lacecap Group) 'Bergfink'

A medium-sized shrub up to 1.5 m (5 feet). The corymbs are large. The ray-flowers form a single ring and are purplish red. The sepals are entire. Fertile flowers are pink. Lateral buds sometimes produce flowers. This lacecap is suitable as a pot plant and is very good for outdoor cultivation. *Bergfink* means "mountain finch." Introduced by Federal Research Institute for Horticulture, Wädenswil, Switzerland, in 1987.

H. macrophylla (Lacecap Group) 'Blanc Bleu Vastérival'

A huge, very vigorous-growing shrub. The leaves are large. The flowerheads are composed of blue fertile flowers surrounded by white florets of four sepals. Raised by Princess Sturdza, France, in 2000 and named for her garden. Introduced by C. Esveld Nurseries.

H. macrophylla (Lacecap Group) 'Blaukehlchen'

A medium-sized shrub about 1.5 m (5 feet) high. The corymbs are large, the single florets forming a ring, sepals are entire, usually four per floret. Flower color is dark lilac to violet, or even pink, depending on soil conditions. Flowering is for a long period, from June to September. Often a second flowering is produced on lateral buds. This cultivar is suitable as a pot plant but not for outdoor cultivation. *Blaukehlchen* means "bluethroat." Introduced by Federal Research Institute for Horticulture, Wädenswil, Switzerland, in 1987.

H. macrophylla (Lacecap Group) 'Bläuling'

A compact shrub up to about 1 m (3 feet). The flowerheads are large, saucer shaped, with a full ring of ray-flowers, somewhat overlapping. sepals are slightly dentate. Flower color is light blue, pink on an alkaline soil. The fertile flowers are blue. This cultivar is very free-flowering and can also flower a second time on well-developed lateral buds. Flowering time is usually from July to September. *Bläuling* means "blue butterfly." Introduced by Federal Research Institute for Horticulture, Wädenswil, Switzerland, in 1984.

Hydrangea macrophylla (Lacecap Group) 'Blaumeise', Boering garden.

Hydrangea macrophylla (Lacecap Group) 'Blaumeise', Maurice Foster garden.

Hydrangea macrophylla (Lacecap Group) 'Blaumeise', Le Vastérival.

Hydrangea macrophylla (Lacecap Group) 'Blaumeise', Maurice Foster garden.

H. *macrophylla* (Lacecap Group) 'Blaumeise'

A strong-growing shrub up to 1.5 m (5 feet) or more, becoming very large. The flowerheads are composed of a ring of florets, usually midblue, sepals slightly dentate. On acid soils with low aluminum, this beautiful plant is, in spite of its name, brilliantly pink, as seen in our own nursery, later turning to a dirty mix of pink and blue; however, when it is well fed with aluminum sulfate, it is one of the best blue lacecaps. It is otherwise a good garden plant. *Blaumeise* means "blue tit" (a small European bird), "blue sky," or "titmouse." Introduced by Federal Research Institute for Horticulture, Wädenswil, Switzerland, in 1979.

H. *macrophylla* (Lacecap Group) 'Bleu Bleu Vastérival'

Very close to 'Blanc Bleu Vastérival'. The center is pale blue with fertile flowers and surrounded by pale blue or pink sepals. Raised by Princess Sturdza, France, in 2000 and named for her garden. Introduced by C. Esveld Nurseries.

Hydrangea macrophylla (Lacecap Group) 'Bleu Bleu Vastérival', Le Vastérival.

Hydrangea macrophylla (Lacecap Group) 'Blue Billow', Holehird Gardens.

Hydrangea macrophylla (Lacecap Group) 'Blue Lagoon', Arboretum de Dreijen.

Hydrangea macrophylla (Lacecap Group) 'Blue Lace', courtesy Wout Kromhout.

H. macrophylla (Lacecap Group) 'Blue Billow'

A seedling selection, grown from wild seed collected in Korea by Richard Lighty. It is a compact midsized bush up to 1.25 m (3.5 feet). Flowers blue to white or pink, usually double. The sterile flowers are long lasting, and the leaves show good autumn colors. Raised at the Mount Cuba Research Station, Delaware, United States.

H. macrophylla (Lacecap Group) 'Blue Lace'

A selected seedling with usually light blue ray-flowers contrasting with the dark green-reddish foliage. Flowering time is in August. Introduced by Darthuizer Nurseries, Netherlands, in 1992.

H. macrophylla (Lacecap Group) 'Blue Lagoon'

Pink or blue sepals partly surround the fertile flowers. The bold foliage is broadly oval with a rounded apex. Origin unknown.

Hydrangea macrophylla (Lacecap Group) 'Buchfink', Arboretum de Dreijen.

Hydrangea macrophylla (Lacecap Group) 'Curtis' Legacy', Rein and Mark Bulk nursery.

Hydrangea macrophylla (Lacecap Group) 'Buntspecht', Arboretum de Dreijen.

H. macrophylla (Lacecap Group) 'Brympton Mauve'

A sturdy shrub up to 1.5 m (5 feet). Flowerheads with ray-flowers in a ring, additional flowers between the fertile flowers, and really large sepals. Flower color is white or with a pink hue. This sport of 'Beauté Vendômoise' is free-flowering but needs shade for good results. Raised by V. Clive, United Kingdom, in 1946.

H. macrophylla (Lacecap Group) 'Buchfink'

A vigorous-growing shrub about 1.5 m (5 feet) high. Flowerheads saucer shaped, with a partly double ring of ray-flowers, sepals rounded, dark rosy red. The fertile flowers are conspicuously bluish. The plant is very free-flowering, midsummer, and sometimes produces flowers from strong lateral buds. It is suitable as a pot plant and for outdoor cultivation. *Buchfink* means "finch." Introduced by Federal Research Institute for Horticulture, Wädenswil, Switzerland, in 1987.

H. macrophylla (Lacecap Group) 'Buntspecht'

A medium-sized shrub up to 1.25 m (3.5 feet), with stout branches. Flowerheads round, ray-flowers in a single ring, sepals entire. The color is a strong rosy red. Strong lateral buds flower a second time. It is suitable as a pot plant and for outdoor cultivation. *Buntspecht* means "woodpecker." Introduced by Federal Research Institute for Horticulture, Wädenswil, Switzerland, in 1987.

H. macrophylla (Lacecap Group) 'Canberra'

A small shrub up to 1 m (3 feet). The leaves are small, dark green and somewhat crinkled. The flowerheads are small, 8 cm (3 inches) across. Many purple fertile flowers are surrounded by white ray-flowers. Flowering time is in June. 'Canberra' is a miniature version of 'Veitchii'. Origin Australia.

H. macrophylla (Lacecap Group) 'Curtis' Legacy'

This name replaces the illegitimate name of *H. japonica* 'Coerulea'. Curtis described it as a variety of *H. japonica* in 1846. The plant is a cultivar and now also treated as such. It is a strong growing with pale pink flowerheads. Origin Japanese.

Hydrangea macrophylla (Lacecap Group) 'Dancing Lady', Darthuizer Nurseries.

Hydrangea macrophylla (Lacecap Group) 'Dart's Songbird', Research Station for Nursery Stock.

H. macrophylla (Lacecap Group) 'Dandenong', courtesy Maurice Foster.

Hydrangea macrophylla (Lacecap Group) 'Dart's Songbird', H. J. van Paddenburgh garden.

Hydrangea macrophylla (Lacecap Group) 'Dart's Romance', courtesy Wout Kromhout.

H. macrophylla (Lacecap Group) 'Dancing Lady'

A medium-sized shrub, probably not more than 1 m (3 feet) high. Flowerheads lilac to pink, a nice color combination. The fertile flowers are lilac. Introduced by Darthuizer Nurseries, Netherlands, in 1992.

H. macrophylla (Lacecap Group) 'Dandenong'

A shrub up to 1.5 m (5 feet). The fertile flowers are violet, the ray-flowers are white, sepals entire. Named after a mountain near Sydney. Origin Australian.

H. macrophylla (Lacecap Group) 'Dart's Romance'

A medium-sized shrub, usually more than 1 m (3 feet). Lilac-pink ray-flowers surround bluish fertile flowers. Introduced by Darthuizer Nurseries, Netherlands, in 1994.

Hydrangea macrophylla (Lacecap Group) 'Dr. Jean Varnier', Maurice Foster garden.

Hydrangea macrophylla (Lacecap Group) 'Eisvogel', PlantenTuin de Oirsprong.

Hydrangea macrophylla (Lacecap Group) 'Eisvogel', C. Esveld Nurseries.

Hydrangea macrophylla (Lacecap Group) 'Elster', Holehird Gardens.

H. macrophylla (Lacecap Group) 'Dart's Songbird'

A dwarf shrub up to about 1 m (3 feet). Flowerheads with a ring of dark pink or blue florets. The sepals are entire. This new plant is very floriferous. Introduced by Darthuizer Nurseries, Netherlands, in 1994.

H. macrophylla (Lacecap Group) 'Dr. Jean Varnier'

A medium-sized shrub up to 1.5 m (5 feet). The flower-heads consist of purple-violet flowers surrounded by pale lilac ray-flowers. This plant is hardy and does not suffer from drought. It is a mutant of 'Lanarth White' and similar to it. The cultivar was found in Dr. J. Varnier's garden in Luneray and shown at the Courson Fair of 1998. Origin French, in 1994.

H. macrophylla (Lacecap Group) 'Eisvogel'

A shrub up to 1.25 m (3.5 feet) or slightly more. The flowerheads are arranged in a semidouble row, single florets large, sepals serrate. Usually the color is blue, but only on a very acid soil. Plants in our nursery grown in sandy-peaty soil flower brilliantly pink, just as 'Blaumeise' does. These cultivars must be fed with aluminum sulfate to get them blue. The foliage is not very attractive and susceptible to chlorosis. *Eisvogel* means "kingfisher." Introduced by Federal Research Institute for Horticulture, Wädenswil, Switzerland, in 1979.

H. macrophylla (Lacecap Group) 'Elster'

A shrub up to 1 m (3 feet), of firm stature. Flowerheads are large, with ray-flowers in a partly double ring, white with a hint of blue, and fertile flowers dark blue. *Elster* means "magpie." Introduced by Federal Research Institute for Horticulture, Wädenswil, Switzerland, in 1983.

Hydrangea macrophylla (Lacecap Group) 'Etoile Violette', Le Thuit Saint-Jean.

Hydrangea macrophylla (Lacecap Group) 'Fasan', Arboretum de Dreijen.

Hydrangea macrophylla (Lacecap Group) 'Fasan', Maurice Foster garden.

Hydrangea macrophylla (Lacecap Group) 'Everdawn', courtesy Wout Kromhout.

H. *macrophylla* (Lacecap Group) 'Etoile Violette'

This Japanese form is very similar to 'Izu no hana'. Found by Corinne Mallet at Izu in Japan and introduced in 1994. It is too tender for outdoor cultivation in colder climates but is suitable as a pot plant.

H. *macrophylla* (Lacecap Group) 'Everdawn'

An untidy shrub up to 1 m (3 feet). The flowers are abundantly produced, sterile flowers dark pink, fertile flowers violet. The leaves are dark green, conspicuous. The plant needs some maintenance to keep it tidy. Introduced by Darthuizer Nurseries, Netherlands, in 1994.

H. *macrophylla* (Lacecap Group) 'Fasan'

A huge shrub about 1.5 m (5 feet) high with sturdy branches. The flowerheads are round, the ray-flowers are large, sepals entire or slightly heart shaped, placed in a semidouble ring. Flower color is clear red. Lateral branches often produce a second flowering period. Suitable as pot

Hydrangea macrophylla (Lacecap Group) 'Fasan', Holehird Gardens.

Hydrangea macrophylla (Lacecap Group) 'Gaku no cyo kanisha', Rein and Mark Bulk nursery.

Hydrangea macrophylla (Lacecap Group) 'Flamingo', Boering garden.

Hydrangea macrophylla (Lacecap Group) 'Geisha', Research Station for Nursery Stock.

plant and for outdoor cultivation. *Fasan* means "pheasant." Introduced by Federal Research Institute for Horticulture, Wädenswil, Switzerland, in 1979.

H. macrophylla (Lacecap Group) 'Flamingo'
A large irregular-shaped shrub up to 2 m (6.5 feet). The flowerheads are large and saucer shaped with ray-flowers in a single ring, sepals broadly acuminate. Flower color is rosy red to purple. Suitable as a pot plant but not for outdoor cultivation. Introduced by Federal Research Institute for Horticulture, Wädenswil, Switzerland, in 1987.

H. macrophylla (Lacecap Group) 'Forget Me Not'
A spreading shrub up to 1 m (3 feet). Inflorescences consist of blue ray-flowers, fertile flowers also blue. Sepals slightly overlapping, usually four, serrate at the upper part. This cultivar produces new flowers after a severe night's frost in April. Bred by de Belder and van Trier, in Belgium, in 1988.

H. macrophylla (Lacecap Group) 'Gaku no cyo kanisha'
A small shrub with ray-flowers scattered over the flowerhead. Leaves long and pointed, light green. Origin Japanese; distributed by Milim Botanical Garden, Korea.

H. macrophylla (Lacecap Group) 'Ganymede'
A medium-sized shrub about 1.5 m (5 feet) high and wide. The flowerheads consist of irregular ray-flowers, pale lilac or very pale pink, surrounding the fertile flowers. Flowering time is early in the season. The plant needs some protection in less favorable locations. Origin French.

H. macrophylla (Lacecap Group) 'Geisha'
An untidy shrub up to 1.5 m (5 feet). The flowerheads are large, lilac-pink, rarely blue. This tender plant needs a sheltered place and also some pruning. Introduced by Cayeux of France in 1967.

Hydrangea macrophylla (Lacecap Group) 'Geoffrey Chadbund', Trelissick Garden.

Hydrangea macrophylla (Lacecap Group) 'Gimpel', Arboretum de Dreijen.

Hydrangea macrophylla (Lacecap Group) 'Geoffrey Chadbund', Stourton House Flower Garden.

Hydrangea macrophylla (Lacecap Group) 'Gimpel', Holehird Gardens.

H. macrophylla (Lacecap Group) 'Geoffrey Chadbund'

A compact shrub up to 1.5 m (5 feet) high and wide. The flowerheads are rounded, and the ray-flowers are arranged in a single ring, occasionally a double ring. Florets are rosy red, or purplish, sepals entire. This cultivar is the "lacecap" counterpart of 'Ami Pasquier'. Flowers and foliage are of the same color, according to Mallet. Origin England; named and introduced by J. Russell, before 1956. RHS Award: AGM 1992.

H. macrophylla (Lacecap Group) 'Gimpel'

A vigorous-growing shrub, 1.25 m (3.5 feet) or more. Flowerheads round, ray-flowers in a single ring, sometimes also some florets between the lilac or violet fertile flowers, sepals large, round and entire, or slightly dentate, pink. The fertile flowers are whitish. Suitable as a pot plant. *Gimpel* means "bullfinch." Introduced by Federal Research Institute for Horticulture, Wädenswil, Switzerland, in 1987.

H. macrophylla (Lacecap Group) 'Gold Dust'

A vigorous-growing, medium-sized shrub. The leaves are golden yellow and quite showy. Flowerheads blue to pink, fertile flowers bluish. Bred by Louisiana Nurseries, United States.

H. macrophylla (Lacecap Group) 'Gold Nugget'

A dwarf shrub, barely exceeding 1 m (3 feet). Free-flowering with white to mauve ray-flowers. Flowers long-lasting. The leaves are dark green with strong yellow blotches but sometimes reverting to fully green. Bred by Louisiana Nurseries, United States.

H. macrophylla (Lacecap Group) 'Goldstrike'

A vigorous-growing shrub up to 1.25 m (3.5 feet). The leaf margins are yellow variegated, leaf-blades also irregularly striped, with a good autumn color. Flowerheads pink to mauve. Bred by Louisiana Nurseries, United States.

Hydrangea macrophylla (Lacecap Group) 'Grant's Choice', Maurice Foster garden.

Hydrangea macrophylla (Lacecap Group) 'Grasmücke', PlantenTuin de Oirsprong.

Hydrangea macrophylla (Lacecap Group) 'Grasmücke', Research Station for Nursery Stock.

Hydrangea macrophylla (Lacecap Group) 'Green Tonic', Stourton House Flower Garden.

H. macrophylla (Lacecap Group) 'Gold Zing'

Leaves golden yellow. Distributed by Gossler Farm, Springfield Nurseries, United States.

H. macrophylla (Lacecap Group) 'Grant's Choice'

A large shrub sometimes exceeding 1.5 m (5 feet), sparsely branched. Flowerheads large, ray-flowers light pink with white, very charming. The fertile flowers are bluish green and contrast well. Sepals large, heavily serrate. The very similar 'J. M. Grant' is not identical as is sometimes stated. Selected by James M. Grant of Grayswood Hill, United Kingdom, before 1940.

H. macrophylla (Lacecap Group) 'Grasmücke'

A slow-growing low shrub. Flowers saucer shaped, ray-flowers are placed in a single ring, florets large, sepals almost entire, rosy red. A good plant for pots and tubs. *Grasmücke* means "white throat." Introduced by Federal Research Institute for Horticulture, Wädenswil, Switzerland, in 1987.

H. macrophylla (Lacecap Group) 'Green Eyes'

A dwarf to semidwarf shrub. The leaves are yellow variegated, flowers white, turning to mauve with age. Bred by Louisiana Nurseries, United States.

H. macrophylla (Lacecap Group) 'Green Tonic'

A medium-sized shrub. Ray-flowers white, sepals large with green spots and stripes, heavily dentate. Fertile flowers lilac-blue, the sepals are arranged in a ring. This mutant from 'Mariesii Grandiflora' was found in Chelsea Physic Garden in London. Raised by Elizabeth Bullivant, United Kingdom, in 1997. Similar to 'Stourton Lace', also from Elizabeth Bullivant.

Hydrangea macrophylla (Lacecap Group) 'Hanabi', C. Esveld Nurseries.

Hydrangea macrophylla (Lacecap Group) 'Hatsu shime', PlantenTuin de Oirsprong.

Hydrangea macrophylla (Lacecap Group) 'Harrow's Blue', Royal Botanic Garden, Edinburgh.

Hydrangea macrophylla (Lacecap Group) 'Hobella', Trelissick Garden.

H. macrophylla (Lacecap Group) 'Hanabi'

A tall vigorous-growing shrub, sometimes exceeding 2.5 m (8 feet). The flowerheads are exceptionally large. The ray-flowers are double, arranged in a ring, and some florets are scattered throughout the fertile flowers. The white florets look like little stars. Flowering time is very long, until October. This remarkable cultivar seems destined to become one of the best newly introduced cultivars. Trademarked names are FIREWORKS, VUURWERK, and FEU D'ARTIFICE. Bred by T. Yamamoto, Japan, in 1960.

H. macrophylla (Lacecap Group) 'Harrow's Blue'

A small plant, flowering profusely with almost pure white florets. Fertile flowers are dark blue. The sepals are not overlapping. Raised at the Royal Botanic Garden, Edinburgh, United Kingdom.

H. macrophylla (Lacecap Group) 'Hatsu shime'

A large shrub, exceeding 1.5 m (5 feet) high and about as wide. Flowerheads large, about 20 cm (8 inches) across. The fertile flowers are violet to greenish, and the relatively small ray-flowers are almost white or light pink. The leaves are variegated and shiny green. Fully green plants can suddenly produce yellow leaves again. Origin Japanese.

H. macrophylla (Lacecap Group) 'Hera'

A large shrub, about 1.75 m (5.75 feet) high and wide. The leaves are large and shiny green. The flowerheads are also large, up to 20 cm (8 inches) across. The fertile flowers are purple, and the ray-flowers, which consist of four sepals, are purple with a small white margin. Bred by August Steiniger, Germany, in 1979.

H. macrophylla (Lacecap Group) 'Hobella'

A compact plant. The flowers are arranged in circles of sterile pale pink sepals. The corymbs are somewhat saucer shaped, later flattened. After a couple of weeks, they turn to greenish and three weeks later change again to dark red. In this way the plant stays attractive for a long time. Also suitable as a pot plant. This cultivar is trademarked under the name HOVARIA. Bred by K. and W. Hofstede, Netherlands, in 1994.

Hydrangea macrophylla (Lacecap Group) 'Holibel', C. Esveld Nurseries.

Hydrangea macrophylla (Lacecap Group) 'Iso chidori', Rein and Mark Bulk nursery.

Hydrangea macrophylla (Lacecap Group) 'Hugh', Maurice Foster garden.

Hydrangea macrophylla (Lacecap Group) 'Izu no hana', Le Vastérival.

H. macrophylla (Lacecap Group) 'Holibel'

A vigorous-growing shrub, found as a branch sport of 'Libelle' but differing by the much larger quantity of sterile flowers. The florets are scattered intensively through the fertile flowers, almost forming a flat corymb. Trademarked name is HOVARIA. Bred by K. and W. Hofstede, Netherlands, in 1996. 'Snow' is a similar sport.

H. macrophylla (Lacecap Group) 'Hugh'

Sepals large, slightly serrate, white. The fertile flowers are green to purple. Raised by Elizabeth Bullivant, United Kingdom, in 1980, but not named until 2000. Possible synonym: 'Stourton Lace'.

H. macrophylla (Lacecap Group) 'Io'

A moderate shrub up to 1.5 m (5 feet). The leaves show clear veins. The flowerheads are white with pointed sepals, and the fertile flowers are greenish white. This plant is surprisingly hardy and easy to cultivate. Origin Japanese.

H. macrophylla (Lacecap Group) 'Iso chidori'

A strong-growing shrub up to 1.5 m (5 feet). The corymbs are large, red to rosy red. Sepals strongly dentate. Fertile flowers have a white center. Name may be wrongly spelled "Iso shidori." Origin Japanese; distributed by Milim Botanical Garden, Korea.

H. macrophylla (Lacecap Group) 'Izu no hana'

A moderate-growing shrub. The flowerheads are formed of many fertile flowers, blue to purplish green, and tightly packed, only a few florets, purple or pink, double, placed in one or more irregular ring. The sepals are on long stalks, which is unusual. This plant was discovered on the Izu Peninsula and is now in cultivation in Europe. Raised by Hisashi Iida, Japan, in 1970.

Hydrangea macrophylla (Lacecap Group) 'James Grant', courtesy Arborealis.

Hydrangea macrophylla (Lacecap Group) 'Jungfrau Picotee', Floriade 2002.

Hydrangea macrophylla (Lacecap Group) 'Jōgosaki', Floriade 2002.

Hydrangea macrophylla (Lacecap Group) 'Juno', Jardin Bellevue.

Hydrangea macrophylla (Lacecap Group) 'Jōgosaki', Trelissick Garden.

H. macrophylla (Lacecap Group) 'James Grant'

Sometimes considered synonymous with 'Grant's Choice', but careful comparison at the Research Station in Boskoop, Netherlands, has shown minor differences. Bred by J. Grant, Grayswood Hill, United Kingdom, before 1962.

H. macrophylla (Lacecap Group) 'Jōgosaki'

A small shrub, rarely 1.5 m (5 feet) high, well branched. The flowerheads have small purple fertile flowers, surrounded by large, double silvery pink florets, consisting of four sepals. This is one of the few double-flowering lacecaps. Also called 'Fireworks', 'Vuurwerk', and 'Feu d'Artifice'. Probable synonym: *H. macrophylla* (Lacecap Group) 'Jōgosaki fuiri'. Origin Japanese.

H. macrophylla (Lacecap Group) 'Jungfrau Picotee'

This small shrub is very similar to the better known 'Love You Kiss'. The flowerheads show a hint of green. Origin Japanese.

Hydrangea macrophylla (Lacecap Group) 'Juno', Maurice Foster garden.

Hydrangea macrophylla (Lacecap Group) 'Kardinal', C. Esveld Nurseries.

Hydrangea macrophylla (Lacecap Group) 'Juno', Trelissick Garden.

H. macrophylla (Lacecap Group) 'Klaveren', courtesy Arborealis.

H. macrophylla (Lacecap Group) 'Juno'

A moderate-growing shrub with pink flowerheads. It needs shade for good results. Similar to 'Mariesii Lilacina'. Synonym: 'Hidcote Pink'. Although some authorities suggest that 'Kaye Leslie' is a synonym, the authors doubt such a relationship exists as the two cultivars strongly differ. Raised by Elizabeth Bullivant, United Kingdom, in 1975.

H. macrophylla (Lacecap Group) 'Kardinal'

A sturdy, vigorous-growing shrub up to 1.5 m (5 feet). The corymbs are saucer-shaped, and the ray-flowers are arranged in a double ring, dark red, the sepals are elongated and entire. The flowers are purplish pink. Flowering time is in July. A second show of flowers is displayed sporadically on strong side shoots. *Kardinal* means "cardinal." Introduced by Federal Research Institute for Horticulture, Wädenswil, Switzerland, in 1987.

H. macrophylla (Lacecap Group) 'Kaye Leslie'

Sepals pink, fertile flowers heavily serrate, ruby red. Present at Le Thuit Saint-Jean. Not a synonym of 'Juno' although some have suggested such.

H. macrophylla (Lacecap Group) 'Klaveren'

A strong-growing shrub up to 1.25 m (3.5 feet). Inflorescences large, up to 20 cm (8 inches) across, usually lilac-pink, and becoming coppery in the autumn. Bred by R. Michel-Kerneur, France, in 1994.

Hydrangea macrophylla (Lacecap Group) 'Komnu Costen', courtesy Arborealis.

Hydrangea macrophylla (Lacecap Group) 'Lemon Wave', C. Esveld Nurseries.

Hydrangea macrophylla (Lacecap Group) 'Lanarth White', Maurice Foster garden.

Hydrangea macrophylla (Lacecap Group) 'Lemon Wave', courtesy Arborealis.

H. macrophylla (Lacecap Group) 'Komnu Costen'

The sepals are almost round and entire, white; fertile flowers blue. A French cultivar from the Mallets.

H. macrophylla (Lacecap Group) 'Lanarth White'

This sturdy, well-growing shrub attains a height of about 1.5 m (5 feet). The flowerheads are rounded, the ray-flowers are pure white, the fertile flowers lilac to lilac-pink. The florets are arranged in several rows. The sepals are ovate to acuminate. Flowering time is from July to August. This cultivar supposedly is a sport of 'Thomas Hogg'. Selected by M. Williams, Lanarth, United Kingdom, before 1949. RHS Awards: AM 1949, AGM 1992.

H. macrophylla (Lacecap Group) 'Lemon Wave'

A medium-sized shrub. The leaves are conspicuously variegated with yellow edges and some hints of white. The flowerheads are white, small, and unimportant. This hydrangea is cultivated solely for its foliage. Origin not known.

Hydrangea macrophylla (Lacecap Group) 'Libelle', Holehird Gardens.

Hydrangea macrophylla (Lacecap Group) 'Maculata', Trelissick Garden.

Hydrangea macrophylla (Lacecap Group) 'Love You Kiss', C. Esveld Nurseries.

Hydrangea macrophylla (Lacecap Group) 'Maculata', C. Esveld Nurseries.

H. macrophylla (Lacecap Group) 'Libelle'

A large shrub up to 1.5 m (5 feet), with weak branches often needing some staking. The leaves are light green with entire margins, bold and saucer shaped. The corymbs are flat and rounded, ray-flowers are pure white arranged in one or two rows, and fertile flowers are blue. The number of sepals varies from a single ring to almost "mophead." This cultivar is excellent as a pot plant but it is too floppy for general planting outdoors. 'Snow' and 'Holibel' may be mutants of 'Libelle'. *Libelle* means "dove" or "dragonfly." Introduced by Federal Research Institute for Horticulture, Wädenswil, Switzerland, in 1964.

H. macrophylla (Lacecap Group) 'Love You Kiss'

A low shrub, usually not exceeding 1 m (3 feet). The flowerheads consist of white fertile flowers, surrounded by ray-flowers, which are white with a pink edge, an unusual combination for lacecaps. Like other cultivars such as 'Mirai', this one is closely related to 'Kiyosumi' (synonym, var. *kiyusumensis*). Trademarked name is HOVARIA. Bred by Yatabe Mototeru of Japan.

H. macrophylla (Lacecap Group) 'Maculata'

A shrubby plant up to 1.25 m (3.5 feet), with sturdy branches. The leaves are acuminate, with irregular white variegation along the margins, which shows up best when the plant is grown in shade. The flowerheads are pinkish white, a few ray-flowers surround the fertile flowers. The plant is a shy flowerer. This is the most variegated cultivar, not to be mistaken with 'Tricolor' or 'Quadricolor'. Origin Japanese.

Hydrangea macrophylla (Lacecap Group) 'Mariesii', Le Thuit Saint-Jean.

Hydrangea macrophylla (Lacecap Group) 'Mariesii Grandiflora', Maurice Foster garden.

Hydrangea macrophylla (Lacecap Group) 'Mariesii Grandiflora', Jardin Bellevue.

Hydrangea macrophylla (Lacecap Group) 'Mariesii Lilacina', Sir Harold Hillier Gardens and Arboretum.

H. macrophylla (Lacecap Group) 'Mariesii'

A sturdy shrub up to 1.5 m (5 feet) or more. The flowerheads are about 15 cm (6 inches) across, saucer shaped. The ray-flowers are blush-pink, sepals round and entire, sometimes scattered over the fertile flowers, but usually in a ring. This plant was imported from Japan to Great Britain in 1879 by Charles Maries, for Messrs. Veitch (United Kingdom). Victor Lemoine was the first hybridizer to successfully propagate it from seed, and he named three seedlings, all starting with "Mariesii." Haworth-Booth renamed some of them to avoid confusion in horticulture. Although horticulturists generally accept this practice, it is not allowed under the ICNCP to change the name of an older cultivar. The true 'Mariesii' is now scarce. RHS Awards: AM 1938, FCC 1965.

H. macrophylla (Lacecap Group) 'Mariesii Grandiflora'

A huge shrub up to 1.5 m (5 feet) or more and about as wide. Flowerheads large, rounded, and about the same size as those of 'Mariesii'. Sepals wavy, pure white and slightly tinged with pale pink. This plant is more robust then 'Veitchii' when planted in less favorable places. Haworth-Booth renamed this cultivar "White Wave," an illegitimate name. Bred by Victor Lemoine, Nancy, France, in 1902.

H. macrophylla (Lacecap Group) 'Mariesii Lilacina'

A medium-sized shrub, but sometimes exceeding 1.5 m (5 feet). The flowers are scattered at the edges of the single ray-flowers, lilac or pink, rarely purplish blue. Sepals strongly dentate. Fertile flowers are blue to pinkish blue. Flowering is exceptionally long, from July to the end of October. Haworth-Booth renamed this cultivar Lilacina', an illegitimate name. Bred by Victoir Lemoine, Nancy, France, in 1904.

H. macrophylla (Lacecap Group) 'Mariesii Perfecta'

A sturdy shrub, with stout branches, up to 2 m (6.5 feet) high and wide. The flowerheads are rounded, the ray-flowers are blush pink, or light blue, sepals round and entire.

Hydrangea macrophylla (Lacecap Group) 'Mariesii Perfecta', Jardin du Mesnil.

Hydrangea macrophylla (Lacecap Group) 'Mariesii Perfecta', Hemelrijk Tuinen.

Hydrangea macrophylla (Lacecap Group) 'Mariesii Silver', Research Station for Nursery Stock.

Hydrangea macrophylla (Lacecap Group) 'Messalina', Floriade 2002.

Flowering time is from July to August. Haworth-Booth renamed this cultivar "Blue Wave," an illegitimate name although one that is in general use and firmly established. Blue-flowering plants are called 'Blue Wave' (synonym, 'Bluewave') and pink ones go under the original name 'Mariesii Perfecta', but it is certain that they are otherwise identical. Selected by Victor Lemoine of France, in 1904. RHS Awards: AM 1965, FCC 1985, AGM 1992.

H. macrophylla (Lacecap Group) 'Mariesii Silver'

This inconspicuously variegated form from 'Mariesii' appeared recently on the market. Although variegated mutants are not rare, this plant could be a renamed version of 'Maculata' or similar cultivars.

H. macrophylla (Lacecap Group) 'Messalina'

A moderate-growing shrub up to 1.25 m (3.5 feet). Flowerheads are flattened lacecaps, usually pale pink to purplish pink. This tender cultivar needs a sheltered place in the garden. Bred by Kientzler of Germany, in 1969.

Hydrangea macrophylla (Lacecap Group) 'Miranda', Maurice Foster garden.

Hydrangea macrophylla (Lacecap Group) 'Mousmée', Research Station for Nursery Stock.

Hydrangea macrophylla (Lacecap Group) 'Miranda', courtesy Arborealis.

Hydrangea macrophylla (Lacecap Group) 'Mousmée', Le Thuit Saint-Jean.

H. macrophylla (Lacecap Group) 'Miranda'

A small shrub, not exceeding 1 m (3 feet), usually less than that, but becoming much wider. Flowers in corymbs, irregularly rounded. The florets are numerous, clear pink, not lasting very long. Sepals rounded, three or four per flower, fertile flowers pinkish orange. Raised by Michael Haworth-Booth, United Kingdom, before 1980.

H. macrophylla (Lacecap Group) 'Morgan Blue'

A compact shrub up to 1 m (3 feet). The florets are pale lilac, sepals serrate, fertile flowers green.

H. macrophylla (Lacecap Group) 'Mousmée'

A strong-growing shrub, occasionally up to 2 m (6.5 feet) in mild conditions. The corymbs are large, up to 20 cm (8 inches) across, the ray-flowers arranged in a scattered ring and colored dark pink to purplish pink with little spots. The fertile flowers are pinkish red, too. Flowering time is in mid-season. Synonym possibly: 'Aduarda'. Bred by R. Talbot, United Kingdom, in 1960.

Hydrangea macrophylla (Lacecap Group) 'Morgan Blue', courtesy Arborealis.

Hydrangea macrophylla (Lacecap Group) 'Möwe', C. Esveld Nurseries.

Hydrangea macrophylla (Lacecap Group) 'Möwe', Cor van Gelderen garden.

Hydrangea macrophylla (Lacecap Group) 'Möwe', Maurice Foster garden.

H. macrophylla (Lacecap Group) 'Möwe'

A vigorous-growing, sturdy shrub up to 1.5 m (5 feet), becoming wider. The saucer-shaped corymbs are covered with irregularly placed red to purple ray-flowers. The sepals are large, slightly dentate. Flowering time is from August to September. Suitable as a pot plant and for outdoor cultivation. It must be fed with aluminum sulfate to turn the flowers blue, even when the plant is grown in acid soil. *Möwe* means "seagull." Introduced by Federal Research Institute for Horticulture, Wädenswil, Switzerland, in 1964.

H. macrophylla (Lacecap Group) 'Mücke'

A compact, low-growing plant with sturdy, short branches. The flowerheads are relatively small, the ray-flowers light pink with almost white, serrate sepals. It is a good plant for forcing and as a pot plant, but it is too tender for outdoor cultivation. *Mücke* means "mosquito." Synonym: 'Shower'. Introduced by Federal Research Institute for Horticulture, Wädenswil, Switzerland, in 1968.

Hydrangea macrophylla (Lacecap Group) 'Mücke', Arboretum Kalmthout.

Hydrangea macrophylla (Lacecap Group) 'Nachtigall', Maurice Foster garden.

Hydrangea macrophylla (Lacecap Group) 'Nachtigall', C. Esveld Nurseries.

H. macrophylla (Lacecap Group) 'München'
A compact plant, suitable for house and patio. Flowerheads pink. Bred by Rampp Nursery, Germany, before 1990.

H. macrophylla (Lacecap Group) 'Nachtigall'
A medium-sized shrub, about 1.5 m (5 feet), with stout, short branches. The flowerheads are circular, the ray-flow-ers in a single ring, dark blue or violet, especially when fed with aluminum. The fertile flowers are also violet. The florets are arranged in a single ring, sepals slightly serrate. This cultivar is derived from 'Enziandom', an equally good blue plant but not a lacecap. *Nachtigall* means "nightingale." Introduced by Federal Research Institute for Horticulture, Wädenswil, Switzerland, in 1979.

H. macrophylla (Lacecap Group) 'Nizza'
A compact plant. Flowerheads pink with yellow center, also available in blue. The fertile flowers are whitish. A member of the CITY-LINE series. Bred by Rampp Nursery, Germany, before 1999.

H. macrophylla (Lacecap Group) 'Ome gaku'
A strong-growing shrub up to 2 m (6.5 feet). The flowerheads are also large, up to 18 cm (7 inches) across. The ray-flowers are light purplish blue or pink, the fertile flowers are blue. This cultivar is not fully hardy and it requires little water. Origin Japanese.

H. macrophylla (Lacecap Group) 'Papagei'
A tall shrub, sometimes exceeding 2 m (6.5 feet) high, with thin branches. The corymbs are medium sized, the ray-

Hydrangea macrophylla (Lacecap Group) 'Papagei', Arboretum de Dreijen.

Hydrangea macrophylla (Lacecap Group) 'Pengwyn', Trelissick Garden.

Hydrangea macrophylla (Lacecap Group) 'Papagei', C. Esveld Nurseries.

flowers large, flat, dark violet to purple but also purplish pink on some acid soils, sepals dentate to entire. Flowering time is in midseason. *Papagei* means "parrot." Introduced by Federal Research Institute for Horticulture, Wädenswil, Switzerland, in 1987.

H. macrophylla (Lacecap Group) 'Pengwyn'

This shrubby plant is a mutant of 'Lanarth White'. The flowerheads are large, the florets and sepals are white. The fertile flowers are also white, not purple as in 'Lanarth White'. Raised by B. Champion, Trelissick Garden, United Kingdom.

H. macrophylla (Lacecap Group) 'Pfau'

A dwarf form, only suitable as a pot plant and not for the garden. Flowerheads about 15 cm (6 inches) across, gentian blue or pink. The sepals are elongated and pointed, margins entire to slightly dentate. One of the few dwarf hortensias. *Pfau* means "peacock." Introduced by Federal Research Institute for Horticulture, Wädenswil, Switzerland, in 1983.

Hydrangea macrophylla (Lacecap Group) 'Pfau', Arboretum de Dreijen.

Hydrangea macrophylla (Lacecap Group) 'Posy Bouquet Elegance', Floriade 2002.

Hydrangea macrophylla (Lacecap Group) 'Posy Bouquet Suzy', Floriade 2002.

Hydrangea macrophylla (Lacecap Group) 'Posy Bouquet Grace', Floriade 2002.

Hydrangea macrophylla (Lacecap Group) 'Quadricolor', Trelissick Garden.

Hydrangea macrophylla (Lacecap Group) 'Posy Bouquet Kaysey', Floriade 2002.

H. macrophylla (Lacecap Group) Posy Series

Four members of this series were shown at Floriade 2002, an international horticultural exposition held in Netherlands. All were developed by Sakamoto, Syoui Seta Gun, Japan. **'Posy Bouquet Elegance'** has flowers with pointed, pure pink and white double sepals with entire margins. It is among the few double-flowered mopheads. **'Posy Bouquet Grace'** has pure white, pointed sepals. **'Posy Bouquet Kaysey'** is a compact shrub with dark blue flowers and double sepals. **'Posy Bouquet Suzy'** has warm pink, broadly pointed sepals.

Hydrangea macrophylla (Lacecap Group) 'Rosewarne Lace', Royal Horticultural Society Garden Wisley.

Hydrangea macrophylla (Lacecap Group) 'Rotkehlchen', C. Esveld Nurseries.

Hydrangea macrophylla (Lacecap Group) 'Rotdrossel', Arboretum de Dreijen.

H. macrophylla (Lacecap Group) 'Quadricolor'

A medium-sized shrub, not exceeding 1.25 m (3.5 feet), and bushy. It is named for the four-colored leaves, which are pale green, dark green, and variegated yellow and white. The flowerheads are loose, light blue or light pink. The leaves do not revert to all green. Propagation is difficult. This very conspicuous plant differs from 'Tricolor' (although frequently confused with it) by having yellow variegation. It differs from 'Maculata', which has white variegation. Finally, it also differs from 'Lemon Wave', which has bold yellow variegation and is, according to Haworth-Booth, a mutant of 'Sea Foam'.

H. macrophylla (Lacecap Group) 'Rosewarne Lace'

This cultivar was found as a chance seedling under a plant labeled 'Domotoi' in Haworth-Booth's garden. The seedling grew faster than the original plant. The correct name of what we call 'Domotoi' is 'Setsuka yae'. Cuttings were made from both plants and became mixed up, causing much confusion. True 'Rosewarne Lace' has light pink ray-flowers, even almost white, sepals heavily serrate, fertile flowers violet with a cream center. It flowers early. The corymbs are about 20 cm (8 inches) across. Sometimes it is suggested that 'Rosewarne Lace' is identical to 'James Grant', but this cannot be correct. Bred by Anthony Bullivant of the United Kingdom.

H. macrophylla (Lacecap Group) 'Rotdrossel'

A tall shrub, sometimes up to 2 m (6.5 feet). The flowerheads are large, brilliant dark red to purple-red. The ray-flowers are large, arranged in one ring, the sepals slightly dentate. Flowering time is from July to August. This cultivar is suitable for forcing and as a pot plant. *Rotdrossel* means "redwing." Introduced by Federal Research Institute for Horticulture, Wädenswil, Switzerland, in 1987.

H. macrophylla (Lacecap Group) 'Rotkehlchen'

A slow-growing shrub up to 1 m (3 feet) or slightly more. The flowerheads are saucer shaped, the ray-flowers are dark red to purple and arranged in a single ring. Fertile flowers are rosy red. The sepals are entire, heart shaped. Flowering time is from July to August. *Rotkehlchen* means "redbreast." Introduced by Federal Research Institute for Horticulture, Wädenswil, Switzerland, in 1979.

Hydrangea macrophylla (Lacecap Group) 'Rotschwanz', Maurice Foster garden.

Hydrangea macrophylla (Lacecap Group) 'Sandra', Plantarium.

Hydrangea macrophylla (Lacecap Group) 'Rotschwanz', Arboretum de Dreijen.

Hydrangea macrophylla (Lacecap Group) 'Sea Foam', Boering garden.

H. *macrophylla* (Lacecap Group) 'Rotschwanz'

This shrub grows up to 1.5 m (5 feet), with thin branches. The flowerheads are large, the florets are starlike, arranged in a single row. The fertile flowers are yellowish pink. The sepals are elongated, entire. Flowering time is from July to August. The form of the flowers, a rare one, is very interesting. This cultivar is considered the best of the Swiss lacecaps. *Rotschwanz* means "red start." Introduced by Federal Research Institute for Horticulture, Wädenswil, Switzerland, in 1987.

H. *macrophylla* (Lacecap Group) 'Sandra'

A medium-sized shrub. The flowerheads are bicolored, the sepals are white with red margins. This cultivar is derived from f. *kiyusumensis* and is a member of the trademarked series DUTCH LADIES. Bred by D. van der Spek, Netherlands, in 2000.

H. *macrophylla* (Lacecap Group) 'San Remo'

A compact plant, with light purple or pink flowerheads and whitish fertile flowers. A member of the CITY-LINE series. Bred by Rampp Nursery, Germany, before 1996.

H. *macrophylla* (Lacecap Group) 'Sea Foam'

A shrub up to 1.5 m (5 feet) or more. The flowerheads are sparsely covered with ray-flowers, usually white to light blue or light pink. The sepals are almost white. This cultivar is tender and needs protection in less suitable places, although it does well in seaside plantings. It supposedly is very close to the wild subspecies, *H. macrophylla* var. *normalis,* which was named by Wilson at the time of the introduction. Origin Japanese.

Hydrangea macrophylla (Lacecap Group) 'Selina', Plantarium.

Hydrangea macrophylla (Lacecap Group) 'Snow', Trelissick Garden.

Hydrangea serrata 'Setsuka yae', C. Esveld Nurseries.

Hydrangea macrophylla (Lacecap Group) 'Snow', Trelissick Garden.

H. macrophylla (Lacecap Group) 'Selina'

A compact shrub, with bold, dark green leaves, brown red when young. The florets are arranged in a single ring, rosy red. Sepals are heart shaped to egg shaped. The fertile flowers are dark pink. One of the trademarked series DUTCH LADIES. Bred by D. van der Spek, Netherlands, in 2002.

H. macrophylla (Lacecap Group) 'Selma'

A compact shrub, free-flowering. The corymbs are large and dark red. This cultivar is a recorded hybrid with 'München'. One of the trademarked series DUTCH LADIES. Bred by D. van der Spek, Netherlands, in 2002.

H. macrophylla (Lacecap Group) 'Setsuka yae'

A moderate-growing shrub just over 1 m (3 feet) and rarely up to 1.5 m (5 feet). It prefers acid soils. Corymbs are small and irregular. The individual sterile flowers are half-double, which is unique in this group of plants. Flowering time is from August to September. The color is usually brilliant

blue. Mr. Domoto, living in the United States, sent a plant to France from Japan. It is an interesting, attractive cultivar. Synonyms: 'Domotoi', 'Taika yae'.

H. macrophylla (Lacecap Group) 'Shamrock'

Almost identical to 'Etoile Violette' but much hardier. Bred by Robert Mallet, France.

H. macrophylla (Lacecap Group) 'Sheila'

A compact shrub with large corymbs, almost round. The sepals are very large, pink and more or less cup shaped. This cultivar is the counterpart of the mophead 'Stella'. One of the trademarked series DUTCH LADIES. Bred by D. van der Spek, Netherlands, in 2002.

H. macrophylla (Lacecap Group) 'Snow'

A branch sport of 'Libelle' found in Great Britain, about 1972. 'Holibel' is a similar sport. The flowerheads have more ray-flowers than 'Libelle', giving the impression of being almost a mophead on some flowers.

Hydrangea macrophylla (Lacecap Group) 'Soraya', Plantarium.

Hydrangea macrophylla (Lacecap Group) 'Sumida no hanabi', Floriade 2002.

Hydrangea macrophylla (Lacecap Group) 'Stourton Lace', Stourton House Flower Garden.

Hydrangea macrophylla (Lacecap Group) 'Tambour Major', courtesy Arborealis.

H. *macrophylla* (Lacecap Group) 'Soraya'

A strong-growing shrub up to 1.25 m (3.5 feet). Leaves very dark green. Flowerheads relatively small, with four or five rounded sepals, light rosy lilac. One of the trademarked series DUTCH LADIES. Bred by D. van der Spek, Netherlands, in 2002.

H. *macrophylla* (Lacecap Group) 'Stourton Lace'

A medium-sized shrub, Flowerheads with white ray-flowers, heavily dentate sepals. Fertile flowers lilac to blue. Very similar to 'Green Tonic'. Raised by Elizabeth Bullivant, United Kingdom, in 1997.

H. *macrophylla* (Lacecap Group) 'Sumida no hanabi'

Almost identical to 'Hanabi' but with more florets, pure white on long stalks. Purple fertile flowers. *Hanabi* means "fireworks." Origin Japanese.

H. *macrophylla* (Lacecap Group) 'Tambour Major'

A shrub up to 1.25 m (3.5 feet). The flowerheads consist of double sepals, light blue, much like 'Hanabi'. A good example of what in Japan is called an Izu hydrangea. All Izu hydrangeas bear double ray-flowers.

Hydrangea macrophylla (Lacecap Group) 'Taube', Boering garden.

Hydrangea macrophylla (Lacecap Group) 'Tricolor', Holehird Gardens.

Hydrangea macrophylla (Lacecap Group) 'Tokyo Delight', Maurice Foster garden.

Hydrangea macrophylla (Lacecap Group) 'Tricolor', C. Esveld Nurseries.

H. macrophylla (Lacecap Group) 'Taube'

A slow-growing shrub, about 1 m (3 feet). Branches sturdy and short. The corymbs are tightly packed with overlapping ray-flowers, carmine red to purplish red. The sepals are round, and slightly dentate. Flowering time is from July to August. Suitable as a pot plant and for outdoor cultivation. *Taube* means "pigeon." Introduced by Federal Research Institute for Horticulture, Wädenswil, Switzerland, in 1979.

H. macrophylla (Lacecap Group) 'Taurus'

A shrub up to 1 m (3 feet). Fertile flowers purplish blue, ray-flowers rounded, four sepals per floret, usually light blue. Leaves light green. Origin French.

H. macrophylla (Lacecap Group) 'Tokyo Delight'

A huge shrub up to 2 m (6.5 feet) in sheltered places. Flowerheads small, 10–15 cm (4–6 inches) across. The ray-flowers are arranged irregularly in one ring. The florets are pure white, maturing light pink. Sepals elongated and dentate. It can be confused with 'Grayswood'. A very beautiful plant, deserving more attention. Origin Japanese, before 1940; introduced by L. de Rothschild.

H. macrophylla (Lacecap Group) 'Tricolor'

A tall vigorous-growing shrub, sometimes up to 2 m (6.5 feet). The leaves are conspicuously variegated with greenish white and yellow. Flowerheads are large, ray-flowers are arranged in an irregular ring, pale pink to white. Flowering time is in August. Very free-flowering. This cultivar needs a protected place in the garden and is grateful for some shade. It has been confused with 'Quadricolor', which is different in the flowerheads. Sometimes regarded as a sport of 'Mariesii' but this is highly questionable as 'Mariesii' was not in cultivation at that time. Bred by Rovere of Pallanza, Italy, before 1860.

Hydrangea macrophylla (Lacecap Group) 'Veitchii', Maurice Foster garden.

Hydrangea macrophylla (Lacecap Group) 'Zaunkoenig', Arboretum de Dreijen.

Hydrangea macrophylla (Lacecap Group) 'Veitchii', Arboretum de Dreijen.

Hydrangea macrophylla (Lacecap Group) 'Zaunkoenig', C. Esveld Nurseries.

H. macrophylla (Lacecap Group) 'Veitchii'
A huge shrub sometimes larger than high, up to 1.5 m (5 feet). The flowerheads have many florets, sometimes 20 or more, irregularly scattered at the edges of the flowers, pure white with pink dots, sepals pointed, fertile flowers greenish. This very strong plant grows in all kinds of conditions. RHS Award: AM 1948. An unnamed variegated plant is found at the Arboretum de Dreijen. This cultivar might be more correctly named 'Rosea', but this is not the place to make that decision. Found in Japan and introduced to the United Kingdom by Charles Maries in 1881.

H. macrophylla (Lacecap Group) 'Wave Hill'
A medium-sized shrub up to 1.25 m (3.5 feet). The foliage is similar to that of 'Tricolor'. Salmon pink ray-flowers surround pink to white fertile flowers.

H. macrophylla (Lacecap Group) 'Yofloma'
A medium-sized, slow-growing shrub. The leaves are golden yellow but need much protection and shade to avoid sunburning. Flowerheads not yet seen. Origin Japanese.

H. macrophylla (Lacecap Group) 'Zaunkoenig'
A compact shrub, not exceeding 1 m (3 feet). Corymbs small, florets arranged in a single regular ring, dark pink, almost luminescent, sepals more or less sharply serrate. The fertile flowers are an attractive pink. This cultivar is a very good pot plant but needs a sheltered place in the garden. *Zaunkoenig* means "wren." Introduced by Federal Research Institute for Horticulture, Wädenswil, Switzerland, in 1979.

H. macrophylla (Lacecap Group) 'Zeisig'
A low-growing, compact shrub with thin branches. Flowerheads have four to six ray-flowers, arranged in a single ring, usually overlapping each other. The florets are slightly serrate or entire, color rosy red. This cultivar is suitable as a pot plant and for outdoor planting. It needs some care. *Zeisig* means "siskin," a type of bird. Introduced by Federal Research Institute for Horticulture, Wädenswil, Switzerland, in 1979.

Hydrangea macrophylla (Lacecap Group) 'Zeisig', courtesy Arborealis.

Hydrangea macrophylla subsp. *stylosa* f. *indochinensis*, Maurice Foster garden.

Hydrangea macrophylla subsp. *stylosa*, Maurice Foster garden.

Hydrangea macrophylla subsp. *stylosa* f. *indochinensis*, Maurice Foster garden.

H. macrophylla subsp. *stylosa* (Hooker & Thomson) McClintock 1956

A thin, small shrublet with upright corymbs. Ray-flowers are 2 cm (0.75 inch) across with slightly serrate sepals. The florets are white, partly overlapping. The fertile flowers are pink or purplish. The leaves are 7–12 cm (2.75–4.75 inches) long, glabrous, and recurved. This subspecies inhabits Sikkim in India and is now in cultivation. It has two formas, f. *indochinensis* and f. *kwangsiensis*, which were reduced to *H. macrophylla* subsp. *stylosa* by McClintock. We feel f. *indochinensis* is distinct enough to be kept as a forma.

H. macrophylla subsp. *stylosa* f. *indochinensis* Merrill 1942

Inflorescences loose. Sepals heavily serrated. Leaves much narrower than in subsp. *stylosa*. The authors think that these differences are important enough for a future new study, when more material is available. Type from Chapa, Vietnam; published in *Journal of the Arnold Arboretum* 23 (1942): 167.

H. mathewsii Briquet 1913

A woody climbing plant with tomentose branchlets. The evergreen leaves are 10–20 cm (4–8 inches) long and half as wide, glabrous above, densely pubescent below. The inflorescences are white, all fertile; there are no ray-flowers. This species inhabits the Andes in Peru. It is related to *H. asterolasia*.

H. oerstedtii Briquet 1919

A woody climbing plant or shrub, growing in tall trees. Branches, stems, pedicels, and inflorescences are pubescent. Leaves ovate to oval, 10–20 cm (4–8 inches) long and 4–10 cm (1.5–4 inches) wide, glabrous above, tomentose below. Flowers pink, with also some pink sterile flowers. This species inhabits the mountains of Costa Rica and reputedly is the most beautiful plant in that country. It is closely related to *H. peruviana*.

Hydrangea paniculata, Crûg Farm Nursery. Taiwanese form wild-collected by Wynn-Jones.

Hydrangea paniculata, Rein and Mark Bulk nursery. Unnamed cross with 'Dharuma' × 'Pink Diamond' and selection from wild-collected material from Praecox group.

Hydrangea paniculata, Crûg Farm Nursery. Taiwanese form wild-collected by Wynn-Jones.

Hydrangea paniculata, Rutten garden. Unnamed cross with 'Dharuma'.

Hydrangea paniculata, Rein and Mark Bulk nursery. Unnamed cross with 'Dharuma' × 'Pink Diamond' and selection from wild-collected material from Praecox group.

Hydrangea paniculata, Rutten garden. Unnamed cross with 'Dharuma'.

Hydrangea paniculata, PlantenTuin de Oirsprong.

Hydrangea paniculata, Rein and Mark Bulk nursery. Unnamed cross with 'Dharuma' × 'Pink Diamond' and selection from wild-collected material from Praecox group.

H. paniculata Siebold 1829

Common name: Peegee hydrangea. A large shrub or even a small tree up to 7 m (23 feet). Branchlets pubescent. Leaves opposite or ternate, often on young plants, 5–15 cm (2–6 inches) long and 3–8 cm (1–3 inches) wide. Inflorescences in pyramidal, compound clusters, or panicles, up to 25 cm (10 cm) long, white or creamy white. The cone-shaped inflorescence distinguishes this species from all other species. Only *H. quercifolia* has more or less similar flowers, but the foliage is different. *Hydrangea paniculata* is closely related to *H. heteromalla*. It is uniform throughout the geographical range of its habitat, occurring in mixed forest in several provinces of southeastern China, in Japan, including Hokkaido, and in Sakhalin in Russia. It has also been found in Taiwan. It seems that the true species is rare in cultivation. The Japanese name is 'Nori utsugi'.

The extensive range of cultivars has been developed primarily by Robert and Jelena de Belder of Arboretum Kalmthout in Belgium. Many cultivars have huge flowers, also suitable for drying for flower arrangements. All entries of *H. paniculata* cultivars are discussed in *Dendroflora* 37 in an intensive survey by this author in the summer of 2000. (*Dendroflora* is the yearbook of the Royal Boskoop Horticultural Society.) The authors are investigating the possibility of establishing a subspecies for three different cultivars, 'Crûg Farm', 'Dharuma', and 'Praecox' because of the differences in flower shape and flowering period, but nothing is yet decided.

H. paniculata 'Ammarin'

A fast-growing shrub up to 2.5–3 m (8–10 ft.). Flower-heads exceptionally large, even larger as than the old peegee hydrangea. A chance seedling, found by Rein and Mark Bulk Nursery in 1999 and named after a friend of the family.

Hydrangea paniculata 'Barbara', Rutten garden.

Hydrangea paniculata 'Big Ben', Hydrangeum.

Hydrangea paniculata 'Bridal Veil', Rutten garden.

Hydrangea paniculata 'Barbara', Rutten garden.

Hydrangea paniculata 'Brussels Lace', Darthuizer Nurseries.

Hydrangea paniculata 'Brussels Lace', Darthuizer Nurseries.

H. paniculata 'Barbara'

A small shrub with very large ray-flowers, pure white and not changing to pink. The branches are weak and can hardly carry the panicles. This novelty is not yet available in Europe and is trademarked in the United States under the name SWAN, licensed by Springfield Nurseries, Massachusetts. Bred by Robert and Jelena de Belder of Arboretum Kalmthout, Belgium, in 1998.

H. paniculata 'Big Ben'

A medium-sized shrub with strong, straight stems, up to 2.5 m (8 feet) high and about 2 m (6.5 feet) wide. The flowering panicles are large, up to 30 cm (1 foot). Ray-flowers open white, turning to pink with age. Flowering time is in July. Bred by Pieter Zwijnenburg, Boskoop, Netherlands, in 1990.

H. paniculata 'Bridal Veil'

A large shrub up to 4 m (13 feet) wide, with weak branches. The white flowers last for a very long time. The ray-flowers are serrate, which is rare in this species. 'Bridal Veil' is a seedling of 'White Moth' and not suitable as an ordinary garden plant. Bred by Robert and Jelena de Belder of Arboretum Kalmthout, Belgium, in 1995.

H. paniculata 'Brussels Lace'

A compact shrub up to 2 m (6.5 feet) high and wide. The flowering period is short, as all flowers open at the same time, in June. Flower color is white and hardly changes in the autumn. 'Brussels Lace' is a seedling of 'Unique'. Bred by Robert and Jelena de Belder of Arboretum Kalmthout, Belgium, in 1975.

Hydrangea paniculata 'Chantilly Lace', courtesy Wout Kromhout.

Hydrangea paniculata 'Burgundy Lace', Royal Horticultural Society Garden Wisley.

H. paniculata 'Burgundy Lace'

A slow-growing shrub, usually wider than high. The small white flower panicles turn to wine red. The flowers cannot be distinguished from those of 'Brussels Lace' during the flowering period, except in the autumn color. Not suitable for drying, as the florets fall easily. Bred by Robert and Jelena de Belder of Arboretum Kalmthout, Belgium, in 1975.

H. paniculata 'Chantilly Lace'

A large shrub up to 2 m (6.5 feet) in 7 to 8 years. Branches strong and erect, dark brown with gray stripes. Flowers in large panicles, sepals glistening white, three or four sepals per floret, turning to pink with age. Size of flowers comparable to the well-known 'Grandiflora'. Container-grown plants produce very large panicles. Flowering time is from June to July. Mentioned by Michael Dirr (1998).

Hydrangea paniculata 'Burgundy Lace', Royal Horticultural Society Garden Wisley.

Hydrangea paniculata 'Darlido', Darthuizer Nurseries.

Hydrangea paniculata 'Degudo', Rutten garden.

Hydrangea paniculata 'Darlido', Darthuizer Nurseries.

H. paniculata 'Darlido'

A small shrub, usually not exceeding 1 m (3 feet) high. Flowers in small corymbs, creamy white and very free-flowering, in July and August. In 1993 it was named 'Greenfinch', but later renamed 'Darlido'. Trademarked name is DART'S LITTLE DOT. Introduced by Darthuizer Nurseries, Netherlands, before 1995.

H. paniculata 'Degudo'

A medium-sized shrub. A detailed description is not available for this seedling of 'Unique'. Bred by F. de Gussem, Belgium, in 2000.

Hydrangea paniculata 'Dharuma', Hydrangeum.

Hydrangea paniculata 'Dharuma', Rutten garden.

Hydrangea paniculata 'Dharuma', Maurice Foster garden.

H. *paniculata* 'Dharuma'

A small shrub up to 1.5 m (5 feet) tall. The flowerheads have many ray-flowers, in flattened panicles, somewhat transparent white and quickly beautifully pink. The leaves are shiny. Flowers appear a month earlier than those of most *H. paniculata* cultivars. 'Dharuma' is used as a parent in hybridizing new *H. paniculata* cultivars, for its relatively small size, interesting flower shape, and the flower's ability to change color very early in the flowering period. This plant may be a hybrid with *H. heteromalla*. In Japan the plant is clearly classified as belonging to *H. paniculata*. Imported from Japan in 1989.

H. *paniculata* 'Dolly'

This form is very similar to the old 'Grandiflora'. The panicles have many sterile ray-flowers, creamy white, and not changing color. Flowering time is from July to August. This plant develops very strong, straight stems and is useful for cultivating half-standards. Bred by Pieter Zwijnenburg, Boskoop, Netherlands, in 1990.

Hydrangea paniculata 'Dolly', Rutten garden.

Hydrangea paniculata 'Dolly', courtesy Arborealis.

Hydrangea paniculata 'Floribunda', Research Station for Nursery Stock.

Hydrangea paniculata 'Everest', PlantenTuin de Oirsprong.

Hydrangea paniculata 'Floribunda', Arboretum Kalmthout.

H. paniculata 'D. V. P. Pinky'

A sturdy shrub of good habit. The panicles are elongated, pure white, changing to nice purplish pink. The sepals are egg shaped. Trademarked name is PINKY WINKY. Bred by Research Station Melle, Belgium, in 2003.

H. paniculata 'Everest'

A strong, large shrub with many firm stems and branches. The panicles carry almost only sterile florets, creamy white, later changing to pink. Synonym: 'Mount Everest'. RHS Award: AGM 1990. Bred by Sir Harold Hillier Gardens and Arboretum, United Kingdom, in 1989.

H. paniculata 'Floribunda'

A well-formed shrub with partly sterile and fertile white flowers, later turning to light pink. The panicles are up to 25 cm (10 inches). This well-known cultivar is distributed throughout Europe by Robert and Jelena de Belder of Belgium. Carl J. Maximowicz introduced this cultivar from Japan to the Botanic Gardens of Saint Petersburg around

1890, and many years later it came from there to Belgium. RHS Awards: AM 1953, AGM 1992.

H. paniculata 'Garnet'

This form has pubescent branches and leaves, which is exceptional. It is related to f. *velutina*, which see. The plant is small, barely exceeding 2 m (6.5 feet). It is very floriferous, flowerheads are small, the ray-flowers pointed, white and turning to ruby red when mature. Flowering time is from August to September. A seedling of 'Pink Diamond' raised by Robert and Jelena de Belder of Arboretum Kalmthout, Belgium, in the 1990s. It is only available in the United States and has been trademarked by Monrovia Nurseries, California, United States.

H. paniculata 'Goliath'

A very fast growing shrub, making very large and strong shoots, easily over 2 m (6.5 ft). The branches seem to be very useful for making standards, as the stems are straight and quite strong. A chance seedling at Rein and Mark Bulk Nursery in 2000.

Hydrangea paniculata 'Grandiflora', Branklyn Garden

Hydrangea paniculata 'Great Escape', Darthuizer Nurseries.

H. paniculata 'Grandiflora'

Common names: PG, Peegee. A large shrub, well branched, with large panicles of sterile ray-flowers. The panicles can reach 30 cm (12 inches) or even more. The flowers are white, turning to pale pink. Flowering time is from July to August. This cultivar is very suitable as a half-standard. Severe pruning in the spring is essential for a rich crop of flowers. This cultivar is mentioned in every publication on hydrangeas. The Japanese name is 'Minazuki'. Originally described by Philipp Franz von Siebold about 1862. RHS Awards: FCC 1869, AGM 1992.

H. paniculata 'Great Escape'

An erect-growing shrub, very vigorous, with strong branches. The flowerheads are small, creamy white, changing to pink, with almost no sterile flowers. Flowering time is from July to September. This cultivar is rare in collections. It is suitable as a half-standard. Introduced by Darthuizer Nurseries, Netherlands, before 1995.

Hydrangea paniculata 'Green Spire', Rutten garden.

Hydrangea paniculata 'Green Spire', Rutten garden.

Hydrangea paniculata 'Kyushu', PlantenTuin de Oirsprong.

Hydrangea paniculata 'Kyushu', Jardin de Valloire.

H. paniculata 'Green Spire'

A very large shrub, up to 5–6 m (16–20 feet) and almost as wide. The branches are more or less pendulous. The leaves are larger than the average cultivar and are shiny green. 'Green Spire' does not flower abundantly and the panicles are small on older plants. Ray-flowers are whitish to light green. This cultivar needs lots of room and is only suitable for larger gardens. It is a seedling of 'Unique'. Raised by Robert and Jelena de Belder of Arboretum Kalmthout, Belgium, in 1975.

H. paniculata 'Kyushu'

A medium-sized shrub with thin but firm branches. The leaves are shiny green, making the plant easy to identify even without flowers. The panicles are not large but abundantly floriferous; fertile flowers are white to greenish white, ray-flowers relatively few. Collingwood Ingram introduced this beautiful plant from Kyushu Island, Japan, to Europe. It is one of the most popular cultivars. Distributed by Robert and Jelena de Belder of Arboretum Kalmthout, Belgium. RHS Award: AGM 1992.

Hydrangea paniculata 'Lammetje', Hemelrijk Tuinen.

Hydrangea paniculata 'Lammetje', Rutten garden.

Hydrangea paniculata 'Lammetje', Rutten garden.

H. paniculata 'Lammetje'

A small slow-growing shrublet. The flowerheads are in firm panicles, almost without fertile flowers, pure white, later very lightly tinged with pink. Flowering time is early in the season. This cultivar is a seedling of 'Pink Diamond'. The name 'Lammetje' means "little lamb" in Dutch. Synonym: 'Klein Schaapje'. The plant is licensed by Springfield Nurseries, Michigan, United States. Bred by Robert and Jelena de Belder of Arboretum Kalmthout, Belgium, in 1995.

H. paniculata 'Last Post'

A shrub up to 1.25 m (3.5 feet). The panicles are large and rosy pink, changing to dark pink. The branches are dark brown. This cultivar is a seedling of 'Pink Diamond'. It seems to be quite useful for extensive borders. Introduced by Darthuizer Nurseries, Netherlands, in 1999.

Hydrangea paniculata 'Last Post', Darthuizer Nurseries.

Hydrangea paniculata 'Last Post', Darthuizer Nurseries.

Hydrangea paniculata 'Mathilde', Le Thuit Saint-Jean.

Hydrangea paniculata 'Mathilde', courtesy J. R. P. van Hoey Smith.

Hydrangea paniculata 'Megapearl', Le Vastérival.

H. paniculata 'Mathilde'

A shrub with large panicles, creamy white with many fertile flowers. Bred by Fréderique Buisson, France, before 1999.

H. paniculata 'Megapearl'

A sturdy shrub with firm, erect branches. The panicles consist mainly of pure white ray-flowers that turn to a good pink at the end of the flowering period. Bred by Pieter Zwijnenburg, Boskoop, Netherlands, in 1990.

H. paniculata 'Melody'

A large shrub with many long branches, up to 4 m (13 feet) high and about as wide. The panicles are very large, up to 35 cm (14 inches), white to pink, and flowering for a long period. This form is poorly known but one of the more attractive cultivars. A seedling of 'Unique'. Raised by Robert and Jelena de Belder of Arboretum Kalmthout, Belgium, in 1985.

Hydrangea paniculata 'Megapearl', courtesy R. Houtman

Hydrangea paniculata 'Melody', courtesy Wout Kromhout.

Hydrangea paniculata 'Phantom', Le Vastérival.

Hydrangea paniculata 'October Bride', Darthuizer Nurseries.

Hydrangea paniculata 'Phantom', PlantenTuin de Oirsprong.

H. paniculata 'Mid Late Summer'

A strong-growing shrub up to 4 m (13 feet), and well-branched. The panicles consist mainly of fertile green flowers surrounded by white ray-flowers, turning to pink when mature. Flowering time is very late in the season and sometimes poor due to bad weather. Bred by Pieter Zwijnenburg, Boskoop, Netherlands, in 1990.

H. paniculata 'Mount Aso'

This clone of wild origin was found on Mount Aso, a volcano on Kyushu in Japan. It is a medium-sized shrub, with many branches. It flowers very late, sometimes until November. The flowerheads are white with some green and have many fertile green flowers. Plants under this name may differ, as there are seedlings in the trade. Synonym: 'Mont Aso'. Note that the name 'Mount Aso' is also attached to a cultivar of *H. serrata*. Raised by Robert and Jelena de Belder of Arboretum Kalmthout, Belgium, in 1967.

H. paniculata 'October Bride'

A medium-sized shrub up to 2.5 m (8 feet). The panicles are large. Flowering time is very late in the season but lasts a long time, until frost comes. This form is not generally available in the trade. It is a seedling of 'Tardiva'. Raised by Robert and Jelena de Belder of Arboretum Kalmthout, Belgium, in 1967.

H. paniculata 'Papillon'

A wide-growing form up to 3 m (10 feet). The panicles are large, colored white to cream. Flowering time is in August. The numerous ray-flowers are butterfly shaped, hence the cultivar name. This plant is quite rare. Bred by Robert and Jelena de Belder of Arboretum Kalmthout, Belgium, in 1970.

H. paniculata 'Phantom'

A large shrub with many long branches. The juvenile leaves are yellowish green. The panicles are large, much like those of 'Grandiflora', creamy white and turning to a good pink in early autumn. Bred by Pieter Zwijnenburg, Boskoop, Netherlands, in 1990.

Hydrangea paniculata 'Pink Briant', Le Vastérival.

Hydrangea paniculata 'Pink Diamond', Von Gimborn Arboretum.

Hydrangea paniculata 'Pink Diamond', Royal Horticultural Society Garden Wisley.

H. paniculata 'Pink Beauty'

Flower color is said to be mauve. May be the same as *H. macrophylla* 'Pink Beauty'.

H. paniculata 'Pink Briant'

Carries long panicles with few ray-flowers and many green fertile flowers. Bred by Briant SA, of France.

H. paniculata 'Pink Diamond'

A vigorous-growing shrub exceeding 3 m (10 feet) high and wide, similar to 'Unique'. The panicles are long and narrowly cone shaped with few ray-flowers, white turning to dark pink. This attractive plant is now generally available in the trade. It is very good for dry flowers and as a parent in hybridizing. Bred by Robert and Jelena de Belder of Arboretum Kalmthout, Belgium, in 1980.

Hydrangea paniculata 'Pink Diamond', courtesy Arborealis.

Hydrangea paniculata 'Praecox', Holehird Gardens.

Hydrangea paniculata 'Praecox', Darthuizer Nurseries.

Hydrangea paniculata 'Ruby', Hemelrijk Tuinen.

H. paniculata 'Pink Lady'

A dwarf shrub, barely more than 1.5 m (5 feet), with short branches. The large flowerheads bear many fertile flowers. The ray-flowers are shell pink and quickly turn to darker pink. Bred by Pieter Zwijnenburg, Boskoop, Netherlands, in 1990.

H. paniculata 'Pink Wave'

A large shrub with many long branches, sparsely beset with leaves. Panicles about 20 cm (8 inches), white to green. Flowering lasts for a long time. Bred by Edouard Avdeew, France, in 1980.

H. paniculata 'Praecox'

A very sturdy shrub up to 5 m (16 feet), with thick, strong branches unlike those of any other cultivar. Leaves large, yellow-green at first, later darker green. Flowering time is early in the season, usually in June. The flattened panicles bear many fertile flowers, white changing to yellow, sepals four or five per floret. This plant was brought from Japan to the United States by Charles Sprague Sargent in 1893. The Japanese name is 'Ezo nori utsugi'. RHS Awards: AM 1956, FCC 1973, AGM 1992.

H. paniculata 'Ruby'

A medium-sized shrub up to 3 m (10 feet). The flowerheads appear early in the season, white at first rapidly changing to pink, later turning to almost claret-red when mature. The flowering period is long, sometimes 10 weeks. This cultivar is a seedling of 'Pink Diamond'. It is very rare outside the United States. The trademarked name is ANGELS BLUSH. Bred by Robert and Jelena de Belder of Arboretum Kalmthout, Belgium, in 1970.

Hydrangea paniculata 'Silver Dollar', PlantenTuin de Oirsprong.

Hydrangea paniculata 'Supreme Pink', Hemelrijk Tuinen.

Hydrangea paniculata "Taiwan form," Rein and Mark Bulk nursery.

Hydrangea paniculata 'Silver Dollar', Rutten garden.

Hydrangea paniculata 'Skylight', Hydrangeum.

Hydrangea paniculata 'Tardiva', Research Station for Nursery Stock.

Hydrangea paniculata 'Tardiva', Research Station for Nursery Stock.

H. paniculata 'Silver Dollar'

An erect-growing shrub up to 4 m (13 feet) and sometimes 2 m (6.5 feet) wide, with long, straight branches. The panicles are pure white, have mostly fertile flowers, and do not turn to pink. This cultivar is still rare in the trade. Bred by Pieter Zwijnenburg, Boskoop, Netherlands, in 1990.

H. paniculata 'Skylight'

Similar to 'Silver Dollar', differing mainly in that the flowers turn to rosy red. Bred by Pieter Zwijnenburg, Boskoop, Netherlands, in 1990.

H. paniculata 'Supreme Pink'

Panicles medium-sized, turning to pure pink. The sepals look like little propellers. Flowering time is early in the summer. This cultivar was bred by Robert and Jelena de

Belder of Arboretum Kalmthout, Belgium, in 1985. It was named but never introduced.

H. paniculata "Taiwan form"

Panicles large, with green fertile flowers and white sterile flowers. This unnamed form is very similar to the species.

H. paniculata 'Tardiva'

A tidy shrub up to 3 m (10 feet). The panicles appear late in the summer, and the flowering period goes well into October. There are almost no fertile flowers in the panicles, but the sepals are not tightly packed. True 'Tardiva' is relatively rare; often plants are mixed or replaced by the much commoner 'Floribunda'. The origin of 'Tardiva' is uncertain. According to Bean (1991), it is a French introduction. Our information states that is was raised by Crown Commissioners, Windsor, United Kingdom, before 1975.

Hydrangea paniculata 'Tender Rose', Rutten garden.

Hydrangea paniculata 'Unique', Darthuizer Nurseries.

H. paniculata 'Tender Rose'

A slow-growing shrub up to 2 m (6.5 feet). The large panicles are white, turning to a beautiful pink in late summer. The fertile flowers are pink when opening. Said to be a hybrid of *H. aspera* subsp. *sargentiana,* but this is very unlikely as not the slightest influence of that species can be seen in this cultivar. Introduced by Darthuizer Nurseries, Netherlands, 1987.

H. paniculata 'Unique'

A medium-sized shrub up to 2.5 m (8 feet) tall and at least as wide. The branches are weak, which is why the plants are often very wide. The flowers are creamy white, in large panicles. 'Unique' is the first introduction of Robert and Jelena de Belder of Arboretum Kalmthout, Belgium, before 1970. It is the parent of several outstanding cultivars. It was named 'Unique' because it was the only plant left after a trainee thoroughly weeded a seedbed.

H. paniculata f. velutina (Nakai) Kitamura 1980

This natural forma from Japan is very similar to the species, but the leaves, branches, and panicles are softly pubescent. Introduced by J. Russell. The plant is tender.

H. paniculata 'Vera'

This old cultivar is probably no longer in cultivation. The flowers are in small panicles, cream, later pink. An old catalog of Arboretum Kalmthout suggests that this is the species itself. Bred before 1900 by de Kort, who preceded Robert and Jelena de Belder at Arboretum Kalmthout.

H. paniculata 'Webb'

Reportedly a sport of 'Grandiflora' and similar to it. Synonym: 'Webb's Variety' (no longer allowed by the ICNCP). Origin United States.

Hydrangea paniculata 'Unique', courtesy Arborealis.

Hydrangea paniculata 'Unique', Arboretum de Dreijen.

Hydrangea paniculata 'White Lace', Rutten garden.

Hydrangea paniculata 'White Lady', Rutten garden.

Hydrangea paniculata 'White Lace', C. Esveld Nurseries.

Hydrangea paniculata 'White Moth', Darthuizer Nurseries.

Hydrangea paniculata 'White Moth', Royal Horticultural Society Garden Wisley.

H. paniculata 'White Lace'

This shrubby plant is very similar to 'Brussels Lace' in habit, foliage, and panicles. The flowers are not as beautiful. Bred by Robert and Jelena de Belder of Arboretum Kalmthout, Belgium, in 1970.

H. paniculata 'White Lady'

A small shrub, similar to 'Pink Lady', a sister seedling. The ray-flowers are serrate, which is not very usual. The flower color is white, later turning to light pink. Bred by Pieter Zwijnenburg, Boskoop, Netherlands, in 1990.

H. paniculata 'White Moth'

A large shrub up to 4 m (13 feet). The plant is very free-flowering, with large panicles, pure white without a trace of pink. Flowering time continues until September. The flowerheads are very large, and for young plants too heavy; such plants have to be staked. This cultivar is readily available. Bred by Robert and Jelena de Belder of Arboretum Kalmthout, Belgium, in 1975.

Hydrangea paniculata 'Zwijnenburg', courtesy Arborealis.

Hydrangea paniculata 'Zwijnenburg', PlantenTuin de Oirsprong.

Hydrangea paniculata 'Zwijnenburg', Rutten garden.

H. paniculata 'Zwijnenburg'

A well-branched medium-sized shrub up to 2.5 m (8 feet) high and wide. The flowers are white to cream and the panicles carry only sterile ray-flowers. The panicles are almost as big as those of the old 'Grandiflora', but 'Zwijnenburg' turns more to pink than does 'Grandiflora'. 'Zwijnenburg' has proven to be one of the best new introductions. The trademarked name is LIMELIGHT. Bred by Pieter Zwijnenburg, Boskoop, Netherlands, in 1990.

H. peruviana Moricand 1830

A shrub or climber. Branchlets pubescent with erect star-like hairs. Leaves evergreen, 5–15 cm (2–6 inches) long and 3–8 cm (1–3 inches) wide, glabrous on both sides, margins remotely denticulate. The few sterile flowers are white, the fertile flowers scattered. This species is very closely related to *H. oerstedtii* and might be merged with that species: the minor differences in the inflorescence suggest that these are two forms of a single species. *Hydrangea peruviana* is very tender.

Hydrangea peruviana × H. serratifolia, Spinners Garden.

Hydrangea quelpartii, Trelissick Garden.

Hydrangea quercifolia, Sir Harold Hillier Gardens and Arboretum.

H. peruviana × H. serratifolia

A climbing plant. Leaves dark green and persistent, ovate with an acuminate apex. Flowers not seen. Young leaves on plants in cultivation have serrate margins on juvenile leaves. This plant is not hardy enough for outside cultivation. It is an artificial hybrid, created before 1995 in the United States by an unknown breeder, and can be seen at Spinners Gardens, owned by P. Chappell.

H. preslii Briquet 1919

A woody shrub or climber up to 4–5 m (13–16 feet). Branchlets and flowerheads pubescent. Leaves evergreen, 10–20 cm (4–8 inches) long and 4–8 cm (1.5–3 inches) wide, petioles 2 cm (0.75 inch). Sterile flowers always absent. This species, the first assigned to section *Cornidia*, has been known since 1794. It inhabits the mountains of Costa Rica, Colombia, and Ecuador.

H. pubinervis Rehder 1907

See *H. heteromalla*. Closely related to 'Xanthoneura', distinguished by its glabrous leaves and pubescent midrib, but not different enough for a rank as cultivar or forma. Leaves are narrower and serrate. Its habitat is Sichuan province, China. It should be treated as a cultivar; McClintock sunk it in synonymy.

H. quelpartii

Closely related to *H. anomala*, with smaller leaves. Flowers not yet seen. It occurs in the vast area of *H. anomala* and does not deserve specific rank. Rather, it is a Korean expression that can be classified under *H. anomala* subsp. *petiolaris*. It originates from Quelpart Island, Korea. The hardiness is sufficient for western Europe. Synonym: *H. quelpartensis*. Author name unknown.

H. quercifolia Bartram 1791

Common name: Oakleaf hydrangea. A sparsely branched shrub, usually not more than 1.5–2 m (5–6.5 feet). Young branches tomentose, brown-red. The leaves are oak shaped, with deep lobes, up to 25 cm (10 inches) across, almost glabrous above, tomentose below. The flowers are arranged in panicles with numerous sterile flowers, creamy white, with fertile flowers scattered through the panicle, which can reach 20 cm (8 inches). A yellow-leaved form has been found by P. Catt in the United Kingdom, named 'Little Honey'. This species inhabits southeastern United States (Georgia, Florida, Alabama, and adjacent regions). In recent years a range of cultivars has been introduced, mainly in the United States. RHS Awards: AGM 1992.

H. quercifolia 'Alice'

A large shrub up to 3 m (10 feet), robust mounding. Leaves deeply lobed with usually a brilliant autumn color. Flowers in very large panicles, white and turning to pink with age. The ray-flowers are scattered all over the panicles. Mentioned by Michael Dirr (1989).

Hydrangea quercifolia 'Applause', Rutten garden.

Hydrangea quercifolia 'Burgundy', PlantenTuin de Oirsprong.

Hydrangea quercifolia 'Brido', Rein and Mark Bulk nursery.

Hydrangea quercifolia 'Burgundy', PlantenTuin de Oirsprong.

H. quercifolia 'Alison'

A large vigorous-growing shrub with splendid dark green leathery foliage that turns to an attractive reddish purple in autumn. The erect panicles can reach 30 cm (12 inches) long. Pure white ray-flowers are scattered throughout the panicles. Mentioned by Michael Dirr (1997).

H. quercifolia 'Applause'

An old shrubby plant, cultivated for a long time without a cultivar name. It is similar to 'Flemygea' and is quite free flowering. Leaves wrinkled, panicles long and white, fertile flowers greenish. Named by Rein and Mark Bulk about 1980.

H. quercifolia 'Back Porch'

This cultivar flowers early in the season, with large white panicles, turning pink when mature. Bred by Louisiana Nurseries, United States.

H. quercifolia 'Brido'

A shrubby plant up to 2 m (6.5 feet), often with an untidy shape. The leaves resemble those of the species. The flowerheads are very interesting: the panicle contains white fertile flowers and very double sterile flowers in abundance. This very spectacular plant needs a sheltered place in the garden, and it can suffer in very cold winters. It originated at Snow Flake Nurseries in Alabama, hence the trademarked name SNOWFLAKE. Bred by Edgar Aldridge and Loren Aldridge, United States, in 1960.

H. quercifolia 'Burgundy'

A moderately strong-growing shrub, sparsely branched, and up to 2 m (6.5 feet). Leaves large and deeply lobed, turning a brilliant deep red in autumn. Flowers in large panicles, white, turning to pink with age. This old clone was longtime propagated without a cultivar name. Bred by Rein and Mark Bulk, Netherlands, in 1995.

Hydrangea quercifolia 'Cloud Nine', Rutten garden.

Hydrangea quercifolia 'Flemygea', C. Esveld Nurseries.

Hydrangea quercifolia 'Flemygea', Rutten garden.

Hydrangea quercifolia 'Flemygea', Darthuizer Nurseries.

Hydrangea quercifolia 'Flemygea', Darthuizer Nurseries.

H. quercifolia 'Camelot'

A vigorous-growing shrub with large leaves and upright conical panicles, white to cream. The leaves turn deep red in autumn. Bred by Louisiana Nurseries, United States, before 1995.

H. quercifolia 'Cloud Nine'

This still unknown plant has very handsome showy white flowers with pointed sepals. It is quite similar to 'Brido'. Bred by Louisiana Nurseries, United States, before 1997.

H. quercifolia 'Emerald Lake'

A medium-sized shrub up to 2 m (6.5 feet), with somewhat weak branches. It is very free-flowering with huge compact panicles but not as large as in 'Harmony'. Bred by Louisiana Nurseries, United States, before 1997.

H. quercifolia 'Flemygea'

A shrubby plant with firm habit, up to 2.5 m (8 feet). The branches tend to bow under the weight of the flowerheads. The flowerheads are panicles, 30 cm (12 inches) long, with very many green fertile flowers and many florets with four or five sepals. The white color turns to pink. Flowering time is from June until September. Trademarked name is SNOW QUEEN. Bred by B. Flemer, Princeton Nurseries, United States, before 1980.

H. quercifolia 'Gloster'

This shrubby form has unique ray-flowers, with five, not four, sepals per sterile flower. Bred by Louisiana Nurseries, United States, before 1997.

Hydrangea quercifolia 'Harmony', Rutten garden.

Hydrangea quercifolia 'John Wayne', Rutten garden.

Hydrangea quercifolia 'Joe McDaniel', courtesy Maurice Foster.

Hydrangea quercifolia 'John Wayne', Darthuizer Nurseries.

H. quercifolia 'Harmony'

A shrub up to 1.5 m (5 feet), with weak branches. Very free-flowering, with huge white panicles, 15–20 cm (6–8 inches) across. The flowering branches need staking, as they cannot carry the weight of the flowerheads. The plant makes a spectacular sight, but the weak branches are a disadvantage. The leaves are much like those of the species itself. Originally found by Th. A. McDaniel, father of plantsman J. C. McDaniel, in a churchyard in Alabama, United States, before 1985.

H. quercifolia HOVARIA

Under this trademark the Hofstede Nursery grows a selection of *H. quercifolia* very similar to 'Brido' but said to be an improvement. The authors found it very difficult to detect any difference. The cultivar name is unclear.

H. quercifolia 'Joe McDaniel'

A vigorous-growing shrub with showy white flowers, borne in large panicles. Autumn color red. Found in the wild by the late plantsman J. C. McDaniel. Raised by Louisiana Nurseries, United States, before 1997.

H. quercifolia 'John Wayne'

A huge shrub up to 2 m (6.5 feet). The leaves are 12–20 cm (4.75–8 inches) across, much like the species. The flowerheads are panicles with very large single ray-flowers, creamy white. Bred by Louisiana Nurseries, United States, before 1997.

H. quercifolia 'Late Hand'

A large vigorous-growing shrub with big handlike leaves. The flowers are snowy white, in large panicles. Flowering time is later than that of most cultivars. Bred by Louisiana Nurseries, United States, before 1997.

Hydrangea quercifolia 'Marshall', Le Thuit Saint-Jean.

Hydrangea quercifolia 'Sike's Dwarf', Royal Horticultural Society Garden Wisley.

Hydrangea quercifolia 'Pee Wee', Royal Horticultural Society Garden Wisley.

H. quercifolia 'Luverne Pink'

An attractive bushy, medium-sized cultivar. Flowers white in large panicles, turning to soft pink with age. Bred by Louisiana Nurseries, United States, before 1997.

H. quercifolia 'Marshall'

A shrubby plant of the normal size. Leaves as in the species. The flowerheads are relatively small, white and turning to pink. Fréderique Buisson does not know the origin of this cultivar.

H. quercifolia 'Patio Pink'

A vigorous-growing shrub with large leaves, coloring well in the autumn. Flowers white, turning to pink. Bred by Louisiana Nurseries, United States, before 1997.

H. quercifolia 'Pee Wee'

A dwarf, broadly mounding shrub with small lobed leaves and small panicles of white ray-flowers. Bred by Louisiana Nurseries (?), United States.

H. quercifolia 'Picnic Hill'

A bushy plant with short internodes, resulting in dense foliage. Flowers medium-sized, white to light pink. Bred by Louisiana Nurseries, United States, before 1997.

H. quercifolia 'Roanoke'

A loose shrub up to 2 m (6.5 feet). The flowerheads are large, loose panicles and more open than in 'Harmony'. Flowering branches bow to the ground unless they are staked. Bred by Louisiana Nurseries, United States, before 1993.

H. quercifolia 'Sike's Dwarf'

This shrub is similar to the species, but does not exceed 1.5 m (5 feet), hence its name. Branches are strong and carry the panicles without staking. Ray-flowers are white to creamy, sepals round and entire. Fertile flowers pinkish, closely packed together. Flowering time is from July to August. This cultivar is an excellent garden plant due to its firm habit. Bred by Louisiana Nurseries, United States, before 1990.

H. quercifolia 'Snowdrift'

A large shrub with many thin branches. The leaves are like those of the species. The panicles are much like those of 'Harmony' but in all respects inferior to that cultivar. Bred in the United States, before 2000.

Hydrangea quercifolia 'Tennessee', Maurice Foster garden.

Hydrangea quercifolia 'Tennessee', courtesy Klaas Verboom.

Hydrangea quercifolia 'Tennessee', Rutten garden.

H. quercifolia 'Snow Giant'

A strong-growing shrub up to 3 m (10 feet). Leaves large, deeply lobed. Flowers white, very much like those of 'Snowflake', possible even larger. Registered with the Canadian Ornamental Plant Foundation. In cultivation in Netherlands. Origin Japanese.

H. quercifolia 'Tennessee'

A medium-sized shrub up to 1.5 m (5 feet). Many sterile florets with four or five sepals, in large panicles. The leaves are large, deeply divided, and wrinkled. Young plants and long branches should be staked. Mature plants are wider than high. Flowering time is from July to August. This cultivar was grown from seed collected in Tennessee. Two or three slighly different clones may be in cultivation. According to the ICNCP, words like *variety, clone,* or *form* are no longer allowed as the name or as a part of the name, so the name 'Tennessee Clone' should not be used. Raised by Jelena de Belder of Arboretum Kalmthout, Belgium, in 1974.

H. quercifolia 'Wade Mahlke'

A compact shrub. The flowers are of strong constitution and similar to those of 'Harmony' or 'Roanoke'. Bred by Louisiana Nurseries, United States, before 1997.

Hydrangea scandens subsp. *scandens*, C. Esveld Nurseries.

Hydrangea scandens subsp. *scandens*, Crûg Farm Nursery.

H. scandens Seringe subsp. **scandens** 1830

A small variable shrub up to 1 m (3 feet) or a little more, sometimes spreading to horizontal. The corymbs are small, about 10 cm (4 inches) across, the ray-flowers are white. This species is very free-flowering, white to yellow, but unfortunately quite rare in cultivation. Its habitat is Honshu Island, Japan, and Taiwan in mountainous regions. The Japanese name is 'Gaku utsugi'.

This species is very complex. McClintock recognizes four subspecies, all of them previously described as species. Hayata, Rehder, and Koidzumi split this species into many more species, subspecies, and varieties. Haworth-Booth maintains some of these former species as formas of *H. scandens* subsp. *chinensis*, without mentioning the authority who did this. That is why in the descriptions that follow Haworth-Booth is mentioned after the new combinations, without proper description. The alternative is to ignore these formas and to consider them as cultivars.

Because we have seen the variability of living material, especially in the wild-collected material of Wynn-Jones, we do not favor lumping all these taxa in one subspecies. Instead, we propose to maintain *H. angustipetala* as a forma. McClintock includes *H. angustipetala* Hayata and *H. angustisepala* Hayata in *H. scandens* subsp. *chinensis* on the basis of herbarium material. Nevertheless, careful comparison of living plants raised from wild-collected seed convinced us that at least a few of those former species reduced to formas by Haworth-Booth deserve more than cultivar rank. Some of them differ strongly from *H. scandens* subsp. *chinensis*. In fact, several photographs of different forms of *H. scandens* subsp. *chinensis* are shown in this volume. Thus, we maintain as formas of *H. scandens* subsp. *chinensis* the following: f. *angustipetala*, f. *formosana*, f. *macrosepala*, and f. *obovatifolia*. There are plenty of differences within this extremely variable complex to explain and defend these changes of rank.

Hydrangea scandens subsp. *chinensis*, Arboretum Kalmthout.

Hydrangea scandens subsp. *chinensis*, Maurice Foster garden.

Hydrangea scandens subsp. *chinensis*, Crûg Farm Nursery.

Hydrangea scandens subsp. *chinensis*, Arboretum de Dreijen.

Hydrangea scandens subsp. *chinensis*, Maurice Foster garden.

H. scandens subsp. *chinensis* (Maximowicz) McClintock 1956

A shrub up to 1.25 m (3.5 feet), with smooth branches and foliage. The leaves are also variable in shape, 5–15 cm (2–6 inches) long and about 4–7 cm (1.5–2.75 inches) wide. The corymbs have few ray-flowers, white or bluish, with four sepals. Sometimes sterile flowers are lacking completely. This subspecies is variable due to its wide geographic distribution. It inhabits large parts of China, Philippine Islands, Ryukyu Islands, Taiwan, and Myanmar. It touches Japan on Yakushima Island. Synonym: *H. lobbii* Maximowicz. The Japanese name is 'Yakushima ajisai'.

Hydrangea scandens subsp. *chinensis*, Jardin Bellevue.

Hydrangea scandens subsp. *chinensis* f. *angustipetala*, Crûg Farm Nursery.

Hydrangea scandens subsp. *chinensis* f. *angustipetala*, Crûg Farm Nursery.

Hydrangea scandens subsp. *chinensis* 'Big White', courtesy Maurice Foster.

Hydrangea scandens subsp. *chinensis* f. *formosana*, Crûg Farm Nursery.

H. scandens subsp. *chinensis* f. *angustipetala* Hayata 1911

A small shrub up to 1 m (3 feet). Leaves oblong, serrate, and somewhat tomentose. Flowers in terminal cymes, creamy yellow, fertile flowers bordered by serrate florets. Leaves evergreen, especially on plants from Taiwan. Habitat is northern Taiwan. Name sometimes misspelled *angustisepala*.

H. scandens subsp. *chinensis* 'Big White'

A more free-flowering form. Bred by Maurice Foster of Kent, United Kingdom.

H. scandens subsp. *chinensis* f. *formosana* Koidzumi

A deciduous shrub with very narrow willowy leaves. Terminal flowers cream, turning to yellow in the summer. Habitat is southern Taiwan.

Hydrangea scandens subsp. *chinensis* f. *macrosepala*, C. Esveld Nurseries.

Hydrangea scandens 'Konterigi ki nakafu', C. Esveld Nurseries.

Hydrangea scandens subsp. *chinensis* f. *obovatifolia*, Crûg Farm Nursery.

H. scandens subsp. *chinensis* f. *macrosepala* Hayata 1903

A deciduous shrub with narrow willowy leaves. Terminal flowers cream, fading to white, about 5 cm (2 inches), flowering in summer and autumn. Requires partial shade. Habitat is southern Taiwan. Synonym: *H. angustipetala* f. *macrosepala* Hayata 1911. (Description supplied by Wynn-Jones.)

H. scandens subsp. *chinensis* f. *obovatifolia* Hayata 1912

A small deciduous shrub with serrate, hairy leaves. Flowers in terminal cymes, surrounded by broad sepals, white changing to yellow in the autumn. Requires some shade and a good moist soil. Habitat is northeastern Taiwan. Synonym: *H. angustipetala* f. *obovatifolia* Hayata 1911.

H. scandens 'Konterigi ki nakafu'

A small shrublet, almost creeping, barely more than 50 cm (20 inches) high. Branchlets thin. The leaves are ovate, 5–9 cm long. The small corymbs have a few sterile white florets. The leaves are inconspicuously variegated with bluish black and tend to revert to green. This delicate plant needs a very sheltered place in the garden. Synonym: *H. scandens* 'Variegata' of Haworth-Booth's book. May need to be classified under subsp. *liukiuensis*. Origin Japanese.

H. scandens subsp. *kwangtungensis* (Merrill) McClintock 1956

A shrub up to 1.5 m (5 feet), branches and stems softly villous. Leaves 8–10 cm (3–4 inches) long and 4–5 cm (1.5–2 inches) wide, villous. The corymbs have numerous fertile flowers, sterile flowers few. This rare plant is only known from herbarium specimens, collected in Guangdong province, China (indicating that distribution is restricted).

Hydrangea scandens subsp. *liukiuensis*, C. Esveld Nurseries.

Hydrangea scandens subsp. *liukiuensis* f. *luteovenosa*, C. Esveld Nurseries.

Hydrangea scandens subsp. *liukiuensis*, 'Fragrant Splash', Rein and Mark Bulk nursery.

Hydrangea seemannii, Stourton House Flower Garden.

H. scandens subsp. **liukiuensis** (Nakai) McClintock 1956

This low-growing, shrubby plant is very closely related to the species itself and differs only by the thicker leaves and by having a few sterile ray-flowers. Leaves are small and often have a yellow band along the midvein and a reddish brown stem. Habitat is on the Ryukyu Islands and in Japan on Kyushu and Shikoku. A few cultivars are available in Japan only: **'Hanagasa'**, firm creamy white corymbs, double sepals, few fertile flowers; **'Han temari'**, loose umbels of creamy white sepals; **'Iyo komon'**, small rounded pink and white corymbs, slightly variegated foliage; **'Iyo temari kogeko'**, rounded corymbs, large white sepals; **'Kogaku yae'**, semidouble sepals; **'Mangetsu'**, rounded white sepals, yellow fertile flowers; **'Renben kogake'**, rounded white sepals, as in a bowl, not pointed; **'Setono tsuki'**, purplish sepals and pink fertile flowers, possibly a hybrid with *H. serrata;* **'Yellow Kogaku'**, yellow sepals, yellow fertile flowers.

H. scandens subsp. **liukiuensis** **'Fragrant Splash'**

Possibly the same as 'Konterigi ki nakafu' although the variegation seems brighter.

H. scandens subsp. *liukiuensis* f. *luteovenosa* Koidzumi 1925

The leaves have pale yellow veins; they are small, leathery, and purplish when young. Flowerheads have about 20 white florets. The material seen was growing on Honshu, Japan. This plant is closely related to *H. scandens* subsp. *liukiuensis,* mainly differing in the flowerheads: those of f. *luteovenosa* are almost without ray-flowers. The differences are not important enough to separate the plants, but it is better to keep the plants in cultivation apart. Plants of f. *luteovenosa* could be treated as cultivars and named 'Kogaku utsugi'.

H. seemannii Riley 1924

A climbing plant or shrubby. Branchlets pubescent with brown hairs. Leaves evergreen, 5–20 cm (2–8 inches) long,

Hydrangea seemannii × H. serratifolia, Spinners Garden.

Hydrangea serrata, Maurice Foster garden.

Hydrangea serrata, Darthuizer Nurseries.

3–8 cm (1–3 inches) wide, glabrous above, slightly pubescent below, on long petioles. Flowerheads corymbose, glabrous fertile flowers white, sterile flowers usually present, white. *Hydrangea seemannii* can be confused with *H. oerstedtii*, but is readily recognized by the white flowers. This rare species inhabits the mountains of Mexico. It is one of the few species of section *Cornidia* in cultivation. It was introduced by Neil Treseder about 1985. There are huge plants in the Strybing Arboretum in San Francisco, California, United States.

H. seemannii × *H. serratifolia*

A strong-growing climbing shrub, with evergreen leathery leaves. Flowers not seen. This cross was made before 1995.

H. serrata (Thunberg) Seringe 1830

A shrubby plant, usually well-branched and up to 1.5 m (5 feet). The leaves are ovate to slightly lanceolate, margins often reddish, usually serrate, rarely entire. Flowerheads in flat corymbs, like the lacecaps of *H. macrophylla*. The true

species is rare in cultivation, but many cultivars are available in the trade. Synonyms: *H. serrata* 'Japonica', *H. japonica* Siebold. The Japanese name is 'Yama ajisai' or 'Yezo ajisai'.

Considerable disagreement exists on the status of *H. serrata*. McClintock and Makino reduce it to a subspecies of *H. macrophylla*. Haworth-Booth divides *H. macrophylla* into several species such as *H. japonica*, *H. maritima*, *H. acuminata*, *H. thunbergii*, *H. serrata*, and finally *H. macrophylla* itself. McClintock lumps the mopheads and the lacecaps of *H. macrophylla* with *H. serrata*, including the taxa presented by Haworth-Booth, into one highly variable species. Finally, Yamamoto (1998) recognizes three varieties: var. *acuminata*, var. *angustata*, and var. *yesoensis*.

Cultivars of *H. serrata* have been around for a long time and have possibly hybridized with others. Until the exact status of these plants can be defined, we maintain *H. serrata* as a separate species. The DNA research of Ben J. M. Zonneveld clearly shows that *H. serrata* is a valid species in itself (see appendix 1), as many other authors like Krüssmann

Hydrangea serrata 'Acuminata', Trelissick Garden.

Hydrangea serrata 'Aigaku', Rutten garden.

Hydrangea serrata 'Azisai', Maurice Foster garden.

(1976–1978), Bean (1991), Mallet, Lawson-Hall and Rothera (1995), Church, and Dussine already suspected. We agree that Haworth-Booth's division of *H. macrophylla* certainly would be helpful in designing a scheme for the division of *H. macrophylla* and *H. serrata* cultivars into cultivar groups. We further feel that many of the characteristics he believes are specific could be recognized. Although these may not be stable or substantial enough to alter the taxonomical status of the species, they could be used to group the cultivars.

Hydrangea serrata has long been in cultivation, and mainly Japanese cultivars are known. In spite to what has been assumed, few if any of these cultivars are hybrids with *H. macrophylla*. We feel the following taxa can be treated as cultivars belonging to *H. serrata* as has been done by other authors.

H. serrata 'Acuminata'

According to Mallet, true 'Acuminata' is a slender shrub up to 1 m (3 feet), with large green fertile flowers, only sparsely surrounded by lilac ray-flowers, the corymbs are small, the leaves are pointed. There is much confusion whether 'Intermedia' is identical to 'Acuminata' as can be found mainly in French nurseries, for example Pépinières Thoby. The plants grown in European nurseries are most probably not the original 'Acuminata', which Siebold introduced as a species. It is quite possible that this taxon no longer exists in Europe. Haworth-Booth named this taxon *H. japonica* 'Intermedia', thus creating the confusion. There is also some confusion with 'Blue Bird', but that cultivar is distinguished by the many more flowerheads. Synonyms: *H. acuminata* Siebold, *H. buergeri* Nakai, *H. fertilis* Nakai, *H. coreana* Lee.

H. serrata 'Azisai'

A shrub up to 1.25 m (3.5 feet), shy-flowering with sterile florets, pinkish or bluish, depending on soil acidity. The sepals are entire and borne on long stalks. This cultivar can be compared with the well-known 'Rosalba'. *Azisai*, also spelled *ajisai*, means "hortensia." According to Haworth-Booth, 'Azisai' looks superficially like 'Blue Bird', which is, however, much later described. Origin Japanese; named by Leopold Dippel before 1900.

H. serrata 'Aigaku'

A low shrublet with blue fertile flowers, surrounded by separate light blue ray-flowers, almost spadelike. Haworth-Booth suggests that this might be the true and much better known 'Blue Bird'. Origin Japanese.

H. serrata 'Airagun yama'

A small shrub, with rounded leaves, flowerheads irregularly formed, with many pink fertile flowers, ray-flowers white, but only a few per floret. Origin Japanese.

Hydrangea serrata 'Akabe yama', Rein and Mark Bulk nursery.

Hydrangea serrata 'Altosa', Stourton House Flower Garden.

Hydrangea serrata 'Amagi amacha', C. Esveld Nurseries.

H. serrata 'Akabe yama'

This attractive, tidy plant came from Korea in 1995. The leaves are almost lanceolate. The flowers are small white lacecaps, eventually blush or pink. The fertile flowers are reddish lilac. The sepals are slightly serrate and arranged four in a floret.

H. serrata 'Akiko'

A well-growing shrub with open habit. The fertile flowers are whitish, ray-flowers are pure white. Leaves dentate. Flowers occur on terminal buds as well as on lower lateral branches. Origin Japanese.

H. serrata 'Akishino temari'

A small shrub with little rounded spherical flowerheads, ray-flowers white, double, and pointed, arranged around the greenish fertile flowers. This flowerhead-shape is called "temari." The plant is remarkable. Origin Japanese.

H. serrata 'Altosa'

Leaves broadly ovate, brownish green with fresh green margins. The sepals are double, the fertile flowers are pink. A conspicuous cultivar bred by the Bullivants, United Kingdom, before 2000.

H. serrata 'Amacha yae'

This shrub belongs to the Amacha Group of cultivars that can be used as tea plants. The flowerheads consist of many sterile flowers with double sepals, light lilac. Origin Japanese.

H. serrata 'Amagi amacha'

A dwarf shrub, not exceeding 1 m (3 feet), well-branched. The leaves are narrow with a yellowish midrib. The flowerheads have large, starlike pure white florets; the fertile flowers are white, too. There are only a few florets per corymb. This plant was discovered by Makino about 1925. It grows

Hydrangea serrata 'Amagi amacha', Rutten garden.

Hydrangea serrata 'Autumn Fire', C. Esveld Nurseries.

abundantly on the Japanese islands of Honshu, Kyushu, and Shikoku. This cultivar can be confused with 'Oamacha' being one of the many Japanese named clones from the Amacha Group. This plant does not deserve varietal rank: the cultivated specimens are a single clone. Mallet states that 'Angustata' might be considered as a forma of *H. serrata*. Interestingly Bertrand gives also 'Pulchra' as a synonym, although 'Pulchra' is more often considered a synonym of the very different 'Prolifera'. Mallet states that it is designated by the name 'Shiro yama'. Synonyms: *H. serrata* var. *angustata* Franchet & Savatier, *H. serrata* var. *angustata* Makino, *H. serrata* subsp. *angustata* Sugimoto.

H. *serrata* 'Ao bano fuji'

A small shrub. The ray-flowers are light lilac, sepals entire, and broadly heart shaped. They surround the yellow fertile flowers. Origin Japanese.

H. *serrata* 'Ao gashima gaku'

An untidy shrub, with large leaves. Flowerheads with pinkish ray-flowers. The fertile flowers are purplish blue. Origin Japanese.

H. *serrata* 'Ao temari'

A medium-sized shrub. Flowerheads are mophead shaped (temari), sepals broadly heart shaped, not dentate. Usually the flowers are blue or lilac. Origin Japanese.

H. *serrata* 'Ao yama'

This shrub carries blue ray-flowers around dark blue fertile flowers. Synonym: 'Hyuga ao'. Origin Japanese.

Hydrangea serrata 'Autumn Fire', C. Esveld Nurseries.

H. *serrata* 'Autumn Fire'

A large shrub up to 1.5 m (5 feet), with conspicuous autumn color. The fertile flowers are small, pinkish; the ray-flowers also pink. Sepals five or six, overlapping each other. Invalid synonym: *H. chinensis japonica*. Bred by C. Esveld Nurseries, Boskoop, Netherlands, in 2000.

H. *serrata* 'Aya ezo yae'

The flowerheads are composed of few florets with long, stalked sepals, creamy white, double, almost spherical (temari). Origin Japanese.

Hydrangea serrata 'Belzonii', Research Station for Nursery Stock.

Hydrangea serrata 'Belladonna', C. Esveld Nurseries.

Hydrangea serrata 'Belzonii', Trelissick Garden.

H. serrata 'Belladonna'

A small shrub, barely more than 60 cm (2 feet) and almost acting as a groundcover. The leaves are small, 5 cm (2 inches) long and maybe 1 cm (0.4 inch) wide. The flowerheads are small mopheads, with few fertile flowers, pink to light blue. This cultivar is easy to grow and is suitable for small gardens. Like several other Japanese cultivars, it was once considered a natural variety. It is distributed here and there as 'Maiko', although two different lacecaps have been given this name. One of them is an introduction by Robert and Jelena de Belder, collected in Hallasan, Korea. The other comes from Japan and was introduced to Europe about 1990 by T. Yamamoto. Synonym: *H. serrata* f. *belladonna* (Kitamura) Hara.

H. serrata 'Belzonii'

A large shrub up to 2 m (6.5 feet) or even more. It has four to six ray-flowers on a flowerhead, light pink or light blue, opening almost white, inconspicuous. The leaves are ternate. This cultivar is possibly of hybrid origin, with one parent being *H. macrophylla*. Synonym: *H. belzonii* Siebold & Zuccarini 1864. Origin Japanese.

H. serrata 'Beni'

A rounded and spreading shrub up to 1.25 m (3.5 feet). The flowerheads are scarlet, becoming dark red with age; the fertile flowers are greenish. This plant is a clone of wild-collected *H. serrata*. The word *beni* means "red." Bred by Heronswood Nursery, Washington, United States, before 2000.

Hydrangea serrata 'Beni gaku', G. A. van Klaveren garden.

Hydrangea serrata 'Beni kansetsu', Rokko Alpine Botanical Garden.

Hydrangea serrata 'Beni gaku', Rein and Mark Bulk nursery.

Hydrangea serrata 'Beni yama', Maurice Foster garden.

H. serrata 'Beni gaku'

A shrub up to 1.25 m (3.5 feet). Flowerheads consist of lilac fertile flowers. The ray-flowers start white, turning to red quickly if the plant is grown in a sunny location. This cultivar is sometimes considered a synonym of 'Rosalba', but such a relationship is highly doubted. For one thing, 'Beni gaku' is more vigorous growing than 'Rosalba', and for another, its flowers are darker red. Origin Japanese.

H. serrata 'Beni henge'

A spreading shrub, very free-flowering with pink ray-flowers, the fertile flowers are light lilac. Origin Japanese.

H. serrata 'Beni kansetsu'

An unusual cultivar with distinct foliage color, mottled creamy white. The young growth contrasts strongly with the glossy dark older leaves. This plant has been photographed in Rokko Gardens, Japan. Flowers not seen. Origin Japanese.

H. serrata 'Beni temari'

A small shrub. The spherical flowerheads consist of many ray-flowers, salmon pink to almost white, gradually turning, reddish, sepals dentate; there are only few fertile flowers. Origin Japanese.

H. serrata 'Beni yama'

Fertile lilac purple flowers, surrounded by light red ray-flowers with a white center. This cultivar has been wrongly distributed as 'Beni gaku'. Origin Japanese.

H. serrata 'Besshi temari'

Rounded flowerheads with many fertile flowers. The ray-flowers are light lilac and also scattered between the fertile flowers, which is unusual. Sepals dentate. Origin Japanese.

Hydrangea serrata 'Blue Bird', H. J. van Paddenburgh garden.

Hydrangea serrata 'Blue Deckle', Jardin du Mesnil.

Hydrangea serrata 'Blue Bird', Maurice Foster garden.

Hydrangea serrata 'Blue Deckle', H. J. van Paddenburgh garden.

H. serrata 'Blue Bird'

A small shrub up to 1 m (3 feet). The foliage is dense, green with reddish ribs. Flowerheads small but long lasting. The florets are bluish pink, the sepals are entire, fertile flowers blue when mature, becoming pink on very alkaline soil. Flowering time is from June to September. This cultivar is sometimes confused with 'Intermedia'. The older Japanese name is 'Aigaku' (which see), but 'Blue Bird' is a fully accepted name. Origin Japanese, before 1940. RHS Awards: AM 1960, AGM 1992.

H. serrata 'Blue Deckle'

A slow-growing shrub, rarely exceeding 1.25 m (3.5 feet), The corymbs are intermediate in shape between the *H. macrophylla* mophead and the *H. serrata* lacecap. Florets are tightly packed, sepals serrate, and sometimes in three circles. The color can vary from pink to light blue. Flowering time is from July to August. This cultivar can flower on side shoots as well as terminals, but one has to take care with late spring frosts. It has a great reputation, but success is not always granted. Bred by Michael Haworth-Booth, United Kingdom, before 1970.

H. serrata f. chinensis

A dwarf plant, barely more than 50 cm (20 inches) high. The leaves are small, 6–7 cm (2.5–2.75 inches). The small corymbs are about 10 cm (4 inches) wide, the few florets are charming, but not conspicuous. The sepals are pink, never blue. This plant needs a lot of shade for good results. It is only interesting for collectors and enthusiastic gardeners who want a challenge. Synonym: *H. serrata* 'Chinensis'. Origin Chinese. Introduced to Europe about 1950.

H. serrata 'Chirifu yama'

A well-branched but small shrub. The leaves are heavily variegated with golden splashes. The flowerheads are small with only a few light blue or pink ray-flowers, surrounding dark blue fertile flowers. Origin Japanese.

Hydrangea serrata 'Diadem', Arboretum de Dreijen.

Hydrangea serrata 'Ezo yoshino' courtesy Arborealis.

Hydrangea serrata 'Ezo yoshino', Le Thuit Saint-Jean.

H. serrata 'Chiri nishiki'

A shrub with variegated leaves and entirely green leaves. Variegated leaves have irregular golden splashes. The flowerheads are composed of many fertile flowers, with few pink ray-flowers, consisting of four sepals. Probably synonym: *H. serrata* 'Chiri san sue' (named after Mrs. Matsumoto). Origin Japanese.

H. serrata 'Chuba amacha'

A compact shrub, with wide dark green leaves. Flowers very small, whitish pink, only a few ray-flowers. This cultivar is a member of the Amacha Group, with sweet-smelling leaves. Origin Japanese.

H. serrata 'Daisen ezo'

Leaves large. Flowerheads consist of many blue fertile flowers, almost without ray-flowers. Origin Japanese.

H. serrata 'Daisen nohsei ezo'

A shrub with strongly dentate leaves. The flowerheads are small and have few bluish sepals. Origin Japanese.

H. serrata 'Diadem'

A dwarf shrub up to 80 cm (32 inches) high and somewhat wider. The flowerheads are irregularly rounded, having only a few florets per corymb. The sepals are dome shaped, with slightly denticulate to entire margins. This hydrangea is attractive in blue and in pink color. The fertile flowers are blue. Flowering time is very long, usually from June to September, but the plant is not free-flowering. A second crop of flowers appears in late summer. RHS Awards: PC 1962, AM 1963. Bred by Michael Haworth-Booth, United Kingdom, before 1962.

H. serrata 'Ezo yoshino'

A small shrub, with more or less lanceolate leaves. Flowerheads are very pale blue to white. Origin Japanese.\

H. serrata 'Forget Me Not'

A low-growing, spreading shrub up to 1 m (3 feet). The florets have three or four pink sepals and overlap each other. Bred by de Belder and van Trier of Belgium, before 2000. A second clone in the trade, with the same name, has white florets in a single ring consisting of four or five sepals. The fertile flowers are blue and the leaves are narrow.

H. serrata 'Fugire gaku'

Leaves narrow. The fertile flowers are lilac, the ray-flowers are white. The leaves should be variegated, but this plant is very unstable. Origin Japanese.

Hydrangea serrata 'Forget Me Not', Rutten garden.

Hydrangea serrata 'Forget Me Not', H. J. van Paddenburgh garden.

Hydrangea serrata 'Forget Me Not', Arboretum Kalmthout.

H. *serrata* 'Fuji no shirayuki'

A small shrub, with narrow, pale green leaves. Ray-flowers are double and white, the fertile flowers are also white. Origin Japanese.

H. *serrata* 'Fuji no taki'

A small shrub, probably not more than 1 m (3 feet). Flowerheads very conspicuous, composed of four or five florets, twice double and pure white. The fertile flowers are invisible. Origin Japanese.

H. *serrata* 'Gaku ajisai'

The very large flowerheads consist mainly of fertile flowers, surrounded by a few florets. Origin Japanese.

H. *serrata* 'Gokano sho yama'

A small shrub with open flowerheads. The yellow fertile flowers are irregularly surrounded by light mauve ray-flowers. May be a natural hybrid. Origin Japanese.

Hydrangea serrata 'Forget Me Not', Darthuizer Nurseries.

Hydrangea serrata 'Golden Sunlight', C. Esveld Nurseries.

Hydrangea serrata 'Grayswood', Holehird Gardens.

Hydrangea serrata 'Grayswood', Trelissick Garden.

Hydrangea serrata 'Grayswood', C. Esveld Nurseries.

H. serrata 'Golden Sunlight'

A shrub up to 1 m (3 feet). The foliage is clear yellow in spring, turning to soft green in late summer; it withstands burning in full sun. Flowerheads as in 'Intermedia', sepals reddish, fertile flowers pink to blue. Shy flowering. This sport of the well-known 'Intermedia' was found in the nursery of H. Kolster (Boskoop). It is a remarkable plant and unique among the cultivars of *H. serrata*. A similar plant is pictured in *Japanese Color Guide of Hydrangeas* (Yamamoto 1998) under the name 'Gold Leaf'. It is almost impossible that the two are identical, as one of the authors was a member of the Trial Committee of the Royal Boskoop Horticulture Society, which granted an AM in 1995 to Kolster's plant. It can also be a renaming to avoid breeder's rights. Bred by H. Kolster, Netherlands, in 1995.

H. serrata 'Gold Leaf'

A yellow-leaved shrub that easily burns in full sun. A mutant from a mophead cultivar. Origin Japanese.

H. serrata 'Grayswood'

A huge shrub, often 2 m (6.5 feet) high or even more. Flowers in large corymbs, the florets have elongated dentate sepals, white with pink edges, later turning entirely red, purplish on acid soils. The sepals do not overlap and are heavily serrate, usually three or four per floret, one being larger than the others. Flowering time is from June to October. This very showy plant needs a bright, sunny place. Origin Japanese. Introduced by Mr. Chambers of Grayswood Hill, United Kingdom, in 1888. RHS Awards: AM 1948, AGM 1992.

H. serrata 'Green Yama'

A large-leaved shrub. The flowers are real mopheads, and the sepals are fully green, which is very conspicuous. It is questionable whether this form belongs to *H. serrata*. See also 'Midori yama'. Origin Japanese.

Hydrangea serrata 'Hakucho', courtesy Arborealis

Hydrangea serrata 'Hakusen', Floriade 2002.

Hydrangea serrata 'Hallasan', C. Esveld Nurseries.

Hydrangea serrata 'Hallasan', Le Vastérival.

H. serrata 'Hachibusa temari'

A shrub of unknown size. The flowerheads are spherical, the sepals not overlapping, purple, blue, or pink. Origin Japanese.

H. serrata 'Hachijō hime gaku'

A shrublet with small white fertile flowers and white ray-flowers.

H. serrata 'Hakka amacha'

An open shrub with loose white ray-flowers and white fertile flowers. Belongs in the Amacha Group. Origin Japanese.

H. serrata 'Hakucho'

A small, low-growing shrublet up to 80 cm (32 inches) at most. The leaves are narrow and light green. Flowerheads are composed of four or five double florets, pure white; sepals are egg shaped, like little stars. Fertile flowers are few. Discovered on Mount Fuji in Japan.

H. serrata 'Hakusen'

A large-leaved shrub, probably more than 1 m (3 feet). The flowerheads are mopheads, pure white in color. May be a cultivar of *H. macrophylla*. Origin Japanese.

H. serrata 'Hallasan'

A dwarf plant, about 80 cm (32 inches) high, with stoloniferous branches. It behaves as a groundcover. The leaves are dark green and ovate. Flowers are pink or bluish with few florets per corymb. The number of sepals varies from three to eight. This plant was collected in the Hallasan National Park, Korea. More than one clone is in cultivation. See more information at 'Spreading Beauty'. Synonym: 'Hallasou'. Raised by Robert and Jelena de Belder of Arboretum Kalmthout, Belgium, in 1976.

H. serrata 'Hana no sasayuki'

An untidy shrub. Flowerheads without sterile flowers. The fertile flowers are violet and numerous. Origin Japanese.

Hydrangea serrata 'Hime amacha', Rein and Mark Bulk nursery.

Hydrangea serrata 'Hondoji wuji yama', Rein and Mark Bulk nursery.

Hydrangea serrata 'Hime gaku', courtesy Arborealis.

H. *serrata* 'Hana yama'

A well-growing plant up to 1 m (3 feet). Abundant fertile flowers are light lilac or pink, with a few dentate light lilac sepals in threes. Origin Japanese.

H. *serrata* 'Hime ajisai'

A large shrub. Flowerheads in firm mopheads, blue or pink. Possibly better classified under *H. macrophylla*. Origin Japanese.

H. *serrata* 'Hime amacha'

A low-growing shrub with very good autumn color. The flowerheads have white sepals and reddish margins. The fertile flowers are the same color. A member of the Amacha Group. Distributed by Milim Botanical Garden, Korea.

H. *serrata* 'Hime beni gaku'

This plant has the same shape and characteristics as 'Beni gaku', but the ray-flowers are pink instead of red. The name was changed by Yamamoto (1998), as several similar plants were named 'Beni gaku'. Origin Japanese.

H. *serrata* 'Hime gaku'

A small shrub up to 1 m (3 feet). Flowerheads small, usually mauve. The florets are arranged in threes or sometimes four. The foliage is light green. This form needs protection from sun and harsh conditions. Origin Japanese.

H. *serrata* 'Hime yuki ezo'

A large shrub up to 1.5 m (5 feet). The flowers are small mopheads, blue to pink. May belong to *H. macrophylla*. Origin Japanese.

H. *serrata* 'Hondoji wuji yama'

Purple fertile flowers with white ray-flowers consisting of two to five sepals. The name may be misspelled. Distributed by Milim Botanical Garden, Korea.

H. *serrata* 'Hoshisaki ezo ajisai'

Starlike semidouble pink florets surround open corymbs of yellow fertile flowers. Origin Japanese.

H. *serrata* 'Hosoba kogaku'

A small shrub with narrow leaves. The fertile flowers are white, surrounded by dark pink ray-flowers. Origin Japanese.

H. *serrata* 'Hoso hime ajisai'

A medium-sized shrub. Flowers in spherical corymbs, usually blue. Origin Japanese.

Hydrangea serrata 'Impératrice Eugénie', Research Station for Nursery Stock.

Hydrangea serrata 'Intermedia', C. Esveld Nurseries.

Hydrangea serrata 'Impératrice Eugénie', C. Esveld Nurseries.

Hydrangea serrata 'Intermedia', Holehird Gardens.

H. *serrata* 'Hyuga yama'

A shrub up to 1 m (3 feet). The fertile flowers are surrounded by florets ranging in color from dark red to light pink. Origin Japanese.

H. *serrata* 'Impératrice Eugénie'

A shrub up to 2 m (6.5 feet), with firm branches. Flowerheads round, about 12 cm (4.75 inches) across, with florets varying from white to pink, very attractive. Sepals overlap in part, fertile flowers are pinkish blue. 'Intermedia' is quite similar but has larger corymbs. Haworth-Booth describes it as a small mophead. Origin before 1868.

H. *serrata* 'Intermedia'

A well-branched shrub up to 1 m (3 feet) or sometimes more, with dark branches. The flowers are borne in corymbs, the ray-flowers usually pink or bluish, with a white center, the fertile flowers lilac. The florets are arranged in one row, sepals ovate to square, slightly overlapping. This valuable plant was formerly named 'Acuminata', but true 'Acuminata' has green (not dark) branches. The plant is common and astonishingly hardy. Probable synonym: *H. japonica* 'Intermedia'. Origin Japanese, before 1860.

H. *serrata* 'Ishizu chino hikari'

This cultivar bears double light lilac sepals on long pedicels. The inflorescences are small. The leaves are strongly dentate. Origin Japanese.

Hydrangea serrata 'Isusai beni gaku', Rein and Mark Bulk nursery.

Hydrangea serrata 'Isusai jaku', Rein and Mark Bulk nursery.

H. serrata 'Isusai beni gaku'

A shrub up to 1 m (3 feet) or slightly more. The flowerheads consist of many ray-flowers with four sepals per floret, white, with red margins; the fertile flowers are reddish to purple. The ray-flowers turn dark red in fall when planted in a sunny position. Origin Japanese; distributed by Milim Botanical Garden, Korea.

H. serrata 'Isusai jaku'

A strong-growing shrub, not unlike 'Intermedia', with many white ray-flowers, four sepals per floret, and dark red fertile flowers. Leaves bold and coarse. Origin Japanese; distributed by Milim Botanical Garden, Korea.

H. serrata 'Itsushi boshi'

The ray-flowers have five sepals per floret, all pure white. The fertile flowers are white also. Origin Japanese.

H. serrata 'Iwano shiratsuyu'

A heavily variegated small shrub. Flowers not seen. A provisional name, given by Yamamoto. Origin Japanese.

H. serrata 'Iyo gashuri'

A medium-sized shrub. The flowerheads have many purple fertile flowers and only a few sterile florets. The sepals are pink, mottled with white, almost striped. Iyo is a region in Japan that has given birth to many selections. Origin Japanese.

H. serrata 'Iyo kansetsu'

A very low-growing shrublet, not exceeding 50 cm (20 inches). The long, narrow leaves are speckled and mottled white. Flowers not seen. Origin Japanese.

H. serrata 'Iyo komachi'

A small shrub. The flowerheads are small and consist of a few fertile flowers. Dark purple sepals are on long pedicels. Branches are dark red. Origin Japanese.

H. serrata 'Iyo nishiki'

A shrub probably not more than 1 m (3 feet). The leaves are mottled and speckled with yellow dots and splashes. Flowerheads are rounded, and lilac fertile flowers are surrounded by lilac ray-flowers. Origin Japanese.

H. serrata 'Iyo no ao gashuri'

A large-leaved shrub with conspicuous flowers, blue or lilac, with white stripes all over the sepals. There are only a few florets per inflorescence. Probably identical to 'Iyo gashuri'. Origin Japanese.

H. serrata 'Iyo no hoshizaki'

A small shrub, with narrow leaves. The flowerheads are small and open. Lilac ray-flowers surround a few fertile flowers. The florets have five broadly pointed sepals. Origin Japanese.

H. serrata 'Iyo no midaregami'

A shrub with narrow leaves. The ray-flowers are blue, with white stripes. This plant is unstable and reverts easily. Origin Japanese.

H. serrata 'Iyo no sakazuki'

A small shrublet, with narrow leaves. The florets are salmon pink with long-stalked sepals. The fertile flowers also are salmon colored. Origin Japanese.

H. serrata 'Iyo no usuzumi'

Sepals are almost black, or at least dark violet becoming darker as the summer goes on. Origin Japanese.

Hydrangea serrata 'Iyo shibori', Floriade 2002.

Hydrangea serrata 'Iyo temari', Maurice Foster garden.

Hydrangea serrata 'Iyo shibori', courtesy Arborealis.

H. serrata 'Iyo no jyujisei'
A low-growing shrub with large leaves. The flowerheads are dark pink, the single florets are lighter pink to rose, sepals narrow. Origin Japanese.

H. serrata 'Iyo shibori'
A shrub up to 1 m (3 feet). Clear pink or blue ray-flowers with whitish speckles surround the fertile flowers. The ray-flowers have four sepals per floret. Very similar to 'Iyo no ao gashuri'. Origin Japanese.

H. serrata 'Iyo temari'
Flowerheads large, more or less umbrella shaped (temari), colored salmon, white, or pink. Origin Japanese.

H. serrata 'Izu no chō'
A shrublet with large leaves. The inflorescence consists of green fertile flowers surrounded by light blue heavily dentate ray-flowers. Origin Japanese.

H. serrata 'Izu no hana temari'
The flowerheads are little mopheads, with strong double pink florets. Origin Japanese.

H. serrata 'Izu no odoriko'
A shrub up to 1.25 m (3.5 feet) and about as wide. The flowerheads are firm corymbs, pale pink or almost white, with four or five double sepals per floret. Origin Japanese.

H. serrata 'Jinaitō gaku'
The inflorescences are large. Bluish fertile flowers are surrounded by almost cup-shaped florets, each consisting of slightly dentate light pink or light blue sepals. The name is probably misspelled; 'Junihitō gaku' seems more correct. Origin Japanese.

H. serrata 'Joyōka'
Fertile and sterile flowers are green due to a virus.

Hydrangea serrata 'Kiyosumi', Maurice Foster garden.

Hydrangea serrata 'Kiyosumi', Holehird Gardens.

H. serrata 'Jungfrau Picotee'

A small shrub with large serrate sepals, white with green hue and red margins. The plant is free-flowering, like 'Mikako', 'Mirai', and related cultivars. It has been found on Hokkaido in Japan. The name is very doubtful. Origin Japanese. Possibly *H. macrophylla* Lacecap Group, which see.

H. serrata 'Kamioka chō yama'

A shrub with large pink to white heart-shaped sepals surrounding the green fertile flowers. Origin Japanese.

H. serrata 'Kanaya no sawa'

The leaves are large. The dentate milky white sepals overlap each other and surround gray-green fertile flowers. Origin Japanese.

H. serrata 'Kifu gaku'

The leaves are variegated, half yellow and half green, but the variegation is unstable. A few white ray-flowers surround the greenish fertile flowers. Origin Japanese.

H. serrata 'Kifu yama'

The variegated leaves have yellow spots and flecks, like that of 'Kifu gaku', but the variegation is unstable. Origin Japanese.

H. serrata 'Kikuzaki hai'

A spreading shrub with large leaves having dentate margins. The flowerheads consist of small double irregular greenish florets and only a few fertile flowers. Origin Japanese.

H. serrata 'Kita ioyhijima gaku'

A shrub with rounded leaves. Florets are white and starlike with sepals not overlapping. The fertile flowers are light pink or lilac. An inconspicuous plant. Origin Japanese.

H. serrata 'Kiyosumi'

A dwarf plant, rarely over 80 cm (32 inches). Leaves sharply serrate. The irregularly placed florets have round white sepals with red margins. The fertile flowers are purple. This population was discovered on Mount Kiyosumi, in the province of Chiba, and was named *H. serrata* var. *kiyusumensis*, a name lacking taxonomic status at present. The author of the name could not be traced. Several cultivars with white florets and red margins are derived from this plant. Bred by Yasaka Hayasha, Japan, in 1950.

H. serrata 'Kizami gaku'

Many dark blue fertile flowers are surrounded by few dark pink florets with dentate sepals. Origin Japanese.

H. serrata 'Ko amacha'

Leaves dentate. Fertile flowers are pink and yellow. The florets have three or four sepals, pink with a white center. Origin Japanese.

H. serrata 'Kochō no mai'

The flowerheads are very loose and show attractive double florets on long stalks, light lilac or pink. Synonym: 'Kochō shigidanka' (preferred by Yamamoto). Origin Japanese.

H. serrata 'Kōa kuchi'

A shrub with loose, open inflorescences. White ray-flowers are sparsely placed around the white fertile flowers. Origin Japanese.

H. serrata 'Kō kansetsu'

A narrow-leaved shrublet. Flowerheads are small and consist of pink florets scattered throughout blue fertile flowers. The terminal leaves turn to white in summer. Origin Japanese.

Hydrangea serrata 'Koreana', G. A. van Klaveren garden.

Hydrangea serrata 'Kurenai', Maurice Foster garden.

Hydrangea serrata 'Kurenai', Floriade 2002.

Hydrangea serrata 'Kurenai nishiki', Rein and Mark Bulk nursery.

H. serrata 'Komo chiama seruka'

A slow-growing shrub, usually not more than 1 m (3 feet). The flowerheads contain mostly greenish pink fertile flowers and only a few heavily serrate sepals, white or very light pink, often only one or two florets per corymb. Origin Japanese; distributed by Milim Botanical Garden, Korea.

H. serrata 'Koreana'

A miniature shrublet, rarely more than 50 cm (20 inches) high, wider than high. The flowers are lilac on alkaline soil, blue in acid conditions. The florets have four or five entire sepals. The fertile flowers are bluish. The cultivar is rare in cultivation. The name is not well documented; it is said to be closely related to *H. serrata* f. *chinensis*. 'Spreading Beauty' and 'Hallasan' come from the same population as 'Koreana'. Origin uncertain, probably Korean.

H. serrata 'Kozu shima gaku'

The leaves show a light variation in color. The fertile flowers are blue and surrounded by white, starlike florets of three or four sepals, separated up to the base. Origin Japanese.

H. serrata 'Kujyu akaeda'

A floriferous shrub with roughly puckered foliage, narrow. The florets are dark pink and scattered through the whitish fertile flowers. Origin Japanese.

H. serrata 'Kurenai'

A small shrub, rarely over 1 m (3 feet). The slender branches show the flowers at their best. The flowerheads are surrounded by an irregular ring of florets. The sepals are white, turning pink to rosy red or red in a sunny spot, starting from the apex. Flowering time is from July to August. Origin Japanese.

H. serrata 'Kurenai nishiki'

Identical to 'Kurenai' except for the leaves, which are margined and speckled with yellow. The plant needs care and a sheltered place in the garden.

Hydrangea serrata 'Kuro hime', C. Esveld Nurseries.

Hydrangea serrata 'Macrosepala', Maurice Foster garden.

Hydrangea serrata 'Kuro hime', Maurice Foster garden.

Hydrangea serrata 'Maiko', Holehird Gardens.

H. serrata 'Kurenai yama'

Leaves dark reddish green in summer. The orange-salmon fertile flowers turn to dark red with age. White florets each consist of three white sepals. The flowers turn to dark red with age. Origin Japanese.

H. serrata 'Kuro hime'

A small plant with light green foliage and black-tipped stems. It is quite free-flowering with small corymbs of about 10 cm (4 inches). Each inflorescence has only a few florets, but they are charming. Sepals are purple or pink. The numerous fertile flowers are fairly large and violet colored. Bred by T. Yamamoto of Japan.

H. serrata 'Kuro shime yama azisai'

A shrublet up to 1 m (3 feet). Flowerheads large, the floret arranged in a single ring, blue or pink depending on soil conditions. Sepals four, margins entire. The name means "black princess." Origin Japanese.

H. serrata 'Macrosepala'

A shrub up to 80 cm (32 inches). Flowerheads with four or five ray-flowers, first white later turning to vivid cherry red under the influence of the sun. Needs a sheltered place and moist soil. Synonym: *H. japonica* f. *macrosepala* Regal 1866.

H. serrata 'Maiko'

A low-growing, spreading shrublet, heavily branched and free-flowering. The loose corymbs contain florets with usually four sepals, pink or purple. The fertile flowers are darker. 'Maiko' comes from Mount Hallasan in Korea and is mistakenly considered by some to be identical to 'Spreading Beauty'. These two cultivars, plus 'Hallasan', were collected in Korea by Robert and Jelena de Belder, of Arboretum Kalmthout, Belgium. Because the three cultivars are similar, they have caused much confusion. Yamamoto sent a Japanese cultivar with the name 'Maiko' to Holehird Gardens, United Kingdom, in the late 1980s. That low-growing cultivar has interesting double-colored ray-flowers, wide dark foliage, and a spreading habit. See also 'Shiro maiko'.

Hydrangea serrata 'Matsu hime nishiki', Rein and Mark Bulk nursery.

Hydrangea serrata 'Midori', Rutten garden.

Hydrangea serrata 'Midori', C. Esveld Nurseries.

H. serrata 'Maiko nishiki'
Like 'Belladonna' but with leaves partly variegated. Origin Korean.

H. serrata 'Matsu hime nishiki'
The foliage is partly variegated light yellow, but the variegation is very unstable. The correct name is sometimes considered 'Matsu hime' in spite of the fact that "nishiki" often refers to variegated plants. Origin Japanese; distributed by Milim Botanical Garden, Korea.

H. serrata 'Megacarpa'
Leaves partially white variegated. Fertile flowers lilac, ray-flowers white. This cultivar does not deserve varietal rank (var. *megacarpa*) and should be treated as a cultivar. Synonym: *H. serrata* var. *yesoensis* Yamamoto. Origin Japanese.

H. serrata 'Midori'
A shrublet about 80 cm (32 inches) high. The flowerheads carry florets with partly or completely green sepals in the form of small mopheads. The sepals do not overlap. Autumn color is good. Mallet suggests a virus is responsible for the green sepals. This plant seems to be very delicate and is not long-lived. See also 'Green Yama'. Bred by Takaki Fujota, Japan, in 1988. Plants in cultivation in Netherlands do not match the description.

H. serrata 'Midori boshi temari'
A shrub about 1 m (3 feet) high and wide. Very free-flowering with corymbs carrying double florets on long stalks, lavender or pink, depending on soil conditions. Flowering time is from June to August. Origin Japanese.

H. serrata 'Midori uzu'
Like 'Midori', but the fully green mopheads are larger. This plant can best be described as a green 'Ayesha'. Origin Japanese.

Hydrangea serrata 'Mihagi nishiki', Rokko Alpine Botanical Garden.

H. serrata 'Midori yama'

This shrub with green inflorescences was discovered on a mountain by the Tenryu River in south central Honshu. See 'Green yama'. Origin Japanese.

H. serrata 'Mihagi nishiki'

A slow-growing shrub, with yellow variegated leaves. Origin Japanese.

H. serrata 'Mihara yae'

Flowers large, the semi double florets standing in a ring around the green-lilac fertile flowers. Origin Japanese.

H. serrata 'Mihara yama'

A shrub with broad leaves. The flowerheads are small and consist mainly of blue fertile flowers, mixed with a few light blue or pink florets, with four sepals. Origin Japanese.

H. serrata 'Mikata yae'

A small shrub. The flowerheads are a splendid blue, the sepals double and broadly lanceolate, the margins entire. Origin Japanese.

H. serrata 'Mikawa chidori'

A plant with strange flowerheads. The blue fertile flowers are abnormal and form a disk on which the partly blue and white florets are scattered. They are short lived; both fertile and sterile flowers tend to die quickly. Possibly the name will be changed to 'Tenryu chidori'. Origin Japanese.

H. serrata 'Mikanba gaku'

A strong-growing shrub up to 2 m (6.5 feet). The foliage is very firm and shiny, evergreen in mild winters. The flowerheads consist mostly of greenish fertile flowers surrounded by a few white ray-flowers. Synonym: 'Mikamba'. Origin Japanese.

Hydrangea serrata 'Miyake yae', courtesy Maurice Foster.

H. serrata 'Mira'

A small shrub up to 1 m (3 feet), with firm branches. Leaves fresh green and serrate. The ray-flowers are usually pink with a whitish center. Fertile flowers are pink also. Origin Japanese.

H. serrata 'Miranda'

A small shrub and very free-flowering. The corymbs are not particularly large and carry four to six florets with round entire sepals in the form of a ring. The color may vary from light blue to pink to purplish red. Fertile flowers are numerous, lilac-blue. Selected by Michael Haworth-Booth of the United Kingdom, before 1980. Possibly *H. macrophylla* Lacecap Group, which see.

H. serrata 'Miyabi ezo'

A medium-sized shrub. The leaves are broadly egg shaped and dentate. The flowerheads consist of blue fertile flowers surrounded by pale lilac ray-flowers. Origin Japanese.

Hydrangea serrata 'Miyama yae murasaki', Rutten garden.

Hydrangea serrata 'Mont Aso', C. Esveld Nurseries.

Hydrangea serrata 'Miyama yae murasaki', Floriade 2002.

Hydrangea serrata 'Mont Aso', C. Esveld Nurseries.

H. serrata 'Miyake jime gaku

A shrub with broadly ovate leaves. The flowerheads consist mainly of fertile flowers, blue or mauve, surrounded by almost-white sepals. Origin Japanese.

H. serrata 'Miyake shin yae'

The green fertile flowers are more or less surrounded by double white ray-flowers, which are slightly dentate. Origin Japanese.

H. serrata 'Miyake temari'

A large shrub, the flattened flowerheads (han temari) are greenish cream and cover the fertile flowers. Origin Japanese.

H. serrata 'Miyake tokiwa'

Like 'Miyake temari' but lacking double flowers. The sepals are white, six or seven per floret. In frost-free situations, this plant is evergreen. Origin Japanese.

H. serrata 'Miyake yae'

A shrub with double ray-flowers consisting of large white sepals on long stalks. Origin Japanese.

H. serrata 'Miyama yae murasaki'

A huge, vigorous-growing shrub. The flowerheads are rounded and the florets are perfectly arranged in a ring, being double, with egg shaped small sepals, salmon pink or blue. A remarkable plant. Bred by Takeshi Seto, Japan, in 1950.

H. serrata 'Mount Aso'

An erect shrub up to 1 m (3 feet), with typical "serrata" leaves. Flowerheads with masses of lilac to pink fertile flowers. Already free-flowering at a young age. Sepals four or five, overlapping, pink fading to white. This cultivar has good autumn color. Bred by Robert and Jelena de Belder of Arboretum Kalmthout, Belgium.

Hydrangea serrata 'Nadeshiko gaku', courtesy Arborealis.

Hydrangea serrata 'Oamacha', courtesy Arborealis.

Hydrangea serrata 'Niji', Maurice Foster garden.

H. *serrata* 'Musume'
Growing in the collection of the Arboretum de Dreijen. Origin Japanese.

H. *serrata* 'Nadeshiko gaku'
This shrub has many blue fertile flowers. The florets have four or five white sepals. Origin Japanese.

H. *serrata* 'Naeba ezo'
A small plant with relatively large leaves. The small flowerheads bear white ray-flowers and bluish fertile flowers. Origin Japanese.

H. *serrata* 'Nagaba amacha'
Foliage elongated. Flowerheads small, lilac. The florets have pointed sepals, four together, and they surround the grayish blue fertile flowers. This plant also belongs to the Amacha Group. Origin Japanese.

H. *serrata* 'Nasu ezo'
The florets have strongly serrate lilac to pink sepals. The fertile flowers are white. Origin Japanese.

H. *serrata* 'Nadeshiko gaku'
A shrub up to 1 m (3 feet). The fertile flowers are dark blue, surrounded by very light purple to white ray-flowers. Each floret has four to six strongly dentate sepals. Origin Japanese.

H. *serrata* 'Niji'
A small shrub with narrow leaves. The flowerheads consist of purple fertile flowers and a few florets that are bicolored from pink through violet to light purple with aging. Most flowers have three or four sepals. Origin Japanese.

H. *serrata* 'Niji ima gaku'
The dark blue fertile flowers contrast strongly against the almost white ray-flowers. Origin Japanese.

H. *serrata* 'Nohsei ezo'
A small shrub with white flowers, consisting of four sepals. Fertile flowers are dark blue. Origin Japanese.

H. *serrata* 'Nose yama'
The foliage turns warm brown-green in summer. The ray-flowers are pink and white, with irregularly speckled sepals. The fertile flowers are pink. Origin Japanese.

H. *serrata* 'Oamacha'
A medium-sized shrub up to 1.25 m (3.5 feet). The corymbs are of usual size, purplish, with three or four sepals per floret. The leaves are sweet and can be used as an infusion. In fact, the plant is grown for that purpose in private gardens and Buddhist temples. The autumn color is often

Hydrangea serrata 'Oamacha', Arboretum de Dreijen.

Hydrangea serrata 'Odoriko amacha', courtesy Arborealis.

dark red. This cultivar is treated as a variety by some authors, but it does not deserve that status. Described by Tomitarō Makino, Japan, in 1928.

H. serrata 'Oda niji'

A large shrub with big leaves. The small flowers have strongly dentate florets that are pink changing to white. The fertile flowers also are pink and white. Origin Japanese.

H. serrata 'Odoriko amacha'

A medium-sized shrub, possibly better placed with the lacecaps, although the other Amacha hybrids are all cultivars of *H. serrata*. Leaves large. The ray-flowers are pure white and slightly pointed, with four or five sepals per floret, and are irregularly scattered among the violet fertile flowers. Bred by T. Yamamoto of Japan.

H. serrata 'Ogonda'

Leaves golden yellow. May be synonymous with 'Gold Leaf'. *Ogon* means "gold," *ha* means "leaf." Origin Japanese.

H. serrata 'Oh beni gaku'

Extremely similar to 'Beni gaku' (which see), but the flowers are white with pink spots instead of red. Origin Japanese.

H. serrata 'Oh ginosen'

A free-flowering shrub with elongated foliage. The flowers are borne on long stalks. The florets do not overlap and are pointed, lilac, light pink, or violet. Flowering is abundant. Origin Japanese.

H. serrata 'Oh ginosen yama'

Identical to 'Oh ginosen' but with more sepals. Origin Japanese.

Hydrangea serrata 'Oh niji', courtesy Arborealis.

Hydrangea serrata 'Otsu hime', C. Esveld Nurseries.

Hydrangea serrata 'Oto hime', C. Esveld Nurseries.

H. serrata 'Oh jiro keikoku yama ajisai'

The sepals are mixed: some have smooth edges, others have dentate margins. Origin Japanese.

H. serrata 'Oh jiro temari'

The flowers are small temari (mopheads) consisting of long stalks with florets, interestingly colored with lilac and white speckles. The sepals are entire. Origin Japanese.

H. serrata 'Oh kan'

A shrub with variegated foliage, the center of the leaf blade is partly yellow. The flowerheads are small. Blue fertile flowers are surrounded by a ring of light blue florets with four sepals. Origin Japanese.

H. serrata 'Oh mimachi ezo'

Flowerheads large with many dark blue fertile flowers surrounded by a few florets with four or five salmon pink sepals. Origin Japanese.

H. serrata 'Oh niji'

Similar to 'Niji', with weaker color and sepals more rounded. Less spectacular than 'Niji'. Origin Japanese.

H. serrata 'Oh sumi yama'

A shrub with large leaves. The flowerheads contain many fertile purple flowers. The sterile white flowers are scattered throughout the fertile flowers. Origin Japanese.

H. serrata 'Oh yama amachi ezo'

A well-growing shrub. The corymbs carry some florets, with almost white sepals. The few fertile flowers are lilac colored. This cultivar can also be classified in the Amacha Group. Origin Japanese.

H. serrata 'Oto hime'

A small shrub. Fertile flowers are pink. Sterile flowers are white, turning to fiery red. Similar to 'Kurenai hime', if not identical. Origin Japanese.

H. serrata 'Otsu hime'

A small shrub, barely more than 80 cm (32 inches). The leaves are small, narrow, and V shaped. The few ray-flowers are mauve, the fertile flowers lilac. Origin Japanese; distributed by Milim Botanical Garden, Korea.

H. serrata 'Panachee'

A variegated mutant from 'Professor Iida'. The word *panachee* is French for "variegated."

H. serrata 'Parusanshain'

Flowerheads usually white, sepals white with a red edge. This cultivar may be similar to other plants from Mototeru, such as 'Love You Kiss'. Bred by Yatabe Mototeru of Japan.

Hydrangea serrata 'Plogastel', courtesy Arborealis.

Hydrangea serrata 'Panachee', courtesy Arborealis.

Hydrangea serrata 'Pretty Woman', Arboretum Kalmthout.

H. serrata 'Pichi hime'

May be a lacecap. Bred by Yatabe Mototeru of Japan.

H. serrata 'Pink ezo'

A shrub, barely more than 1 m (3 feet). Leaves large, broadly lanceolate. The flowerheads stand on long stalks, pink, sepals entire, fertile flowers few.

H. serrata 'Pink Yama'

A shrub with narrow leaves. The florets are salmon pink with white striped. The fertile flowers are also white. Origin Japanese.

H. serrata 'Plogastel'

A shrub with nettlelike leaves, heavily variegated yellow. Flowers not seen. A French cultivar from the Mallets.

H. serrata 'Pretty Woman'

A spreading shrub, belonging to the Hallasan group from Korea. The flowerheads are composed of florets of white sepals with purple fertile flowers. Raised by Robert and Jelena de Belder of Arboretum Kalmthout, Belgium, in 1970.

Hydrangea serrata 'Preziosa', Spinners Garden.

Hydrangea serrata 'Professor Iida', courtesy Arborealis.

Hydrangea serrata 'Preziosa', C. Esveld Nurseries.

Hydrangea serrata 'Prolifera', Le Vastérival.

H. serrata 'Preziosa'

A shrub up to 1.25 m (3.5 feet), densely branched. The leaves are green with reddish veins and margins. Flowerheads carry pink fertile flowers, surrounded by pink to red florets with round sepals. This is one of the best cultivars. Remarkably, the flowers do not turn blue, even on very acid soils. May be a hybrid between *H. macrophylla* and *H. serrata* (Haworth-Booth). It can be confused with 'Impératrice Eugénie', but this plant has smaller flowers and is much rarer. Bred by G. Ahrends, Germany, in 1961. RHS Awards: PC 1961, AM 1963, FCC 1964, AGM 1992.

H. serrata 'Professor Iida'

A shrub up to 1 m (3 feet). The flowerheads are composed of white pointed sepals, three or four per floret, slightly dentate. Origin Japanese.

H. serrata 'Prolifera'

A dwarf shrub up to 1 m (3 feet). Leaves small. Flowerheads are small, with four to six florets, and small double pink sepals. The fertile flowers are pink, falling off soon. Carl J. Maximowicz brought this cultivar to Saint Petersburg in 1864, but the plant is much older. It can be confused with 'Stellata' and 'Shichidanka', which are both similar but not identical. Sometimes considered a natural variety. Synonyms: 'Pulchra' (an undocumented name), *H. serrata* 'Pulchella', *H. acuminata* f. *pulchella*. Origin Japanese, 1864.

H. serrata 'Pubescens'

A strong-growing shrub with large pubescent, velvety leaves. It is shy-flowering with a few pale pink florets. According to Haworth-Booth, it is not worthy of cultivation except for a few collectors. Origin before 1865.

Hydrangea serrata 'Prolifera', C. Esveld Nurseries.

Hydrangea serrata 'Ramis Pictis', Rutten garden.

Hydrangea serrata 'Ramis Pictis', C. Esveld Nurseries.

H. serrata 'Ramis Pictis'

A much-branched shrub up to 1.5 m (5 feet). The foliage is interesting for its reddish veins and petioles. The corymbs of this free-flowering plant are small and carry only four to six florets, light pink to whitish, sepals round, the fertile flowers are blue. Sometimes confused with *H. macrophylla* 'Nigra', which is quite different. Synonym: 'Cyanoclada'. Origin Japanese, before 1890.

H. serrata 'Renben gaku'

This plant has spoon-like florets on long stalks. The sepals are lilac and grow together, the fertile flowers are dark purple. *Renben* means "grown" or "joining together." Origin Japanese.

H. serrata 'Renben yama'

The florets are pink, sepals pointed, joined together, also light pink. Fertile flowers few and scattered. Origin Japanese.

H. serrata 'Rokko yama'

A low and spreading shrub. The flowerheads are small, florets lilac to pink. The plant occurs in the wild (Yamamoto 1998). Origin Japanese.

Hydrangea serrata 'Rosalba', Maurice Foster garden.

Hydrangea serrata 'Rosalba', Research Station for Nursery Stock.

Hydrangea serrata 'Sabashi ezo', courtesy Arborealis.

H. serrata 'Rosalba'

This shrubby plant grows up to 1.25 m (3.5 feet) and is densely branched. The corymbs are small, but numerous, the fertile flowers are pink, surrounded by sterile ray-flowers with four pinkish white sepals that turn crimson. The leaves are matt-green and covered with bloom. The origin and history of this cultivar are somewhat complicated. In Japan the name is 'Beni gaku', but there seem to be several slightly different clones, at least according to Ohwi (1965), who named one of them 'Rosea'. Dutch research suggested that the European plants of 'Beni gaku' are identical to 'Rosalba'. Other synonyms are 'Hinoshime', 'Lindleyi', 'Lindleyana,' 'Versicolor', *H. japonica roseo-alba* 1898. Origin Japanese; imported by Philipp Franz von Siebold and introduced by Louis van Houtte of Belgium, before 1850. RHS Awards: AM 1939, AGM 1992.

H. serrata 'Sabashi ezo'

Pale blue sepals form florets, surrounding masses of dark blue fertile flowers. Origin Japanese.

H. serrata 'Sapphirine'

A seedling, grown by Michael Haworth-Booth from Japanese seed. It has white, pointed sepals on lilac fertile flowers. Maurice Foster of Kent, United Kingdom, received cuttings, which he named 'Aquarelle' but later changed to 'Sapphirine' in 1985.

H. serrata 'Secchi'

A shrub up to 1.5 m (5 feet), with rounded leaves. The ray-flowers are blue to lilac, the fertile flowers are violet, and the sepals are rounded, three to four per floret. Origin Japanese.

H. serrata 'Sekka yae kuro jiko'

A shrub with very dark branches. Plant stems are often enlarged and flattened as if fused together. The flowerheads are small, semi double, white. Origin Japanese.

Hydrangea serrata 'Sapphirine', Maurice Foster garden.

Hydrangea serrata 'Sensuku ku', courtesy Maurice Foster.

Hydrangea serrata 'Sekka', courtesy Maurice Foster.

Hydrangea serrata 'Shichidanka', C. Esveld Nurseries.

H. serrata 'Sekka'

A small shrub of about 1 m (3 feet) with dark green foliage. The ray-flowers are rosy lilac and the fertile flowers are purple. Flowering time is as early as June. Free-flowering. According to the name, the plant should have twisted branches, but this is hardly the case. Origin Japanese.

H. serrata 'Sekka yae ajisai'

Branches, leaves, and flowers are all slightly flattened and fused together, making an untidy impression. The ray-flowers are white with a hint of lilac or pink and irregularly shaped. Origin Japanese.

H. serrata 'Sensuku ku'

A small shrub. The small light blue ray-flowers have four sepals, and the fertile flowers are blue. Origin Japanese.

H. serrata 'Settsu komon'

This cultivar has no sterile flowers at all. The fertile flowers are whitish. Origin Japanese.

H. serrata 'Shibori ezo'

This plant has large lilac sepals, heavily striped white. The fertile flowers are white. Origin Japanese.

H. serrata 'Shichi danka'

A small shrublet up to 75 cm (30 inches). The leaves are narrowly lanceolate, dark green. The flowerheads are open, with a few pink florets on long stalks; they look little stars. Sometimes considered synonymous with 'Prolifera', but that plant becomes much taller. 'Shichi danka' is also close to 'Stellata'. The correct spelling of the name may be 'Hichidanka'. Origin Japanese.

H. serrata 'Shichidanka nishiki'

A very small shrublet, barely more than 50 cm (20 inches). The narrow leaves are irregularly variegated with yellow; sometimes half the leaf blade is yellow. The corymbs are small. The few fertile flowers are lilac colored. The florets have five or six sepals and are quite small, broadly acuminate, and lilac-pink in color. Origin Japanese.

Hydrangea serrata 'Shira kuzu', courtesy Maurice Foster.

Hydrangea serrata 'Shiro fuiri', Rutten garden.

H. serrata 'Shiiba temari'

Numerous florets have lilac sepals, in spherical form. Fertile flowers are only few. Origin Japanese.

H. serrata 'Shidare yama'

A broadly spreading plant, possibly useful as a ground cover. Flowers small, florets white. Origin Japanese.

H. serrata 'Shingu temari'

A small mophead hortensia with tiny lilac balls, but not a macrophylla. Origin Japanese.

H. serrata 'Shinkura'

Blue sepals on long stalks. Origin Japanese.

H. serrata 'Shinonome'

Florets consist of double, white sepals with blue tinges scattered throughout the few fertile flowers. Origin Japanese.

H. serrata 'Shin ozaki'

A small shrub with flattened small corymbs. The pointed sepals are light blue or pink and surround the fertile flowers in a single ring. Origin Japanese; distributed by Milim Botanical Garden, Korea. Possibly *H. macrophylla* Lacecap Group, which see.

H. serrata 'Shira kuzu'

A small shrub with dark purple conspicuous leaves. Flowerheads are pink with slightly serrate sepals. The name is alternatively spelled 'Shiro kuzu'.

H. serrata 'Shirasagi'

This cultivar has medium-sized foliage and large flowerheads, mainly with fertile, greenish flowers. The sepals are partly pink and white. Origin Japanese.

H. serrata 'Shiro amache'

A medium-sized shrub. Flowerheads are composed of green-lilac fertile flowers, surrounded by almost white rayflowers with four sepals. Belongs to the Amacha Group. Origin Japanese.

H. serrata 'Shirobana'

A small shrublet with white flowerheads in temari form. Synonym: 'Shirobana hime ajisai'. Origin Japanese.

H. serrata 'Shirobana amache'

Similar to 'Shirobana'. According to Yamamoto (1998), it is indeed identical. Sepals may be more pointed. Origin Japanese.

H. serrata 'Shirobana yama'

A shrub of the usual size, about 1 m (3 feet). The flowerheads have many florets scattered throughout the dark pink fertile flowers. The sepals are pure white with slightly dentate margins. Distributed by Milim Botanical Garden, Korea.

H. serrata 'Shirobana gaku'

A well-branched shrub with small leaves. Fertile flowers are greenish, ray-flowers white. Origin Japanese.

H. serrata 'Shiro fuiri'

A small shrublet up to 75 cm (30 inches). Leaves are more or less variegated with white. The flowers are pure white, with fully double florets, surrounding small heads of fertile flowers. The plant needs a protected place in the garden. Origin Japanese.

Hydrangea serrata 'Shiro gaku', C. Esveld Nurseries.

Hydrangea serrata 'Shiro tae', Holehird Gardens.

Hydrangea serrata 'Shiro tae', C. Esveld Nurseries.

Hydrangea serrata 'Shishiba', Holehird Gardens.

H. serrata 'Shiro gaku'

A small shrub not more than 1 m (3 feet). Florets consist of four or five pointed white sepals. The fertile flowers are green. The name is misspelled 'Chigo gaku'. Origin Japanese.

H. serrata 'Shiro maiko'

A slow-growing small shrub with narrow leaves. The sterile and fertile flowers are pure white. The florets are fully double. A common pot plant in Japan. The plant needs a protected place in the garden. Origin Japanese and Korean.

H. serrata 'Shiro tae'

A dwarf shrub up to 50 cm (20 inches), with attractive pure white flowers. The leaves are small and narrow. The fertile flowers are white, and the few sterile flowers on the corymb have fully double sepals. The plant needs a sheltered place in the garden. Bred by S. Okamoto in 1950.

H. serrata 'Shiro temari'

The spherical flowerheads consist of almost only sterile flowers, white with oval sepals, on long stalks. Origin Japanese.

H. serrata 'Shishiba'

A free-flowering shrub. Pinkish blue fertile flowers are surrounded by rosy pink sterile florets. The plant grows in full sun in a protected site. Origin Japanese.

H. serrata 'Shizaki'

This shrub has huge leaves and fertile flowers in temari form. There are no ray-flowers. The fertile flowers are a dirty lilac color. Origin Japanese. Possibly *H. macrophylla* Hortensia Group, which see.

Hydrangea serrata 'Shōjō', courtesy Arborealis.

Hydrangea serrata 'Spreading Beauty', C. Esveld Nurseries.

Hydrangea serrata 'Spreading Beauty', H. J. van Paddenburgh garden.

Hydrangea serrata 'Spreading Beauty', courtesy Arborealis.

H. serrata 'Shōjō'

A small shrub. Sepals are white with a red band; fertile flowers are white. The three to five florets per flowerhead later turn to reddish. Origin Japanese.

H. serrata 'Showa oshima'

A small shrub, with rounded corymbs in small mopheads. Flower color light blue or pink. May be a mophead cultivar of *H. macrophylla*. Origin Japanese.

H. serrata 'Sōfuren'

A small shrub, with attractive flowerheads consisting of 10 to 12 florets; the sepals are light lilac, winged. The few fertile flowers are lilac also. Origin Japanese.

H. serrata 'Spica'

A shrub 1 m (3 feet) high and wide, with an irregular habit. The fertile flowers are whitish, ray-flowers are white, double, and elongated. Leaves are small. This cultivar is similar to 'Shiro tae'. According to Dussine, it is a larger sibling. Origin Japanese.

H. serrata 'Spreading Beauty'

One of three clones growing from plants collected by Robert and Jelena de Belder at Hallasan in Korea. 'Spreading Beauty' is sometimes regarded as synonymous with 'Hallasan' or 'Maiko'. It was an exclusive plant for a Dutch nursery, but when the other two clones were distributed almost simultaneously to other nurseries, they were mistaken as 'Spreading Beauty'. Now it seems impossible to keep the three clones apart, due to their extreme similarity.

H. serrata 'Stellata'

A plant of uncertain origin, sometimes considered a species, subspecies, or garden form. According to McClintock and Mallet, it is closely related to *H. macrophylla* and to *H. serrata*. The true plant, once lost to cultivation, was rediscovered by Corrine Mallet in a French collection in

1991. It is now back to cultivation. The flowerheads carry sparse sterile flowers and are quite small. See also 'Prolifera'. Synonym: *H. stellata* Siebold & Zuccarini 1840 (double flowers, usually blue).

H. serrata 'Suzukayama yama'

A medium-sized shrub. The flowerheads consist of fertile blue flowers, surrounded by small florets, nicely blue. Each floret carries three or four sepals. Origin Japanese.

H. serrata 'Takao san yama'

A large-leaved shrub. The fertile flowers are green, surrounded by white florets, each with four or five sepals. Origin Japanese.

H. serrata 'Tango ezo temari'

A floriferous shrub, with mophead (temari) flowers, sepals frilled, light blue or light pink. Origin Japanese.

H. serrata 'Tango kaizaki'

Flowerheads consists of only a few light pink dentate florets with many greenish pinkish fertile flowers. Origin Japanese.

H. serrata 'Tango maiko'

A strong-growing shrub, with small mophead flowers, light lilac to shell pink. Origin Japanese.

H. serrata 'Tanigawadake ezo'

A shrub with large leaves. Ray-flowers light pink, few, and small. Origin Japanese.

H. serrata 'Tanoji yama'

A small shrub, with dark purplish brown leaves turning to green with age. Small white florets surround the violet fertile flowers.

H. serrata 'Tappisaki'

A shrub to 1 m (3 feet), with pale pink flowerheads (temari). Once thought to grow wild on Mount Tappisaki, but according to Yamamoto (1998) this is not possible; the many plants must have been planted a long time ago. Origin Japanese.

H. serrata 'Taren beni gaku'

One of several clones of 'Beni gaku' differing only in minor characteristics. Origin Japanese.

Hydrangea serrata 'Taren beni gaku', Rein and Mark Bulk nursery.

H. serrata 'Tate yama ezo'

A small shrub. The flowerheads are small; ray-flowers are white with pink edges, fertile flowers green.

H. serrata 'Temari'

A medium-sized shrub. Flowerheads mopheads or temari shaped, light lilac to light blue. Sepals pointed and heavily serrate. Origin Japanese.

H. serrata 'Temari ezo'

A medium-size shrub, similar to 'Temari', but the flowerheads are somewhat larger and have duller bluish sepals. Origin Japanese.

H. serrata 'Tenuifolia'

This cultivar has very conspicuous foliage. The leaves are narrow, heavily veined, green to reddish, and sharply bent backwards. Flowers not seen. In cultivation in France. Origin Japanese.

Hydrangea serrata 'Thunbergii', Hemelrijk Tuinen.

Hydrangea serrata 'Tiara', Maurice Foster garden.

Hydrangea serrata 'Thunbergii',
Rein and Mark Bulk nursery.

Hydrangea serrata 'Thunbergii',
Rein and Mark Bulk nursery.

Hydrangea serrata 'Tiara', C. Esveld Nurseries.

H. serrata 'Thunbergii'

A shrubby plant up to 1.5 m (5 feet), now included in *H. serrata*. Three clones, with incomplete description and no well-defined living plants, are in cultivation. The first has a few white sepals with pink margins and green fertile flowers (de Belder). The second has many more ray-flowers, and the sepals are white (Dutch nurseries). The third has purple foliage and pink flowerheads with a white center (Lawson-Hall and Rothera 1995). Philipp Franz von Siebold named the original plant in 1840 and treated it as species, but his description was incomplete and based on cultivated material.

H. serrata 'Tiara'

A healthy shrub up to 1 m (3 feet). The leaves are green with crimson when in full sun, producing a beautiful red autumn color. The plant is very free-flowering and the corymbs are abundantly produced. The fertile flowers are bluish, the sterile ray-flowers are arranged in a row, opening mauve, turning blue or pink. A promising novelty. The flowering period is very long, from June to August, and old flowers remain attractive for months. Bred by Maurice Foster of Kent, United Kingdom, 1992.

H. serrata 'Togari gaku'

A shrub with pale variegated leaves. The florets consist of creamy strongly pointed sepals. Origin Japanese.

H. serrata 'Tō gasa yama'

A small shrub. The leaves are lanceolate and similar to those of 'Amagi amacha'. The flowerheads are flat; white sepals surround the creamy fertile flowers. Origin Japanese.

H. serrata 'Tsurugi no mai'

An elegant shrub about 1 m (3 feet) high. The flowers are borne on long stalks, the florets are soft lilac and they form a ring around the fertile flowers. Origin Japanese.

Hydrangea serrata 'Wilsonii', Rutten garden.

Hydrangea serrata 'Yae no amacha', C. Esveld Nurseries.

Hydrangea serrata 'Woodlander', Jardin Bellevue.

H. *serrata* 'Unazuki ōsen ezo'
A shrub with large leaves. The large white sepals form florets and surround the fertile flowers. Origin Japanese.

H. *serrata* 'Usami azisai'
A large shrub, with large leaves and large flowerheads. Light blue florets surround light blue fertile flowers. Origin Japanese.

H. *serrata* 'Warabe'
A small low-growing shrublet, with small and narrow leaves Flowers not seen. Origin Korean; distributed by Milim Botanical Garden, Korea.

H. *serrata* 'Wase amacha'
This shrub has almost round leaves with slightly dentate margins. The florets are rounded, with four or five light pink sepals per flowerhead. The fertile flowers are pink. Origin Japanese.

H. *serrata* 'Wilsonii'
A robust shrub with narrow light green leaves. Sterile flowers are light pink, as are fertile flowers. Not to be confused with *H. heteromalla* 'Wilsonii'.

H. *serrata* 'Woodlander'
A small shrub with small leaves and pinkish mauve flowers. Autumn color is long lasting. Bred by Louisiana Nurseries, United States.

H. *serrata* 'Wryneck'
A shrub up to 1.25 m (3.5 feet), with slender stems. Probably derived from *H. serrata* subsp. *yesoensis*. The flowerheads are intermediate in shape between *H. serrata* and *H. macrophylla*, but the fertile flowers are arranged in the center as in *H. serrata*. Flowering time is from June to July, like it is for the other *H. serrata* cultivars. Possibly from wild origin. See 'Temari ezo'.

H. *serrata* 'Yae no amacha'
A shrub up to 1.25 m (3.5 feet). Flowers in flat corymbs, with florets of double sepals, white or light pink, and a few sterile flowers irregularly arranged like in 'Domotoi' (which see) or 'Oamacha'. Bred by S. Tada of Japan, in 1960.

H. *serrata* 'Yae no ezo'
Large V shaped pointed semidouble sepals on light blue ray-flowers. Origin Japanese.

Hydrangea serrata var. yesoensis, Holehird Gardens.

Hydrangea serrata 'Yoshibori', Floriade 2002.

Hydrangea serrata var. yesoensis, Holehird Gardens.

Hydrangea serrata var. yesoensis, C. Esveld Nurseries.

H. serrata var. *yesoensis* Yamamoto 1998

A low-growing shrub with narrow leaves. The sepals are arranged in threes and are pointed, blue or pink; fertile flowers are bluish. The autumn color can be very good. Native to northern Japan, including Hokkaido, it is the northerly expression of the species. Nuclear DNA content could suggest that it actually belongs to *H. macrophylla* Lacecap Group. *Hydrangea yesoensis* Makino 1926 is a basionym.

H. serrata 'Yoshibori'

Leaves long and narrow, with an acuminate apex. Ray-flowers light pink, sepals entire, fertile flowers green. Origin Japanese.

H. serrata 'Yuki sarasha'

Yellow fertile flowers surrounded by light lilac florets. Origin Japanese.

Hydrangea serratifolia, Trelissick Garden.

Hydrangea serratifolia, Crûg Farm Nursery.

Hydrangea sikokiana, Crûg Farm Nursery.

H. serratifolia (Hooker & Arnott) Philippi 1881

A woody climbing plant. The young branches, inflorescences, and leaves are pubescent or bristly with erect hairs. Leaves are evergreen, 7–15 cm (2.75–6 inches) long and 3–7 cm (1–2.75 inches) wide, with entire or slightly serrate margins. Flowerheads consist of white fertile flowers, almost none sterile. This species inhabits the Andes mountains in Chile and Argentina. Another name for this species, *H. integerrima,* is more appropriate since the leaves of this hydrangea are not serrate; however, according to the rules of the ICBN, the name *H. serratifolia* must be used.

H. sikokiana Maximowicz 1887

A shrub about 1.5 m (5 feet) high. Branches, stems, inflorescences, and flower stalks are pubescent. The leaves slightly resemble those of *H. quercifolia* and are deeply lobed, up to 15–20 cm (6–8 inches) wide. Flowerheads consists of predominantly white fertile flowers, with some sterile florets on long stalks scattered over the corymb.

Native to Honshu and Kyushu islands in Japan, this species is rare in cultivation. Japanese name is 'Yahaze ajisai'.

H. steyermarkii Standley 1940

A climbing plant with branches covered with felty brown hairs. Leaves evergreen, glabrous, dark green, 5–15 cm (2–6 inches) long and about 6–8 cm (2.4–3 inches) wide, ovate, margins slightly serrate. Flowerheads consist of white fertile flowers, none sterile. The species is native to Guatemala, in mountainous regions, at 1500 to 2500 m (4950–8250 feet) altitude.

H. tarapotensis Briquet 1919

A shrub or climbing plant with pubescent branches and inflorescences. Leaves ovate, 9–15 cm (3.5–6 inches) long and 4–9 cm (1.5–3.5 inches) wide, evergreen, glabrous above and below. Flowerheads consist exclusively of white fertile flowers, none sterile. This species is endemic in the Andes of Colombia, Bolivia, and Peru

Hydrangea villosa, C. Esveld Nurseries.

Hydrangea villosa, Crûg Farm Nursery.

Hydrangea villosa, C. Esveld Nurseries.

Hydrangea villosa, courtesy J. R. P. van Hoey Smith.

H. villosa Rehder 1911

A huge shrub up to 2.5 cm (8 feet) with age. Leaves narrow and pointed, about 10–15 cm (4–6 inches) long, somewhat tomentose below, slightly bristly above. Flowerheads large, fertile flowers lilac to purple, ray-flowers white, sepals entire or slightly serrate. Several cultivars formerly classified in *H. aspera* are now included in *H. villosa*. The DNA research of Ben J. M. Zonneveld provides very good reasons to maintain *H. villosa* as a species (see appendix 1). RHS Awards: AM 1950, AGM 1992.

H. villosa 'Anthony Bullivant'

A medium-sized densely branched shrub. The flowers are similar to those of the species but darker colored, an unusual feature. One of the best cultivars of the species. Raised at Stourton House Flower Garden, United Kingdom, in 1993.

H. villosa "Branklyn"

This very beautiful form is not yet named, but already included in this book for its beauty. Raised at Branklyn Garden, Perth, United Kingdom.

Hydrangea villosa 'Anthony Bullivant', Le Vastérival.

Hydrangea villosa 'Anthony Bullivant', Stourton House Flower Garden.

Hydrangea villosa 'Anthony Bullivant', Stourton House Flower Garden.

Hydrangea villosa 'Highdown', Jardin Bellevue.

Hydrangea villosa 'Mauvette' variegated sport, Rein and Mark Bulk nursery.

Hydrangea villosa 'Joelle', Le Thuit Saint-Jean.

Hydrangea villosa 'Le Thuit Saint Jean', Le Thuit Saint-Jean.

Hydrangea villosa 'Mauvette', Maurice Foster garden.

H. *villosa* 'Highdown'

A medium-sized shrub. The leaves are long and broadly acuminate. Flowerheads bear fertile flowers in the center, green at first. The ray-flowers are lilac, the sepals are pale pink. Bred by Sir Frederick Stern, United Kingdom.

H. *villosa* 'Joelle'

Leaves broadly ovate. Ray-flowers pale pink, fertile flowers violet. A selection from seedlings. Raised by Fréderique Buisson, France.

H. *villosa* 'Le Thuit Saint-Jean'

A shrub about 1.5 m (5 feet) high. Leaves long and narrow. The flowerheads are dark pink, with four sepals per floret. This cultivar needs a shady place in the garden. It is a seedling from Fréderique Buisson, France, and was named after her home.

H. *villosa* 'Lionel Fortescue'

A shrub about 2 m (6.5 feet) high. Leaves rounded without a sharp apex. Much the same as other forms in this species. The inflorescences are profusely produced, with white ray-flowers and light lilac fertile flowers.

H. *villosa* 'Mauvette'

A huge shrub up to 2 m (6.5 feet), with sturdy branches, resembling *H. aspera* 'Macrophylla'. The leaves are smaller and much narrower than in that cultivar and more acuminate. It is a very free-flowering plant. The numerous flowerheads have purple fertile flowers and lilac ray-flowers arranged in a circle. The flowering time is from July to August. This cultivar grows faster than do most cultivars of *H. villosa*. It was formerly traded as the species *H. villosa*, which is a different plant. The origin of this cultivar is not well known. Named by the president of the Royal Boskoop Horticulture Society Trial Committee, H. J. Grootendorst. Raised by J. van der Smit Reeuwijk, Netherlands, in 1973.

Hydrangea villosa 'Sam McDonald', Le Thuit Saint-Jean.

Hydrangea villosa 'Trelissick', Stourton House Flower Garden.

Hydrangea villosa 'Spinners', Le Vastérival.

Hydrangea villosa 'Velvet Lace', courtesy Maurice Foster.

H. villosa 'Sam McDonald'

This relatively new plant has conspicuous, very dark lilac-violet fertile flowers. The leaves are grayish green, broadly ovate, and slightly bristly. Bred by Peter Chappell, United Kingdom, before 1996.

H. villosa 'Spinners'

A well-branched shrubby plant, with strong-growing stems. The ray-flowers are very similar to those of 'Mauvette', the fertile flowers are greenish. Bred by Peter Chappell, United Kingdom, and named for his garden.

H. villosa 'Stäfa'

A huge shrub up to 2 m (6.5 feet). Leaves large, acuminate, somewhat velvety. The flowerheads are huge, and pure white florets are scattered throughout purple fertile flowers. Grows more strongly than do most *H. villosa* cultivars. According to L. Ziegler, it might be a hybrid of subsp. *sargentiana* and *H. villosa*. The plant was found by Frikart Brothers about 1970 and has been traded as *H. villosa*. It is no longer propagated. A group of old, unlabelled plants in the Botanical Garden Grueningen may be the real cultivar. Named for the city in Switzerland where the Frikart nursery was situated.

H. villosa 'Trelissick'

A dense shrub. The ray-flowers are lilac to pale lilac, the fertile flowers violet. The flowerheads are quite large. Raised by Elizabeth Bullivant, United Kingdom, in 2002.

H. villosa 'Velvet Lace'

A huge shrub up to 4–5 m (13–16 feet). Leaves long, narrow, and somewhat velvety. Flowerheads large with lilac florets surrounding the purple fertile flowers. A splendid novelty. Bred by Maurice Foster of Kent, United Kingdom, before 2000.

Hydrangea macrophylla, Arboretum Kalmthout.

Genome Size in Hydrangea

BEN J. M. ZONNEVELD

Institute of Molecular Plant Sciences, Clusius Laboratory, Leiden, Netherlands

Summary: Genome size (the size of a basic chromosome set = Cx-value) is used as a new criterion to investigate 71 species and cultivars of the genus *Hydrangea* Linnaeus. The nuclear DNA contents (2Cn) range from 2.17 picograms (pg) in *H. quercifolia* Bartram to 5.36 pg in *H. involucrata* Siebold for the diploid species and 7.00 pg in the tetraploid *H. paniculata* Siebold. The nuclear DNA contents, as measured by flow cytometry with propidium iodide, differ by about 3 pg, implying that the largest genome contains roughly 3 x 10^9 more base pairs than the smallest. Twenty-five cultivars of *H. macrophylla* Seringe and 18 of *H. serrata* (Thunberg) Seringe were also investigated. A small but clear difference between the two taxa confirms that *H. serrata* is a separate species and not a subspecies of *H. macrophylla.* If the large-sized *H. serrata* plants are set apart, they turn out to have on average a DNA content that is intermediate between *H. macrophylla* and *H. serrata.* This seems to indicate that at least some of them are hybrids. The 25 cultivars of *H. macrophylla* that were investigated turned out to consists of two groups: 16 cultivars with a nuclear DNA content of 4.54 pg and 9 cultivars that are presumably triploids with an average of 6.67 pg. The *H. aspera* D. Don group showed different DNA values, suggesting that more than one species is involved. The taxon collected in Taiwan clearly is different from other taxa of *H. aspera*, having nearly 50% more DNA. It could be a new species. Also the three forms of *H. scandens* Seringe measured are heterogeneous with respect to their DNA content. Together it shows that nuclear DNA content as measured by flow cytometry is a relevant trait to throw light on the relationships between *Hydrangea* species and cultivars.

INTRODUCTION

Hydrangea Linnaeus (Hydrangeaceae), containing about 23 species (McClintock 1957), is of interest for its distribution over two continents. Moreover, it has been a popular garden and florist's plant since the importation of *H. macrophylla* Seringe into England by Joseph Banks in 1879. The species can be divided in two sections (McClintock 1957): *Cornidia* with 12 species mainly from tropical South America, and section *Hydrangea* with 13 species from temperate regions of eastern Asia and two species of eastern North America. Several articles have appeared covering part or the whole of the genus *Hydrangea* (Wilson 1923, McClintock 1957, Haworth-Booth 1984, Ohba 1989). The genus is gaining renewed interest, and many new cultivars are introduced. The lacecap types, with a more natural look, developed especially in Wädenswil, Switzerland, seem especially suitable for the garden. The taxonomy is generally considered difficult since the species vary considerably depending on growing circumstances and geographical origins. McClintock (1957) states that especially leaf size and shape and hairiness are extremely variable characters.

Genome size is receiving more attention (Bennett 1972, Grime and Mowforth 1982, Ohri 1998). Zonneveld and Van Iren (2000, 2001) used flow cytometry successfully to investigate the genera *Hosta* Trattinick, *Helleborus* Linnaeus (Zonneveld 2001), and *Galanthus* Linnaeus (Zonneveld et al. in press). In this study the total amount of nuclear DNA as measured by flow cytometry was introduced as a novel criterion in *Hydrangea*. Moreover, it can be used to calculate the DNA content of parents of hybrids. In this article I have determined in 71 species and cultivars the range of nuclear DNA involved, to get an indication about the relationship between the species and the differences, if any, between the cultivars.

MATERIALS AND METHODS

Plant Material

One of the authors of this book, D. M. van Gelderen from Esveld Nurseries, Boskoop, Netherlands, provided plants. They are maintained as a living collection in his nursery.

Flow Cytometric Measurement of Nuclear DNA Content

For the isolation of nuclei, about 0.5 cm^2 of adult leaf, or equivalent amount of petiole or wintered, was chopped together with a piece of *Agave americana* Linnaeus as internal standard. The nuclear DNA content (2C-value) of *A. americana* was measured as 15.9 pg per nucleus with human leucocytes (= 7 pg, Tiersch et al. 1989) as the standard. The chopping was done with a new razor blade in a petri dish in 0.25 ml nuclei-isolation buffer as described by Johnston et al. (1999). After adding 2 ml propidium iodide (PI) solution (50 mg PI/l in isolation buffer) the suspension with nuclei was filtered through a 30 ?m nylon filter. The fluorescence of the nuclei was measured, half an hour and one hour after addition of PI, using a Partec CA-II flow cytometer. The more DNA in a nucleus, the higher the intensity of the fluorescence. The 2Cn DNA content of the sample was calculated as the sample peak mean, divided by the *Agave* peak mean, and multiplied with the amount of DNA of the *Agave* standard. In most cases, two different samples, and at least 5000 nuclei, were measured twice for each clone. Most histograms revealed a CV of around 5%.

Results and Discussion

All available *Hydrangea* species and cultivars were investigated experimentally by flow cytometry. The latter method was not applied earlier to *Hydrangea*. Genome size complements the work based mainly on morphological characters of earlier works. Based also on our earlier results with other plants, it is not illogical to assume that related taxa have similar amounts of DNA, but the reverse is not always true. In Table 1 the investigated species and cultivars of *Hydrangea* are arranged alphabetically with their nuclear DNA contents. They all belong to section *Hydrangea* with the exception of *H. integrifolia* Hayata, which belongs to section *Cornidia*. The genome size in the investigated species varies between 2.17 and 7.00 pg. The difference between the largest DNA content and the smallest one is about 4.8 pg, equivalent to nearly 4.8×10^9 base pairs. This means that millions of years must have elapsed since they separated. The results clearly show that some species are a heterogeneous assemblage.

In *Hydrangea aspera* the nuclear DNA contents of 3.4, 3.5, 3.7, and 4.2 are found. The latter taxon, *H. aspera* 'Villosa', could be better given the original name again: *H. villosa* Rehder. A plant grown from seed collected in Taiwan is suggested to be *H. aspera*, but turns out to have about 50% more DNA. As it is grown from collected seed, it seems unlikely that it is a triploid and in fact it could constitute a new species. *Hydrangea scandens* Seringe is also a mixed assemblage with the nuclear DNA contents of 4.0, 4.1, and 4.8. Here also f. *angustipetala* seems to be a species separate from *H. scandens*. The three American species *H. quercifolia* Bartram, *H. arborescens* Linnaeus, and the only species of section *Cornidia* measured, *H. integrifolia* Hayata, have by far the lowest amounts of nuclear DNA. It is not clear whether the American species show a decrease of their nuclear DNA content or the Asiatic species have an increase in their DNA content, since their geographical separation. The question about why these differences evolved could not be answered here.

The nuclear DNA content of 12 cultivars of *Hydrangea paniculata* (see Table 1) averages 7 pg, despite the fact that, based on chromosome numbers, diploids, tetraploids, and hexaploids have been recorded. If the measured plants are all tetraploids, only these seem to have been introduced in the garden.

Table 1 also shows the DNA content of 25 cultivars of *Hydrangea macrophylla*. Several remarkable facts emerge from it. Nine of the 25 cultivars turn out to be triploids. This was confirmed by counting their chromosomes from root tips (Zonneveld unpublished). These were probably selected for having a more luxurious growth (van Gelderen pers. comm.). They produce less seed than the diploids of *H. macrophylla*, and most of the seedlings are slow growing (Zonneveld unpublished). The triploids seem to be recognizable morphologically as having coarsely serrated leaves, whereas the diploids have finely serrated leaves. There is no connection with the type of the flowerheads, that is, lacecap (L) or globose (G).

Measurements of the percentage of stainable pollen in selected diploid and triploid *Hydrangea* cultivars yielded the following results:

Diploids

'Alpenglühen'	95%
'Holstein'	86%
'King George V'	80%
'Tiara'	89%

Triploids

'Admiration'	95%
'Blaumeise'	89%
'Gerda Steiniger'	45%
'Nachtigall'	10%
'R. F. Felton'	90%
'Sybilla'	87%

This data shows that even the triploids can have high pollen stainability, in accordance with the fact that they make a fair amount of good seed.

Equally interesting in Table 1 is the clear difference in nuclear DNA content of about 10% between *Hydrangea macrophylla* and *H. serrata*. They have repeatedly been separated as being two different species (Wilson 1923, Haworth-Booth 1984) or united again into a single species (see Makino in Hara 1955, McClintock 1957). Morphologically they are clearly different (Table 2) and even McClintock (1956) states that they can usually be distinguished without difficulty on the basis of the difference in leaf texture. *Hydrangea macrophylla* is a robust coastal plant with large glabrous, thick leaves and a limited distribution. *Hydrangea serrata* is a much more slender woodland plant, with much smaller usually hairy, thin leaves and a distribution in most of Japan.

Some of the plants under *Hydrangea serrata* are supposed to be hybrids with *H. macrophylla* like 'Preziosa' and 'Tiara'. Based on their DNA content 'Preziosa' is indeed a hybrid with a DNA content intermediate between *H. macrophylla* and *H. serrata*, but 'Tiara' is not. *Hydrangea serrata* is very variable in plant size. When the large plants ('Acuminata', 'Blue Bird', f. *chinensis*, 'Japonica', 'Miranda', 'Oamacha', 'Yae no amacha', and var. *yesoensis*) are set aside, the average nuclear DNA content for the remaining 10 plants drops from 4.28 to 4.23 pg. More relevant is that all these large cultivars of *H. serrata* have a higher DNA value with an average nuclear DNA content of 4.38 pg, actually intermediate between *H. serrata* in the narrow sense and *H. macrophylla*. Also McClintock (1956) remarks that in some specimens of *H. macrophylla* and *H. serrata* the difference in leaf texture is not clearly marked, pointing in my opinion to the hybrid nature. It cannot be excluded that they are indeed hybrids. If so, they could be more inclined to make unreduced gametes. If these were fertilized by gametes of *H. macrophylla* it would explain the source of the triploid "*H. macrophylla.*" This also explains why the values for the triploid are a bit short for a triploid. Based on 4.54 pg for the diploid *H. macrophylla*, triploids with 6.81 pg would be expected. The slightly lower value of 6.67 pg could be due to *H. serrata* influence, but this is highly speculative. Lastly, the nuclear DNA content of *H. serrata* var. *yesoensis* could suggest that it actually belongs to *H. macrophylla* and is not a synonym of *H. serrata* as suggested by McClintock (1957).

The above conclusions are based on the data as measured from the available species. I am the first to admit that some of my suggestions could be considered as speculative. Still, the DNA contents clearly separate *Hydrangea macrophylla* from *H. serrata* and show that many *H. macrophylla* cultivars are triploid. The data also suggest that several *H. serrata* taxa could be hybrids. Moreover, *H. aspera* and *H. scandens* turn out to be heterogeneous and some of their cultivars might be new species. The results can give a firm footing to what earlier were mainly educated guesses. To conclude, it is shown here that flow cytometry can be used to circumscribe the cultivars and to show (absence of) relationships between species. Therefore flow cytometry can be a very useful tool to investigate the relationships between members of the genus *Hydrangea*.

REFERENCES

Bennett, M. D. 1972. Nuclear DNA content and minimum generation time in herbaceous plants. *Proceedings of the Royal Society, London* 181: 109–135.

Grime, J. P., and M. A. Mowforth. 1982. Variation in genome size—an ecological interpretation. *Nature* 299: 151–153.

Hara, H. 1955. Critical notes on some type specimens of east Asiatic plants in foreign herbaria. *Journal of Japanese Botany* 30: 271–278.

Haworth-Booth, M. 1984. *The Hydrangeas.* London: Constable.

Johnston, J. S., M. D. Bennett, A. L. Rayburn, D. W. Galbraith, and H. J. Price. 1999. Reference standards for determination of DNA content of plant nuclei. *American Journal of Botany* 86(5): 609–613.

McClintock, E. 1956. The cultivated hydrangeas. *Baileya* 4: 165–175.

McClintock, E. 1957. A monograph of the genus *Hydrangea*. *Proceedings of the California Academy of Sciences* 29: 147–256.

Ohba, H. 1989. *Hydrangea*. In Y. Satake et al., eds., *Wild Flowers of Japan: Woody Plants.* Tokyo: Heibonsha Company. 166—172.

Ohri, D. 1998. Genome size variation and plant systematics. *Annuals of Botany* 82 (supp. A): 750–812.

Tiersch, T. R., R. W. Chandler, S. S. M. Wachtel, and S. Elias. 1989. Reference standards for flow cytometry and application in comparative studies of nuclear DNA content. *Cytometry* 10: 706–710.

Wilson, E. H. 1923. The hortensias: *H. macrophylla* Seringe and *H. serrata* (Thunberg) Seringe. *Journal of Arnold Arboretum* 4: 233–246.

Zonneveld, B. J. M. 2001. Nuclear DNA contents of all species of *Helleborus* discriminate between species and sectional divisions. *Plant Systematics and Evolution* 229: 125–130.

Zonneveld, B. J. M., J. M. Grimshaw, and A. P. Davis. In press. The systematic value of nuclear DNA content in *Galanthus* L. *Plant Systematics and Evolution*.

Zonneveld, B. J. M., and F. Van Iren. 2000. Flow cytometric measurement of DNA content in *Hosta* reveals ploidy chimeras. *Euphytica* 111: 105–110.

Zonneveld, B. J. M., and F. Van Iren. 2001. Genome size and pollen viability as taxonomic criteria: Application to the genus *Hosta*. *Plant Biology* 3: 176–185.

Table 1. Nuclear DNA Content of Selected *Hydrangea* Species and Cultivars

	Nuclear DNA content (pg)	Standard deviation
H. anomala subsp. petiolaris	**3.06**	0.13
H. anomala subsp. petiolaris 'Cordifolia'	**3.00**	0.10
H. arborescens	**2.64**	0.14
H. aspera subsp. aspera 'Nepal Beauty'	**3.50**	0.16
H. aspera subsp. aspera 'Taiwan'	**5.18**	0.17
H. aspera 'Macrophylla'	**3.72**	0.13
H. aspera subsp. robusta var. longipes	**3.50**	0.17
H. aspera subsp. sargentiana	**3.36**	0.14
H. heteromalla	**3.70**	0.21
H. hirta	**3.63**	0.31
H. integrifolia	**2.25**	0.14
H. involucrata 'Hortensis'	**5.36**	0.25
H. macrophylla diploids	**4.54**	0.05
'Alpenglühen' (G)	4.56	
'Ayesha' (G)	4.53	
'Bodensee' (G)	4.62	
'Jōgosaki' (L)	4.59	
'Joseph Banks' (G)	4.60	
'Hobella' (L)	4.52	
'Holstein' (G)	4.41	
'King George V' (G)	4.57	
'Mariesii Perfecta' (L)	4.55	
'Nigra' (G)	4.56	
var. *normalis* (L; collected in Japan)	4.60	
'Otaksa' (G)	4.53	
'Quadricolor' (L)	4.52	
'Renate Steiniger' (G)	4.54	
'Sea Foam' (L)	4.49	
'Veitchii' (L)	4.47	
H. macrophylla triploids	**6.67**	0.11
'Admiration' (G)	6.77	
'Blaumeise' (L)	6.57	
'Eisvogel' (L)	6.48	
'Europa' (G)	6.76	
'Gerda Steiniger' (G)	6.61	
'Möwe' (L)	6.79	
'Nachtigall' (L)	6.67	
'R. F. Felton' (G)	6.60	
'Sybilla' (G)	6.73	
H. paniculata	**7.00**	0.24
'Brussels Lace'	6.66	
'Floribunda'	7.03	
'Grandiflora'	7.19	
'Green Spire'	7.24	
'Kyushu'	6.84	

Table 1. (continued)

	Nuclear DNA content (pg)	Standard deviation
'Megapearl'	7.26	
'Pink Diamond'	7.05	
'Pink Lady'	6.90	
'Silver Dollar'	7.25	
'Tardiva'	7.22	
'White Lace'	6.82	
'Zwijnenburg' (LIMELIGHT)	6.57	
H. quercifolia 'Tennessee'	**2.17**	0.10
H. scandens	**4.16**	0.27
H. scandens subsp. chinensis f. angustipetala	**4.76**	0.25
H. scandens subsp. chinensis f. liukiuensis	**4.02**	0.15
H. serrata	**4.29**	0.24
'Acuminata'	4.46	
'Beni gaku'	4.27	
'Blue Bird'	4.39	
f. chinensis	4.17	
'Grayswood'	4.28	
'Intermedia'	4.19	
'Japonica'	4.22	
'Miranda'	4.24	
'Oamacha'	4.37	
'Preziosa'	4.36	
'Prolifera'	4.11	
'Rosalba'	4.23	
'Shiro gaku'	4.30	
'Shiro tae'	4.18	
'Spreading Beauty' (collected in Korea)	4.34	
'Tiara'	4.20	
'Yae no amacha'	4.38	
var. yesoensis	4.56	
H. villosa	**4.23**	0.21

G = Globose; L = Lacecap

Table 2. Comparison of *H. macrophylla* and *H. serrata*

	H. serrata	*H. macrophylla*
plant height	0.6–1.5 m (2–5 feet)	2 m (6.5 feet)
stem slender	massive	
stem color	red spots	green
leaf width	2–5(–8) cm (0.75–2[–3] inches)	6–10 cm (2.4–6 inches)
ratio length/width	>2	<2
petiole color	red	green
leaf surface	dull	shiny
leaf upperside	reddish	green
leaf hairiness	hairy	glabrous
flowering time	early/medium	late
place of flowers	tip + side shoots	stem tip
diameter of flowerhead	4–8 cm (1.5–3 inches)	10–15 cm (4–6 inches)
form of sepals	irregular	regular
number of sepals	3(–4)	4
outline of sepals	mostly serrated	mostly entire
anther color	white	blue/pink (white)
locality	woods of Japan/Korea	coastal Japan
chromosome number	$2x = 36$	$2x = 36$
nuclear DNA content	4.23 pg	4.54 pg

Hydrangea macrophylla, Trebah Garden.

Names without Descriptions

The names listed here have been used for hydrangeas at one time or another, although we often could find no information about the plants themselves. Some names refer to plants no longer in cultivation. Other names have appeared in various plant lists but otherwise remain unknown. Still other names refer to plants known and described in China, but their descriptions (in Chinese) are not yet available to English speakers. A few names refer to plants belonging to genera other than genus *Hydrangea!* We are recording these names here for reference purposes. They should not be reused.

SCIENTIFIC NAMES

H. acuminata Siebold & Zuccarini 1842. Siebold (1840) states that this taxon represents *H. serrata* (Thunberg) Seringe in nature. Said to grow in the mountains of Honshu and Kyushu, Japan. Siebold's description of the species was made from an illustration in *Flora Japonica*. The cultivar 'Acuminata' must not be confused with 'Intermedia', which is very often traded as 'Acuminata'. It is not known if the true variety is still in cultivation. See *H. serrata* 'Intermedia' and *H. serrata* var. *acuminata* Siebold.

H. alaskana Hollick. A fossil.

H. alba Reinwart. Originally named *H. oblongifolia* Blume 1824, it is an expression of *H. aspera*. Native to Java in Indonesia. Not in cultivation.

H. alternifolia Siebold 1829. Not a hydrangea, but *Cardiandra alternifolia*.

H. amagiana Makino 1932. A hybrid between *H. hirta* and *H. scandens* subsp. *chinensis*. It has not been seen by McClintock, nor is it available in the trade. The leaves are coarsely dentate. In 2002 Corrine Mallet discovered in Japan a hybrid between *H. hirta* and *H. scandens* f. *luteovenosa*. It is a shrub of about 75 cm (30 inches). This hybrid may be different from *H. hirta* 'Amagi', which see.

H. amplifolia Rafinesque before 1820. Not included in McClintock's thesis, but mentioned in *Index Kewensis*. See *H. arborescens* subsp. *arborescens*.

H. angustifolia Hayata 1911. Synonym: *H. scandens* subsp. *chinensis* f. *angustipetala*. A misspelling. The type was said to come from Taiwan, but no specimen was cited. The English description is based on the Latin diagnosis of *H. angustipetala* Hayata. There is no description, only a plate, representing the type. Not in the *Flora of Taiwan*.

H. angustipetala f. *formosanum* Hayata 1911. No description, but mentioned in the *Flora of Taiwan*. Collected on Taiwan by B. Wynn-Jones. Whether the material found in nature is different enough from the related forms of *H. scandens* subsp. *chinensis* to maintain this forma is difficult to establish now.

H. angustipetala var. *major* W. T. Wang 1981. No description. Status unknown.

H. angustipetala var. *subumbellata* Hayata 1981. No description available. Reduced to a forma of *H. scandens* by W. T. Wang in 1991 (*Index Kewensis*). See *H. scandens* subsp. *scandens*.

H. anomala var. **sericea** C. C. Yang 1982. No description available. Mentioned in *Index Kewensis*.

H. arborescens var. *canescens* Nicholls before 1830. Leaves smaller than the species, grayish below. See *H. arborescens* subsp. *discolor*.

H. aspera var. *angustifolia* Hemsley 1887. Native to Hubei province in China. See *H. aspera* subsp. *strigosa*.

H. aspera var. *cordata* Pampanini 1910. May have heart-shaped leaves.

H. aspera f. *emasculata* Chun 1954.

H. aspera f. *fulvescens* Rehder 1911. Basionym is *H. fulvescens* Rehder 1907. Closely allied to the now restored name *H. aspera* subsp. *robusta* var. *longipes*. The main difference lies in the tomentum. See *H. aspera* subsp. *aspera*.

H. aspera f. *glabripes* Rehder 1911. Basionym *H. glabripes* Rehder 1907. Closely related to *H. aspera* var. *longipes*, with leaves somewhat broader, covered with stiff hairs above, and villous below. Now included in *H. aspera* subsp. *aspera*, which see.

H. aspera var. *macrophylla* Hemsley 1887. Native to northwestern Hubei province, China. Probably no longer in cultivation as it isn't hardy outdoors.

H. aspera subsp. *robusta* f. *rosthornii* Diels 1901. This form differs slightly from the subspecies by larger leaves and longer petioles. These differences, however, are not distinct enough for restoring the status of a forma. See *H. aspera* subsp. *robusta*.

H. aspera var. *scabra* Rehder 1911. Leaves shaped like those of *H. aspera* subsp. *robusta* f. *rosthornii*, but with villous pubescence below and with shorter petioles. Now included in *H. aspera* subsp. *aspera*, as all these characteristics are unstable and unreliable.

H. aspera var. *sinica* Diels 1900. A Chinese expression. No description available. See *H. aspera* subsp. *strigosa*.

H. aspera var. *strigosior* Diels 1900. Differs slightly from *H. aspera* subsp. *strigosa* (which see) by a less villous tomentum, but the difference is not stable enough to maintain this taxon as a variety.

H. aspera f. *velutina* Rehder 1911. A forma between *H. aspera* and *H. villosa* with dull brownish yellow hairs. Close to subsp. *strigosa*. Now merged with *H. aspera* subsp. *aspera*.

H. asterolasia Diels 1941. A woody climber, with tomentose branchlets and inflorescences. The evergreen leaves are oval, 5—10 cm (2—4 inches) long and 3—5 cm (1—2 inches) wide, glabrous above, tomentose below, petioles tomentose also. Fertile flowers white, sterile flowers usually present. Inhabits the mountains of Costa Rica and Panama to the Andes in Columbia and Ecuador. This tropical species is classified in section *Cornidia*. Not in cultivation.

H. azisai Siebold & Zuccarini 1839. *Azisai*, also spelled *ajisai*, means "hortensia." Siebold wrongly interpreted this name as a species.

H. belzonii Siebold & Zuccarini 1864. Siebold wrongly interpreted this name as a species. See *H. serrata* 'Belzonii'.

H. bendirei (Ward) Knowlton. A fossil.

H. bretschneideri var. *giraldii* (Diels) Rehder 1911. Basionym is *H. giraldii* Diels 1900. According to McClintock, not in cultivation, and known only from a photo. See *H. heteromalla*.

H. bretschneideri var. *lancifolia* Rehder 1911. Extremely close to *H. heteromalla* 'Xanthoneura' and *H. heteromalla* 'Wilsonii'. Now included in *H. heteromalla* (which see) and, when in cultivation, considered to be a cultivar.

H. bretschneideri var. *setchuenensis* (Diels) Rehder 1911. Plants from Sichuan and Hubei provinces differ slightly in foliage. Now merged with *H. heteromalla* (which see).

H. brevipes Chun 1954. A new Chinese species without description. Mentioned in *Index Kewensis*.

H. buergeri Siebold & Zuccarini 1839. Used by Siebold for a garden plant. See *H. serrata*.

H. californica McGinnitie. A fossil.

H. candida Chun 1954. Mentioned in *Index Kewensis*. Habitat: Guanxi province, China.

H. ×canescens Kirchner before 1860. This plant is of little value. It has no showy sterile flowers. Parentage: *H. arborescens* subsp. *arborescens* × *H. arborescens* subsp. *discolor*.

H. caudatifolia W. T. Wang & M. X. Nie 1981. Mentioned in *Index Kewensis*.

H. chinensis var. *formosana* Koidzumi. A deciduous shrub with very narrow, willowy leaves. Terminal cymes cream, turning to yellow in summer. Habitat: southern Taiwan. See *H. scandens* subsp. *chinensis* f. *formosana*.

H. chinensis var. *lobbii* Kitamura 1974. Habitat: Philippines and Java. Now included in *H. chinensis* subsp. *chinensis*, which see.

H. coacta C. F. Wei 1994. Mentioned in *Index Kewensis*. Habitat: Shaanxi province, China.

H. coenotialis Chun 1954. Mentioned in *Index Kewensis*. Habitat: Guangdong province, China.

H. coenotialis var. **acutidens** Chun 1954. Mentioned in *Index Kewensis*.

H. cuspidata Makino 1912. Not a hydrangea, but *Viburnum cuspidatum*.

H. davidii Franchet 1885. A taxon closely allied to *H. scandens* subsp. *chinensis* and now merged with it. Differs mainly in the number of sepals. Treated as a cultivar when in cultivation.

H. discocarpa C. F. Wei 1994. Mentioned in *Index Kewensis*. Habitat: Sichuan province, China.

H. discolor Rafinesque before 1900. Basionym of *H. arborescens* subsp. *discolor* (which see). Differs mainly in the color of the leaf underside.

H. dumicola W. W. Smith 1917. Inflorescences are rough. Closely related to *H. heteromalla* 'Dumicola' (which see). Has to be treated as a cultivar.

H. durifolia Briquet 1919. Habitat: Colombia. See *H. oerstedtii*.

H. ecuadoriensis Briquet 1919. Habitat: Ecuador. See *H. preslii*.

H. epiphytica Morton 1950. Habitat: Costa Rica. See *H. asterolasia*.

H. fargesii Hort. ex F. Weber 1931. Mentioned in *Index Kewensis*.

H. florida Salisbury. Mentioned in *Index Kewensis*. See *H. macrophylla*.

H. fraxinifolia (Lesquereux) Brown. A fossil.

H. fulvescens Rehder 1911. Habitat: Hubei and Sichuan provinces, China. See *H. aspera* subsp. *aspera* f. *fulvescens*.

H. giraldii Diels 1900. Basionym for *H. bretschneideri* var. *giraldii* (which see). Habitat: Shaanxi province, China.

H. glabrifolia Hayata 1913. Habitat: Taiwan. See *H. scandens* subsp. *chinensis*.

H. glabripes Rehder 1911. Habitat: Hubei province, China. See *H. aspera* subsp. *aspera*.

H. goudottii Briquet 1919. Habitat: Colombia. See *H. oerstedtii*.

H. gracilis W. T. Wang & M. X. Nie 1981. Mentioned in *Index Kewensis.*

H. grossiserrata Engler 1918. Habitat: Yakushima, Japan. Basionym of *H. scandens* subsp. *chinensis* f. *grossiserrata* (which see).

H. hedyotidea Chun 1954. Mentioned in *Index Kewensis.* Habitat: Guangdong province, China.

H. heteromalla var. *glabrata*. No information available.

H. ×hortentiolaris H. Cayeux 1922. Parentage: *H. macrophylla* 'Rosea' × *H. anomala* subsp. *petiolaris*. Origin French. Now extinct.

H. hypoglauca Rehder 1911. Rehder classified it as closely related to var. *xanthoneura*, but now that the variety is only considered a cultivar, *H. hypoglauca* is merged with *H. heteromalla* (which see).

H. hypoglauca var. *giraldii* (Diels) C. F. Wei 1994. Mentioned in *Index Kewensis.* See *H. heteromalla.*

H. indochinensis Merrill 1942. This very rare plant is closely related to *H. macrophylla* subsp. *stylosa* and sunk into synonymy of that subspecies by McClintock. The florets carry three strongly dentate sepals. The species is endemic to Vietnam and has been re-introduced to Europe. It is worthy of classification as a forma. See *H. macrophylla* subsp. *stylosa* f. *indochinensis.*

H. inornata Standley 1927. Habitat: Costa Rica. See *H. diplostemona.*

H. involucrata f. **idzuensis** Hayashi. This forma is in cultivation in Japan. It is mentioned in *Wild Flowers of Japan* with a short text in Japanese.

H. involucrata subsp. **tokarensis** M. Hotta & T. Shiuchi 1996. Mentioned in *Index Kewensis.*

H. involucrata 'Yasaku yae'. Origin Japanese. Mentioned in the 1999 catalog of Milim Botanical Garden, Korea. Must be double flowered as *yae* means "double."

H. jiangxiensis W. T. Wang & M. X. Nie 1981. Mentioned in *Index Kewensis.*

H. kamienskii Léveillé 1903. Sargent (1913) doubts that this species is a synonym of *H. paniculata*. It could be a synonym of *H. heteromalla.*

H. kwangsiensis Hu 1931. Habitat: Guangdong province, China. See *H. macrophylla* subsp. *stylosa.*

H. laevigata Cels before 1800. According to K. Koch (before 1800), this species had longer, narrower leaves. No other information available. See *H. arborescens* subsp. *arborescens.*

H. lingii C. Hu 1951. Habitat: Fujian province, China.

H. linkweiensis Chun 1954. Mentioned in *Index Kewensis.* Habitat: Guangxi province, China.

H. linkweiensis var. *subumbellatum* (W. T. Wang) C. F. Wei 1994. No information available.

H. liukiuensis Nakai 1911. Leaves small, often with a yellow band along the midvein, on reddish brown stems. These are the only differences between it and the closely related *H. scandens* subsp. *chinensis* f. *luteovenosa*. The Japanese name is 'Ryukyu konterigi'.

H. longialata C. F. Wei 1994. Mentioned in *Index Kewensis.* Habitat: Yunnan province, China.

H. longifolia Hayata 1908. Habitat: Taiwan. See *H. involucrata.*

H. luteovenosa Koidzumi 1925. The Japanese name is 'Kogaku utsugi'. McClintock sinks this species in *H. scandens* subsp. *liukiuensis*, mainly because Koidzumi did not designate a type and thus the species name is illegitimate (see also McClintock 1957, p. 206). Plants in cultivation come from Japan, apparently in the wild (Bean 1970—1988). The leaves are very small, blotched with yellow, and the inflorescences have about 20 white florets. Milim Botanical Garden in Ky?nggi, Korea, lists two cultivars without description: 'Fuiri' and 'Hana gasa'. See also *H. amagiana* for information about the supposed hybrid with *H. hirta.*

H. macrocarpa Handel-Mazzetti 1925. Based on a plant from Sichuan province, China. See *H. heteromalla,*

H. macrocephala Hort. ex Dippel 1893. Description based on a garden plant clearly belonging to *H. macrophylla*, with very large inflorescences.

H. macrophylla subsp. **chungii** (Rehder) McClintock 1956. A small shrub up to 1.25 m (3.5 feet). Its branches and stems are pubescent, which is unusual in this species. The leaves are egg shaped, with serrate margins, downy below. The corymbs are 15 cm (6 inches) across, purple, with five or six ray-flowers arranged around the fertile flowers. The florets have four round sepals. This subspecies was collected in the Fujian province of China. It is not in cultivation in the Western world.

H. macrophylla subsp. *serrata* Makino 1926. This combination of Makino is not accepted in this volume, just as it is not accepted in practically all publications on this subject since 1956. All references cited choose *H. serrata*, except McClintock in her monograph. The DNA research by Ben J. M. Zonneveld (see appendix 1) shows that *H. serrata* is a good species on its own.

H. macrosepala Hayata 1913. Habitat: Taiwan. See *H. scandens* subsp. *chinensis.*

H. mangshanensis C. F. Wei 1954. Mentioned in *Index Kewensis.* Habitat: Hunan province, China.

H. maximowiczii Léveillé 1903. Resembles *H. lobbii*, but differs in pubescence. This "lobbii" cannot be separated from 'Rosthornii'. Another "lobbii" comes from the Philippines. See *H. aspera* subsp. *robusta.*

*H. **minnanica*** W. D. Han 1994. Mentioned in *Index Kewensis*.

*H. **nebulicola*** Neve & Pompa 1968. Mentioned in *Index Kewensis*.

H. nivea Michaux 1803. Differs from *H. arborescens* subsp. *radiata* (which see) by having more whitish tomentose leaves.

H. oblongifolia Blume 1826. Habitat: Java. See *H. aspera* subsp. *aspera*.

H. obovatifolia Hayata 1913. Habitat: Taiwan. See *H. scandens* subsp. *chinensis* and *H. angustipetala*.

H. opuloides Lamarck 1789. Based on a plant cultivated on Mauritius and sent to the Jardin des Plantes in Paris. See *H. macrophylla* subsp. *macrophylla*.

H. paniculata 'National Arboretum' U.S. National Arboretum, Washington. Plate 12242. Not the name of a cultivar but the place of origin. It is available in the trade. It has huge panicles with many fertile yellowish flowers and scattered white ray-flowers with three or four sepals.

H. platyphylla Briquet 1919. Habitat: Colombia. See *H. oerstedtii*.

H. pottingeri Prain 1869. Habitat: India, see *H. scandens* subsp. *chinensis*.

H. pubescens Zippelius ex Miquel. Not a hydrangea, but *Dichroa pubescens*.

H. reticulata McGinnitie. A fossil.

H. rosthornii Diels 1901. Closely related to *H. aspera* subsp. *robusta*, differing mainly in longer and larger leaves and petioles. McClintock sunk this former species in synonymy, but it might better placed under *H. aspera* subsp. *robusta* var. *longipes* (which see).

H. rotundifolia C. F. Wei 1994. Mentioned in *Index Kewensis*. Habitat: Xizang province (Tibet), China.

H. russellii Chaney & Sandborn. A fossil.

H. sachalinensis Léveillé 1910. Habitat: Sakhalin Island, off eastern Russia. See *H. paniculata*.

H. schindleri Engler 1930. Habitat: Guangdong province, China. See *H. paniculata*.

H. serrata var. *angustata* Makino. See *H. serrata* 'Angustata'.

H. serrata var. *buergeri* Siebold & Zuccarini 1840. A garden form in Japan. See *H. serrata*.

H. serrata var. *minamitanii* Ohba 1989. Mentioned in *Index Kewensis* and in *Wildflowers of Japan*, both without description.

*H. **shaochingii*** Chun 1954. Habitat: Guangdong province, China.

H. speciosa Persoon 1829. Once a common garden plant in Japan and so well known that it was not illustrated in *Flora Japonica*.

H. sprucei Briquet 1919. Habitat: Peru and Colombia. See *H. diplostemona*.

H. stellata Siebold & Zuccarini 1840. Flowers double, usually blue. According to McClintock, a cultivar. See *H. serrata* 'Stellata'.

H. strigosa var. *angustifolia* Rehder 1911. Leaves 20 cm (8 inches) long and 4 cm (1.5 inches) wide. These characters not sufficient to maintain the taxon as a variety. See *H. aspera* subsp. *strigosa*

H. sungpanensis Handel-Mazzetti 1931. Habitat: Sichuan province. See *H. heteromalla*.

*H. **taiwaniana*** Y. C. Lin & F. Y. Liu 1977. Habitat: Taiwan.

H. taquetii Léveillé 1910. Habitat: Korea.

H. umbellata Rehder 1911. Habitat: Guanxi province, China. See *H. scandens* subsp. *chinensis*.

*H. **verticillata*** W. H. Gao 1987. Mentioned in *Index Kewensis*.

H. vestita Wallich 1826. Habitat: northeastern China. See *H. heteromalla*.

*H. **warszewiczii*** Vatke 1872. Mentioned in *Index Kewensis*.

H. xanthoneura var. *setchuenensis* (Diels) Rehder 1912. Habitat: Sichuan province, China. See *H. heteromalla*.

*H. **zhewanensis*** Hsu & Zhang 1987. Mentioned in *Index Kewensis*.

CULTIVAR NAMES

'**Abel Chatenay**' (*H. macrophylla* Hortensia Group) Mouillère 1914. France. Probably no longer in cultivation.

'**Abendrot**' (*H. macrophylla* Hortensia Group). According to the Shamrock list, no longer in cultivation.

'**Abondance**' (*H. macrophylla* Hortensia Group) Draps-Dom 1962. Belgium. Mentioned in the Checklist.

'**Adventsglocke**' (*H. macrophylla* Hortensia Group). Germany. Mentioned in the Checklist.

'**Adolf Paasch**' (*H. macrophylla* Hortensia Group) A. Paasch, Gretdorf in Holstein 1955. Germany. Mentioned in the Checklist.

'**Adonis**' (*H. macrophylla* Hortensia Group) Mouillère 1963. France. Probably lost to cultivation.

'**Albis**' (*H. macrophylla* Hortensia Group) Federal Research Institute for Horticulture 1951. Switzerland. Parentage: 'Bachtel' × 'Ami Pasquier'. According to the Shamrock list, no longer in cultivation.

'**Albury Purple**' (*H. macrophylla* Hortensia Group)

'**Altenburg**' (*H. macrophylla* Hortensia Group) E. Haller 1964. Switzerland. According to the Shamrock list, lost to cultivation.

'**Amaranthe**' (*H. macrophylla* (Hortensia Group) Mouillère 1920. France. A slow-growing shrub with stout, short branches. Flowers large, flattened, amaranth pink. According to the Shamrock list, lost to cultivation.

'**Ambrosiana**' (*H. macrophylla* Hortensia Group). Mentioned in Checklist.

'**Amethyst**' (*H. quercifolia*). Mentioned by Michael Dirr (1989).

'**Andenken an Ferdinand Fischer**' (*H. macrophylla* Hortensia Group) Fischer, 1952. Germany. Mentioned in Checklist.

'**Anderson 1**' (*H. macrophylla* Hortensia Group) M. Anderson 1991. Mentioned in Checklist. Trademark is PINK PARFAIT.

'**Anni Feron**' (*H. macrophylla* Hortensia Group) Dublanchet 1964. France. Mentioned in Checklist.

'**Anni Rampp**' (*H. macrophylla* Hortensia Group) Rampp Nursery 1963. Germany. Mentioned in Checklist.

'**Apollo**' (*H. macrophylla* Hortensia Group) H. Cayeux 1932. France. Maybe J. Wintergalen 1933; Germany. A medium-sized to tall shrub. Corymbs large, flowers crimson and easily turned blue. Flowering time is from July to August. Probably lost to cultivation.

'**Atlas**' (*H. macrophylla* Hortensia Group). Mentioned in Checklist.

'**Attraction**' (*H. macrophylla* Hortensia Group) Foucard 1912. France. A strong-growing shrub, free-flowering with pale pink corymbs. According to the Shamrock list, it is extinct in cultivation.

'**Aurore**' (*H. macrophylla* Hortensia Group) Draps-Dom 1950. Belgium. According to the Shamrock list, lost to cultivation.

'**Autumn Green**' (*H. macrophylla* Hortensia Group). Mentioned in Checklist.

'**Avenir**' (*H. macrophylla* Hortensia Group) Cayeux 1921. France. Mentioned in Checklist.

'**Baby Rimbenet**' (*H. macrophylla* Hortensia Group) Mouillère 1910. France. A small shrub up to 1 m (3 feet), with stout, short branches. Flowers pink or blue. An old cultivar that probably is no longer in cultivation.

'**Bachtel**' (*H. macrophylla* Hortensia Group) Federal Research Institute for Horticulture 1947. Switzerland. A shrub up to 1.5 m (5 feet). Flowerheads large, about 15 cm (6 inches) across, usually salmon pink. Suitable as a pot plant. One of the first introductions of the Federal Research Institute for Horticulture.

'**Baroness Schröder**' (*H. macrophylla* Hortensia Group) K. Wezelenburg & Sons 1927. Netherlands. A weak-growing plant, apt to sunburning and also tender. Flowerheads large, usually pink. Lost to cultivation.

'**Bastei**' (*H. macrophylla* Lacecap Group) Dresdner Zierpflanzenbau 1992. Germany. Mentioned in the Checklist.

'**Beauté de Tours**' (*H. macrophylla* Hortensia Group) Barillet 1923. France. Mentioned in the Checklist.

'**Bellikon**' (*H. macrophylla* Hortensia Group) E. Haller 1975. Switzerland. Named for a village in northern Switzerland. Lost to cultivation.

'**Benidorm**' (*H. macrophylla* Hortensia Group) Dr. Bosse, Versuchsanstalt Friesdorf. Germany. Mentioned in Checklist.

'**Biberstein**' (*H. macrophylla* Hortensia Group) E. Haller 1970. Switzerland. According to the Shamrock list, lost to cultivation.

'**Big Bridget**' (*H. macrophylla* Hortensia Group) G. van der Knaap, Rijsenhout, 2002. Netherlands.

'**Birgit**' (*H. macrophylla* Hortensia Group) Matthes. Germany. Mentioned in University of Dresden-Pirna list.

'**Blackbird**' (*H. macrophylla* Hortensia Group). Mentioned in *Le Monde des hortensias* (Dussine).

'**Blanc de Gaujacq**' (*H. macrophylla* Lacecap Group). No description in the catalog of French nurseryman Jean Thoby. It is certainly white-flowering.

'**Blaufrüh**' (*H. macrophylla* Hortensia Group). Mentioned in the Shamrock list.

'**Blue Fringe**' (*H. macrophylla* Hortensia Group). Mentioned in the Checklist.

'**Blue Lady**' (*H. macrophylla* Hortensia Group). Mentioned in the Shamrock list.

'**Blue Mac**' (*H. macrophylla* Hortensia Group). Seems to be in cultivation in Belgium and is also in the Shamrock collection.

'**Blue Pac**' (*H. macrophylla* Hortensia Group). May be in the Shamrock collection.

'**Blue Rain**' (*H. macrophylla* Hortensia Group) Milim Botanical Garden, Korea.

'**Blue Rain**' (*H. macrophylla* Lacecap Group). Mentioned in the 1999 catalog of the Milim Botanical Garden, Korea.

'**Blushing Pink**' (*H. macrophylla* Hortensia Group). Mentioned by Michael Dirr.

'**Bosahan**' (*H. serrata*) Pépinières Thoby, France. Mentioned in the Shamrock list.

'**Boskoop**' (*H. macrophylla* Hortensia Group) D. A. Koster. Netherlands. According to Koster, the flowers are fiery pink and appear late in the season. Lost to cultivation.

'**Candeur**' (*H. macrophylla* Hortensia Group) Lemoine 1921. France. Pure white flowerheads and serrate sepals. According to the Shamrock list, no longer in cultivation.

'**Candide**' (*H. macrophylla* Hortensia Group) L. F. Cayeux 1967. France. No longer in cultivation. Mentioned in the Checklist.

'**Caprice**' (*H. macrophylla* Hortensia Group) Cayeux 1920. France. Mentioned in the Checklist.

'**Capitaine Nemo**' (*H. macrophylla* Hortensia Group). In the Shamrock collection.

'**Carnea**' (*H. macrophylla* Hortensia Group) L. F. Cayeux 1967. France. Lost to cultivation.

'**Caroline**' (*H. macrophylla* Hortensia Group). A tall shrub with large leaves and flowerheads. Flowers usually bright pink, easily turning a good blue. According to the Shamrock list, no longer in cultivation.

'**Champion**' (*H. macrophylla* Hortensia Group) Cayeux 1927. France. Mentioned in the Checklist.

'**Charme**' (*H. macrophylla* Hortensia Group) H. Cayeux 1932. France. A shrub with large dark pink flowers. Probably lost to cultivation.

'**Charming**' (*H. macrophylla* Hortensia Group) E. Draps 1938. Belgium. Flowerheads red to gentian blue. Probably lost to cultivation.

'**Chazili**' (*H. macrophylla* Hortensia Group) Challet-Herault 1993. France. Mentioned in the Checklist.

'**China Boy Blue**' (*H. serrata*). Souji Sakamoto, Japan. Mentioned in the *Japanese Color Guide*.

'**Clouet-Hamel**' (*H. macrophylla* Hortensia Group) 1956.

'**Cocarde**' (*H. macrophylla* Hortensia Group) H. Cayeux 1932. France. A shrub of the usual size with long-lasting corymbs. Flowers usually reddish pink. According to the Shamrock list, lost to cultivation.

'**Colonel Durham**' (*H. macrophylla* Hortensia Group) K. Wezelenburg & Sons 1927. Netherlands. Corymbs large, pink or blue. Lost to cultivation.

'**Colonel Lindbergh**' (*H. macrophylla* Hortensia Group) D. Baardse 1927. Netherlands. A slow-growing shrub. Flowerheads large, pink or lilac. Flowering time is from August to September. No longer in cultivation. Synonym: 'Lindbergh'.

'**Création**' (*H. macrophylla* Hortensia Group) Cayeux 1933. France. According to the Shamrock list, lost to cultivation.

'**D. B. Crane**' (*H. macrophylla* Hortensia Group) H. J. Jones 1927. United Kingdom. A dwarf shrub. Flowerheads large, slightly serrate, usually pink. Introduced by K. Wezelenburg & Sons, Boskoop, but now lost to cultivation. RHS Award: AM 1927.

'**Dante**' (*H. macrophylla* Hortensia Group) Draps-Dom 1958. Belgium. Mentioned in the Checklist.

'**David Ingamelles**' (*H. macrophylla* Hortensia Group) H. J. Jones 1927. United Kingdom. A dwarf compact shrub. Flowerheads a good pink. Probably lost to cultivation. RHS Award: AM 1928.

'**Dayspring**' (*H. quercifolia*). Mentioned by Michael Dirr before 1997.

'**Decatur Blue**' (*H. macrophylla* Hortensia Group). Mentioned in the Shamrock list.

'**Déesse**' (*H. macrophylla* Hortensia Group) Draps-Dom 1950. Belgium. According to the Shamrock list, lost to cultivation.

'**Delice**' (*H. macrophylla* Hortensia Group) Cayeux 1921. France. Mentioned in the Checklist.

'**Dentelle**' (*H. macrophylla* Hortensia Group) Lemoine 1908. France. A slow-growing shrub, up to 1 m (3 feet). Flowers large, creamy pink, sepals serrate. Available in Netherlands in 1915, but now probably lost to cultivation.

'**Deutschland's Ehre**' (*H. macrophylla* Hortensia Group) Rosenkrantzer 1918. Germany. Mentioned in the University of Dresden list.

'**Devon Panachee**' (*H. macrophylla* Hortensia Group). Mentioned in the Shamrock list.

'**Diamant**' (*H. macrophylla* Hortensia Group) Draps-Dom 1955. Belgium. Mentioned in the Checklist.

'**Diane**' (*H. macrophylla* Hortensia Group) Lemoine 1910. France. A medium-sized shrub. The corymbs are large and composed of crimped flowers, in palest pink to almost white. Lost to cultivation.

'**Die vom Niederrhein**' (*H. macrophylla* Hortensia Group). Germany. According to the University of Dresden list, should be present in the botanical garden of Krefeld.

'**Diskus**' (*H. macrophylla* Lacecap Group). Mentioned in the Checklist.

'**Dlabskas Beste**' (*H. macrophylla* Hortensia Group). Introduced by Dlabska, Berlin Zehlendorf. Germany.

'**Dôme Fleuri**' (*H. macrophylla* Hortensia Group) Lemoine 1911. France. Flowerheads bun shaped, pale pink. Lost to cultivation.

'**Dompfaff**' (*H. macrophylla* Lacecap Group) Federal Research Institute for Horticulture 1979. Switzerland. Mentioned in the Checklist.

'**Doris**' (*H. macrophylla* Hortensia Group). Binz. Germany. Introduced by van Dijk, De Lier, Netherlands. Mentioned in the Checklist.

'Dortmund' (*H. macrophylla* Hortensia Group) A. Steiniger 1959. Germany. Mentioned in the University of Dresden list.

'Draps Champion' (*H. macrophylla* Hortensia Group) Draps-Dom 1955. Belgium. Mentioned in the Checklist.

'Draps Supreme' (*H. macrophylla* Hortensia Group) Draps-Dom 1938. Belgium. Mentioned in the Checklist.

'Drusberg' (*H. macrophylla* Hortensia Group) Federal Research Institute for Horticulture 1964. Switzerland. Parentage: 'Henri Cayeux' × ('King George' × 'Säntis'). Lost to cultivation.

'Duchesse' (*H. macrophylla* Hortensia Group) Cayeux 1964. France. Mentioned in the Checklist.

'Dundalk' (*H. macrophylla* Hortensia Group). Mentioned in the Checklist.

'Early Red' (*H. macrophylla* Hortensia Group) K. Wezelenburg & Sons 1967. Netherlands. Synonym: 'Vörsters Frührot'.

'Easter Star' (*H. macrophylla* Hortensia Group) K. Wezelenburg & Sons 1967. Netherlands. Flowers deep pink, in midseason. Lost to cultivation.

'Edelweiss' (*H. macrophylla* Hortensia Group) P. Flores 1931. Germany. A slow growing shrub, up to 1.5 m (5 feet). Corymbs creamy to greenish white. Possibly lost to cultivation.

'Edison' (*H. macrophylla* Hortensia Group) K. Wezelenburg & Sons 1936. Netherlands. A strong-growing shrub, with stout branches. The flowerheads are large, the sepals are fringed and pink to rose. Lost to cultivation.

'Edith Binz' (*H. macrophylla* Hortensia Group) W. Binz. Germany. Should be in the Shamrock collection. Also mentioned in the Dutch Woody Plantnames List.

'Elégance' (*H. macrophylla* Hortensia Group) H. Cayeux 1937. France. A slow-growing cultivar. Flowerheads small, compact, purple-pink or blue. According to the Shamrock list, lost to cultivation.

'Elfe' (*H. macrophylla* Hortensia Group) Tempel Brothers. Quadlinsburg, Germany. Mentioned in the University of Dresden list.

'Elisabeth Jackertz' (*H. macrophylla* Hortensia Group) Jackertz. Unterbach, Germany. Mentioned in the University of Dresden list.

'Emblême' (*H. macrophylla* Hortensia Group) H. Cayeux 1926. France. A weak-growing plant. Flowerheads crimson. Lost to cultivation.

'Eric Pellerin' (*H. macrophylla* Hortensia Group). Mentioned in the Shamrock list.

'Espoir' (*H. macrophylla* Hortensia Group) Cayeux 1931. France. Mentioned in the Checklist.

'Etincelant' (*H. macrophylla* Hortensia Group) Lemoine 1915. France. A medium-sized shrub, sometimes dwarf. Corymbs large, usually pink. Free-flowering, August to September. May not be in cultivation. Mentioned in the Koster & Sons (Boskoop) nursery catalog of 1936. RHS Award: AM (year unknown).

'Etzel' (*H. macrophylla* Hortensia Group) Federal Research Institute for Horticulture 1947. Switzerland. A hybrid between 'Holstein' and 'Giselher'. Bred by Haller.

'Eugénie Tabart' (*H. macrophylla* Hortensia Group) Mouillère 1909. France. Flowers pink. Lost to cultivation.

'Extase' (*H. macrophylla* Hortensia Group) L. F. Cayeux 1938. France. Flowerheads fresh pink. According to the Shamrock list, lost to cultivation.

'Fanal' (*H. macrophylla* Hortensia Group) H. Cayeux 1935. France. A dwarf shrub, neat and compact. The corymbs are large, usually crimson. Lost to cultivation.

'Feuerball' (*H. macrophylla* Hortensia Group) A. Steiniger 1967. Germany. Mentioned in the Checklist.

'Filibuster' (*H. macrophylla* Hortensia Group). Mentioned in the Shamrock list.

'Flora Gand' (*H. macrophylla* Hortensia Group). Flowers deep pink. Mentioned in the 1967 nursery catalog of K. Wezelenburg and Sons, Netherlands.

'Ford Abbey' (*H. aspera*). United Kingdom. Mentioned in the Checklist.

'Fraicheur' (*H. macrophylla* Hortensia Group) before 1915. Flowers white blushed pink. Cultivated in several Dutch nurseries but probably not in cultivation.

'Frans Hals' (*H. macrophylla* Hortensia Group) K. Wezelenburg & Sons 1927. Netherlands. A dwarf shrubby plant. Flowerheads rather small, usually pink and free-flowering. Probably lost to cultivation. Named for a famous painter and a pupil of Rembrandt.

'Frau A. Rosenkrantzer' (*H. macrophylla* Hortensia Group) Rosenkrantzer. Germany. Mentioned in the University of Dresden list.

'Frederica' (*H. macrophylla* Hortensia Group). Mentioned in the Checklist.

'Freifrau von Stumm' (*H. macrophylla* Hortensia Group) Rosenkrantzer. Germany. Mentioned in the Checklist.

'Freya' (*H. macrophylla* Hortensia Group) J. Wintergalen 1926. Germany. Flowers dark rose, sepals serrate, purple in acid soils. Can be confused with 'Parzifal'. Once available in several Dutch nurseries (D. A. Koster, M. Koster and Sons).

'Friedrich Matthes' (*H. macrophylla* Hortensia Group) F. Matthes 1923. Germany. A dwarf shrub, with stout, sturdy branches. Flowerheads warm pink and very strong. Once available in several Dutch nurseries (D. A. Koster, M. Koster and Sons).

'Frühlingserwachen' (*H. macrophylla* Hortensia Group) H. Schadendorff before 1932. Germany. Flowers deep pink, early in the season. Formerly offered by D. A. Koster nursery of Boskoop.

'Galathée' (*H. macrophylla* Hortensia Group) Lemoine 1911. France. Flowers pure white, sepals serrate. Probably lost to cultivation.

'Gärtnerfreude' (*H. macrophylla* Hortensia Group) A. Steiniger 1964. Germany. Mentioned in the Checklist.

'General Eisenhower' (*H. macrophylla* Hortensia Group). Mentioned in the Checklist.

'General Valhubert' (*H. macrophylla* Hortensia Group) 1927. Mentioned in the Checklist.

'Ginette' (*H. macrophylla* Hortensia Group) Cayeux 1924. France. According to the Shamrock list, lost to cultivation.

'Giselher' (*H. macrophylla* Hortensia Group) J. Wintergalen before 1930. Germany. A slow-growing, weak plant, flowering in July with pink sepals. Formerly available at several Dutch nurseries, but now lost to cultivation.

'Glanzblatt' (*H. macrophylla* Hortensia Group) W. Heinsmann 1969. Germany. Mentioned in the Checklist.

'Gloire de Boissy-Saint Leger' (*H. macrophylla* Hortensia Group) Nonin. France. Flowers pink per Haworth-Booth. According to the Shamrock list, lost to cultivation.

'Gloire de Bruxelles' (*H. macrophylla* Hortensia Group) Draps-Dom 1963. Belgium. Mentioned in the Checklist.

'Gloire de Vanves' (*H. macrophylla* Hortensia Group) 1933. France. Mentioned in the Checklist.

'Glyn Church' (*H. macrophylla* Hortensia Group). Glyn Church is the author of a book on *Hydrangea*.

'Gracieuse' (*H. macrophylla* Hortensia Group) Lemoine 1920. France. Flowers pink, serrate. Synonym: 'Gracieux'.

'Grand Mont' (*H. macrophylla* Hortensia Group). Mentioned in the Shamrock list.

'Groseille' (*H. macrophylla* Hortensia Group) Cayeux 1964. France. Lost to cultivation.

'Gruga' (*H. macrophylla* Hortensia Group) A. Steiniger 1966. Germany. Named after the Gruga park in Dortmund, Germany. Lost to cultivation.

'Gwenlin' (*H. macrophylla* Hortensia Group). Mentioned in the Shamrock list.

'H. C. Zwart' (*H. macrophylla* Hortensia Group) D. Baardse. Netherlands. Mentioned in the Checklist.

'H. Gerritse' (*H. macrophylla* Hortensia Group) D. Baardse 1920. Netherlands. Mentioned in the Checklist. Lost to cultivation.

'Hadsbury' (*H. macrophylla* Lacecap Group). United Kingdom. Mentioned in the Checklist.

'Haku mai hime' (*H. serrata*). Origin Japanese. Milim Botanical Garden, Korea.

'Hallwyl' (*H. macrophylla* Hortensia Group) E. Haller 1969. Switzerland. Mentioned in the Shamrock list and the Checklist. Might be in cultivation.

'Harmonie' (*H. macrophylla* Hortensia Group) Lemoine 1911. France. Corymbs large, blushed white. Lost to cultivation.

'Heidegg' (*H. macrophylla* Hortensia Group) E. Haller 1978. Switzerland. Mentioned in the Shamrock list and the Checklist. Lost to cultivation.

'Heiderösel' (*H. macrophylla* Hortensia Group) before 1935. Germany. A dwarf form, size not known. The flowerheads are deep pink or blue, with serrate sepals. Offered by several Dutch nurseries (D. A. Koster, M. Koster and Sons, C. Esveld), but probably now lost to cultivation.

'Helen Merritt' (*H. macrophylla* Hortensia Group) Kluis and Koning before 1935. Netherlands. Mentioned in the Checklist.

'Helen Rankin' (*H. macrophylla* Hortensia Group) Rotherr 1994. Germany. Mentioned in the Checklist.

'Helge' (*H. macrophylla* Hortensia Group) J. Wintergalen 1921. Germany. A medium-sized shrub, with cherry red or eventually blue flowers, in June to July. Offered by several Dutch nurseries before 1935, but now probably lost to cultivation.

'Hercule' (*H. macrophylla* Hortensia Group) Cayeux 1926. France. Mentioned in the Checklist. Lost to cultivation.

'Hildegard Königer' (*H. macrophylla* Hortensia Group) Brügger 1961. Germany. Mentioned in the Checklist.

'Hiro hen' (*H. serrata*)

'Hollandia' (*H. macrophylla* Hortensia Group) D. Baardse. Netherlands. A strong-growing shrub with sturdy, strong branches. The foliage is heavily serrate. The flowerheads are pink. Offered by Dutch nurseries before 1935, but now lost to cultivation.

'Hondoji aka' (*H. serrata*)

'Hortulanus Budde' (*H. macrophylla* Hortensia Group) D. Baardse 1920. Netherlands. Mentioned in the Checklist. Lost to cultivation.

'Hortulanus Cuneus' (*H. macrophylla* Hortensia Group) D. Baardse 1920. Netherlands. Mentioned in the Checklist. Lost to cultivation.

'Hortulanus Fiet' (*H. macrophylla* Hortensia Group) D. Baardse 1920. Netherlands. Hortulanus Fiet was a curator of the Botanic Gardens of the University of Leiden, Netherlands.

'Hortulanus Van Laren' (*H. macrophylla* Hortensia Group) D. Baardse 1920. Netherlands. Hortulanus Van Laren also worked for the University of Leiden.

'Hortulanus Wilke' (*H. macrophylla* Hortensia Group) D. Baardse 1920. Netherlands. Hortulanus Wilke once worked for the University of Leiden.

'Howaito Dayamondo' (*H. serrata*) Yatabe Mototeru. Japan. Mentioned in the Checklist.

'Hyuga konjou' (*H. serrata*). Japan. Milim Botanical Garden, Korea.

'Iberg' (*H. macrophylla* Hortensia Group) E. Haller 1978. Switzerland.

'Ideal' (*H. macrophylla* Hortensia Group) Cayeux 1924. France. According to the Shamrock list, lost to cultivation.

'Idole' (*H. macrophylla* Hortensia Group) Draps-Dom 1950. Belgium. Mentioned in the Checklist.

'Innocence' (*H. macrophylla* Hortensia Group) Lemoine 1910. France. Flowers creamy white, sepals serrate. Most probably lost to cultivation.

'Islettes' (*H. macrophylla* Hortensia Group) E. Mouillère 1910. France. Flowers pink, long lasting. According to the Shamrock list, lost to cultivation.

'Izu no temari' (*H. serrata*). Probably synonymous with 'Izu no hana temari'.

'J. C. de Lange' (*H. macrophylla* Hortensia Group). Dutch origin. Mentioned in the Checklist.

'Jacques C. Grönewegen' (*H. macrophylla* Hortensia Group) D. Baardse 1920. Netherlands. Named for a well-known but now defunct Dutch nursery.

'Jan Steen' (*H. macrophylla* Hortensia Group) K. Wezelenburg & Sons 1936. Netherlands. Flowers pink. A sibling of 'Frans Hals'. Named for a 17th-century Dutch artist. Most probably lost to cultivation.

'Joconde' (*H. macrophylla* Hortensia Group) Lemoine 1912. France. Flowerheads white, sepals serrate.

'Johann Berger' (*H. macrophylla* Hortensia Group) Berger 1937. Vienna, Austria. Mentioned in the University of Dresden list.

'Johannna Baardse' (*H. macrophylla* Hortensia Group) D. Baardse, 1920. Netherlands. Flowers large, pale pink flowers. Offered by D. A. Koster nursery, Boskoop, in 1932, but now lost to cultivation.

'John C. Mensing' (*H. macrophylla* Hortensia Group) D. Baardse 1918. Netherlands. A dwarf shrub. Flowers usually deep pink. Offered by D. A. Koster nursery, Boskoop, in 1932, but now lost to cultivation.

'John van den Berg' (*H. macrophylla* Hortensia Group) D. Baardse 1915. Netherlands. A tall shrub with pale pink flowers. Lost to cultivation.

'Jonkheer van Tets' (*H. macrophylla* Hortensia Group) D. Baardse 1924. Netherlands. A miniature plant that hardly grows and thus has been discarded. The flowers, if any, were warm red to crimson pink.

'Josef Keller' (*H. macrophylla* Hortensia Group) A. Steiniger 1960. Germany. Mentioned in the Checklist.

'Josef Wintergalen' (*H. macrophylla* Hortensia Group) J. Wintergalen 1943. Germany. Flowers "warm pink" according to Haworth-Booth.

'Joseph Israels' (*H. macrophylla* Hortensia Group) K. Wezelenburg & Sons 1936. Netherlands. A sibling of 'Frans Hals' and 'Jan Steen' with pink flowers. Named for a 17th-century Dutch artist.

'Josephine Charlotte' (*H. macrophylla* Hortensia Group) Draps-Dom 1940. Belgium. Mentioned in the Checklist.

'Jubilaeum' (*H. macrophylla* Hortensia Group) Brügger 1951. Germany. Mentioned in the Checklist.

'Jubilee' (*H. macrophylla* Hortensia Group) H. J. Jones 1927. United Kingdom. A dwarf shrub with stout branches, not exceeding 1 m (3 feet). Flowers fuchsia pink. Lost to cultivation.

'Junbureto hamoni' (*H. serrata*). Yatabe Mototeru. Japan.

'Junbureto merodi' (*H. serrata*). Yatabe Mototeru. Japan.

'K. Hartlieb' (*H. macrophylla* Hortensia Group) D. Baardse 1920. Netherlands. Mentioned in the Checklist.

'Karl Spitteler' (*H. macrophylla* Hortensia Group) Moll Brothers 1945. Germany. Mentioned in the Checklist.

'Ken no mai' (*H. serrata*). Origin Japanese. Milim Botanical Garden, Korea.

'Kifuri yama' (*H. serrata*). Origin Japanese. Mentioned in the Checklist.

'Kirsten' (*H. macrophylla* Hortensia Group) Kientzler 1962. Germany. According to the Shamrock list, still in cultivation.

'**Kluis Superior**' (*H. macrophylla* Hortensia Group) E. M. Kluis of Kluis and Koning 1945. Netherlands.

'**Kölner Bauer**' (*H. macrophylla* Hortensia Group) Graetz 1930. Germany. Mentioned in the Checklist.

'**Kölner Jungfrau**' (*H. macrophylla* Hortensia Group) Graetz 1928. Germany. Mentioned in the Checklist.

'**Komachi**' (*H. serrata*). May be a lacecap.

'**Komet**' (*H. macrophylla* Hortensia Group) J. Wintergalen. Germany. Mentioned in the Checklist.

'**Koralle**' (*H. macrophylla* Hortensia Group) A. Steiniger 1964. Germany. Mentioned in the Checklist.

'**Krimhilde**' (*H. macrophylla* Hortensia Group) J. Wintergalen 1924. Germany. A dwarf shrub. Corymbs have fringed sepals, usually salmon pink. Offered before 1940 by some Dutch nurseries.

'**Lacewing**' (*H. macrophylla* Lacecap Group). Mentioned in the Checklist.

'Lady in Blue' (*H. macrophylla* Lacecap Group). Not a hydrangea, but *Dichroa febrifuga*.

'**Landrat von Miquel**' (*H. macrophylla* Hortensia Group) Rosenkrantzer 1920. Germany. Mentioned in the University of Dresden list.

'**La Neige**' (*H. macrophylla* Hortensia Group) Cailleux 1925. France. Mentioned in the Checklist.

'**Le Loir**' (*H. macrophylla* Hortensia Group) Mouillère 1909. France. Corymbs large, soft salmon pink. Lost to cultivation.

'**Le Loiret**' (*H. macrophylla* Hortensia Group) Foucard 1913. France. Corymbs large, pink or purplish. Most probably not in cultivation.

'**Lemon Zest**' (*H. macrophylla* Hortensia Group). United Kingdom (?). Mentioned in the Shamrock list.

'**Lenzburg**' (*H. macrophylla* Hortensia Group) E. Haller 1967. Switzerland. Named for a small city in central Switzerland. Lost to cultivation.

'**Le Printemps**' (*H. macrophylla* Hortensia Group) Mouillère 1933. France. Mentioned in the Checklist.

'**Les Pins**' (*H. macrophylla* Hortensia Group) Touchaud 1912. France. Mentioned in the Checklist. Lost to cultivation.

'**Liberté**' (*H. macrophylla* Hortensia Group) Lemoine 1912. France. Flowers pale pink with serrate sepals. Lost to cultivation.

'**Lilie Mouillère**' (*H. macrophylla* Hortensia Group) Mouillère 1914. France. A compact shrub with purple or deep blue flowers. Suitable as a pot plant. Most probably lost to cultivation. RHS Award: AM 1914.

'**Lilliputte**' (*H. macrophylla* Hortensia Group). Mentioned in the Checklist.

'**Linda**' (*H. macrophylla* Hortensia Group) A. Steiniger 1927. Germany. Mentioned in the Checklist.

'**Loreley**' (*H. macrophylla* Hortensia Group) J. Wintergalen 1924. Germany. A sturdy semidwarf shrub, freeflowering, with crimson or blue flowerheads. In cultivation at D. A. Koster nursery, Boskoop, before 1932, but now lost to cultivation.

'**Louis Foucard**' (*H. macrophylla* Hortensia Group) Foucard 1912. France. Flowers pink. Lost to cultivation.

'**Lucifer**' (*H. macrophylla* Hortensia Group). According to Haworth-Booth, sepals are red, flowering is early.

'**Luisenburg**' (*H. macrophylla* Hortensia Group) Nieschütz 1983. Germany. Mentioned in the Shamrock list and in the Checklist.

'**Lumina**' (*H. macrophylla* Hortensia Group) H. Cayeux 1934. France. Flowerheads large, pink.

'**Lumineux**' (*H. macrophylla* Hortensia Group) L. Mouillère 1946. France. A sturdy shrub with stout branches, vigorous-growing. Flowering time is from August to September. Corymbs large, flattened, fuchsia pink. Lost to cultivation.

'**Lusatia**' (*H. macrophylla* Hortensia Group). According to the Shamrock list, it is still in cultivation.

'**Lynn Lowrey**' (*H. quercifolia*). Mentioned in the Checklist.

'**Macrosepala**' (*H. macrophylla* Lacecap Group). A large shrub with big, broadly ovate leaves. Flowerheads up to 15 cm (6 inches) across, fertile flowers carmine red, sepals very large and almost white. This old cultivar is probably no longer in cultivation. According to Bertrand it should be variegated, but Regel's description (of f. *macrosepala* in 1866) does not mention this.

'**Madame A. Rosenkrantzer**' (*H. macrophylla* Hortensia Group) Rosenkrantzer 1912. Germany. Mentioned in the Checklist.

'**Madame Albert-Labrun**' (*H. macrophylla* Hortensia Group) Mouillère 1936. France. Mentioned in the Checklist. Lost to cultivation.

'**Madame Auguste Nonin**' (*H. macrophylla* Hortensia Group) E. Mouillère 1911. France. One of many forgotten cultivars bred by Mouillère. Mentioned in the Checklist.

'**Madame Blumhack**' (*H. macrophylla* Hortensia Group). Origin Japanese. Mentioned in the Checklist.

'**Madame Bouvet**' (*H. macrophylla* Hortensia Group) Mouillère 1935. France. Mentioned in the Checklist.

'**Madame Ch. Legoux**' (*H. macrophylla* Hortensia Group) E. Mouillère 1911. France. Mentioned in the Checklist.

'**Madame Charpentier**' (*H. macrophylla* Hortensia Group) E. Mouillère 1911. France. Mentioned in the Checklist.

'**Madame de Fürst**' (*H. macrophylla* Hortensia Group) E. Mouillère 1911. France. Mentioned in the Checklist.

'**Madame Deperier**' (*H. macrophylla* Hortensia Group) Touchard 1912. France. Mentioned in the Checklist. Probably lost to cultivation.

'**Madame E. Tabar**' (*H. macrophylla* Hortensia Group) E. Mouillère 1924. France. Mentioned in the Checklist.

'**Madame Gustave Renault**' (*H. macrophylla* Hortensia Group) Mouillère 1911. France. Mentioned in the Checklist.

'**Madame Jules Busson**' (*H. macrophylla* Hortensia Group). Mentioned in the Checklist.

'**Madame L. Pierre Barillet**' (*H. macrophylla* Hortensia Group) Barillet 1923. France. Mentioned in the Checklist.

'**Madame Louis Dutrie**' (*H. macrophylla* Hortensia Group) Barillet. France. Mentioned in the Checklist.

'**Madame M. F. Morney**' (*H. macrophylla* Hortensia Group) Mouillère 1936. France. Mentioned in the Checklist.

'**Madame Mezard**' (*H. macrophylla* Hortensia Group) M. Mezard 1870. France. Mentioned in the Checklist.

'**Madame P. Marchandeau**' (*H. macrophylla* Hortensia Group) Mouillère 1935. France. Mentioned in the Checklist.

'**Madame Raoult**' (*H. macrophylla* Hortensia Group) Mouillère 1924. France. Mentioned in the Checklist.

'**Madame Renée Jacquet**' (*H. macrophylla* Hortensia Group) E. Mouillère 1912. France. Mentioned in the Checklist.

'**Madame Renée Plessier**' (*H. macrophylla* Hortensia Group) Mouillère 1911. France Mentioned in the Checklist.

'**Madame Raymond**' (*H. macrophylla* Hortensia Group) Mouillère 1909. France. Flowers transparent white flowers, later becoming pinkish. Mentioned in the Checklist.

'**Madame Renault**' (*H. macrophylla* Hortensia Group) E. Mouillère 1910. France. A moderate-growing shrub. Corymbs pink with rounded sepals. Mentioned in the Checklist.

'**Madame Touchard**' (*H. macrophylla* Hortensia Group) Touchard 1912. France. Mentioned in the Checklist.

'**Mademoiselle De Tremault**' (*H. macrophylla* Hortensia Group) E. Mouillère 1911. France. A very old and forgotten cultivar.

'**Mademoiselle Eleonore Novello**' (*H. macrophylla* Hortensia Group) Barillet 1923. France. Mentioned in the Checklist.

'**Mademoiselle Jacqueline Bemin**' (*H. macrophylla* Hortensia Group) Barillet 1923. France. Mentioned in the Checklist.

'**Mademoiselle Marie Barillet**' (*H. macrophylla* Hortensia Group) Barillet. France. Mentioned in the Checklist.

'**Maebach Street**' (*H. macrophylla* Hortensia Group). Mentioned in the Shamrock list.

'**Magenta**' (*H. macrophylla* Hortensia Group) Lemoine 1913. France. Mentioned in the Checklist.

'**Majestic**' (*H. macrophylla* Hortensia Group) Draps-Dom 1951. Belgium. Mentioned in the Checklist.

'**Malva**' (*H. macrophylla* Hortensia Group) A. Steiniger 1952. Germany. Mentioned in the Checklist.

'**Marconi**' (*H. macrophylla* Hortensia Group) K. Wezelenburg & Son 1936. Netherlands. Flowers pink with serrate sepals. Probably lost to cultivation.

'**Marie Berger**' (*H. macrophylla* Hortensia Group) Berger 1937. Vienna, Austria. Mentioned in the University of Dresden list.

'**Marie Matthes**' F. Matthes 1924. France. A vigorous-growing shrub exceeding 1.5 m (5 feet). The corymbs are pink or light blue, with serrate sepals. Offered by Dutch nurseries before 1935, now lost to cultivation.

'**Marie Pierre Flips**' (*H. macrophylla* Hortensia Group) E. Mouillère 1927. France. Mentioned in the Checklist.

'**Marmorprinzessin**' (*H. macrophylla* Hortensia Group) A. Steiniger 1973. Germany. Mentioned in the Shamrock list. Lost to cultivation.

'**Mastodonte**' (*H. macrophylla* Hortensia Group) Chaubert 1920. France. The name suggests a huge plant. Mentioned in the Checklist.

'**Max Schäfer**' (*H. macrophylla* Hortensia Group) Schäfer 1959. Rastatt, Germany

'**Meissner Porzellan**' (*H. macrophylla* Hortensia Group) Nieschütz. Germany. Mentioned in the Checklist.

'**Memoire de M. Arthur Barillet**' (*H. macrophylla* Hortensia Group) Travouillon 1923. France. Mentioned in the Checklist.

'**Merritt's Pink**' (*H. macrophylla* Hortensia Group). Louisiana Nurseries. United States. Mentioned in the Louisiana Nurseries catalog and by Michael Dirr (1997). Available in the United States.

'**Merritt's Pride**' (*H. macrophylla* Hortensia Group). Louisiana Nurseries. United States. Mentioned by Michael Dirr (1997).

'Merveille Blanc' (*H. macrophylla* Hortensia Group) Dumas 1937. France. A branch sport of 'Merveille', differing in the white color of the flowers. Possibly lost to cultivation.

'Merveille Rose' (*H. macrophylla* Hortensia Group) Dumas 1937. France. Like 'Merveille Blanc' but with pink flowers.

'Meteor' (*H. macrophylla* Hortensia Group) J. Wintergalen 1934. Germany. A moderate-growing shrub up to 1.25 m (3.5 feet). The flowers are dark red or crimson, the sepals are serrate. Lost to cultivation.

'Mistress A. Rich' (*H. macrophylla* Hortensia Group) E. Mouillère 1911. France. Mentioned in the Checklist.

'Monique Mouillère' (*H. macrophylla* Hortensia Group) Mouillère 1960. France. Mentioned in the Checklist.

'Monsieur G. Renault' (*H. macrophylla* Hortensia Group) E. Mouillère 1911. France. Lost to cultivation.

'Mont Blanc' (*H. macrophylla* Hortensia Group) Cayeux 1927. France. Flowers certainly white.

'Mont Rose' (*H. macrophylla* Hortensia Group) Lemoine 1909. France. Mentioned in the Checklist.

'Morgenröte' (*H. macrophylla* Hortensia Group) Rosenkrantzer. Germany. Possibly synonymous with 'Morgenrot'.

'Moritzburg' (*H. macrophylla* Hortensia Group) Dresdner Zierpflanzenbau 1991. Germany. Mentioned in the Checklist.

'Mrs. Charles Mills' (*H. macrophylla* Hortensia Group) K. W. Wezelenburg & Son. Netherlands. A low-growing shrub, not exceeding 1 m (3 feet), with warm pink flowerheads. Now lost to cultivation.

'Mrs. F. Huggett' (*H. macrophylla* Hortensia Group) H. J. Jones 1927. United Kingdom. A vigorous-growing shrub. It bears large corymbs, usually pink. Doubtful whether this plant is still in the trade.

'Mrs. Norman Luff' (*H. macrophylla* Hortensia Group). Of Dutch origin, as a deciduous rhododendron with that name has been introduced by M. Koster and Sons nursery, Boskoop.

'Muttertag' (*H. macrophylla* Hortensia Group) Schäfer. Rastatt, Germany. Mentioned in the University of Dresden list.

'Mythen' (*H. macrophylla* Hortensia Group) Federal Research Institute for Horticulture 1964. Switzerland. Named after twin mountains in central Switzerland. According to the Shamrock list, lost to cultivation.

'Nanping' (*H. macrophylla* Hortensia Group) S. van der Schie Anjers BV 2002. Aalsmeer, Netherlands.

'Nanping' (*H. macrophylla* Lacecap Group) Eveleens 1996. Aalsmeer, Netherlands. Mentioned in the Checklist.

'Neige Orléanaise' (*H. macrophylla* Hortensia Group) Chaubert 1922. France. A tall vigorous-growing shrub up to 2 m (6.5 feet). The flowerheads are pure white and long lasting. This cultivar is tender. RHS Award: AM 1925. Lost to cultivation.

'Nikolaus Lambert' (*H. macrophylla* Hortensia Group) J. Lambert and Sons 1933. Trier, Germany. A strong-growing shrub with pink flowers.

'Nixe' (*H. macrophylla* Hortensia Group) J. Wintergalen 1928. Germany. A dwarf shrub, with stout, short branches. Flowerheads medium-sized, dark crimson red. The flowers can be made to turn intense blue but the color does not last long. Offered by a few Dutch nurseries before 1940, but now lost to cultivation.

'Normandie' (*H. macrophylla* Hortensia Group) H. Cayeux 1927. France. Corymbs large, with cherry pink florets. Lost to cultivation.

'Nouvelle Europe' (*H. macrophylla* Hortensia Group) Draps-Dom 1950. Belgium. Mentioned in the Checklist.

'Odin' (*H. macrophylla* Hortensia Group) J. Wintergalen 1932. Germany. A compact, short-branched shrub. The corymbs are large and round, rosy crimson to shining red. Flowering time is from July to August. Offered by Dutch nurseries before 1940 but now lost to cultivation.

'Olympia' (*H. macrophylla* Hortensia Group) A. Steiniger 1952. Germany. Mentioned in the Shamrock list and in the Checklist.

'Opale' (*H. macrophylla* Hortensia Group) Foucard 1910. France. A medium-sized shrub. The large corymbs are opalescent white. Lost to cultivation.

'Orient' (*H. macrophylla* Hortensia Group) H. Cayeux 1964. France. Mentioned in the Shamrock list.

'Osning' (*H. macrophylla* Hortensia Group) J. Wintergalen 1917. Germany. Flowers crimson pink.

'Ostergruss' (*H. macrophylla* Hortensia Group) Haller. Switzerland 1968. According to the Shamrock list, lost to cultivation.

'Ozora' (*H. macrophylla* Hortensia Group). Not in cultivation.

'Panda Pinku' (*H. macrophylla* Hortensia Group). Mentioned in the Checklist.

'**Papillon**' (*H. macrophylla* Hortensia Group) Mouillère 1913. France. A shrub up to 1.5 m (5 feet). Flowerheads yellowish white with green dots. Probably no longer in cultivation. Not to be confused with *H. paniculata* 'Papillon'.

'**Parure**' (*H. macrophylla* Hortensia Group) H. Cayeux 1932. France. A sturdy shrub with pink flowerheads and crimped sepals. A seedling of 'Merveille'. According to the Shamrock list, it is lost to cultivation.

'**Patio White**' (*H. quercifolia*). Louisiana Nurseries before 1997. United States.

'**Patriote**' (*H. macrophylla* Hortensia Group) H. Cayeux 1935. France. A compact shrub up to 1.25 m (3.5 feet). The flowerheads are crimson pink. Free-flowering. According to the Shamrock list, it is lost to cultivation.

'**Paul Kipke**' (*H. macrophylla* Hortensia Group) Kipke. Wismar, Germany. Mentioned in the University of Dresden list.

'Peach hime' (*H. serrata*). Misspelling of 'Pichi hime'. From Miyoski and Company, Japan.

'**Peer Gynt**' (*H. macrophylla* Hortensia Group) J. Wintergalen 1921. Germany. A sturdy shrub with stout, short branches, usually not more than 1.25 m (3.5 feet) high. Corymbs large, pale pink or lavender blue, sepals serrate. Flowering time is from July to August. Offered by some Dutch nurseries before 1940 but now probably lost to cultivation.

'**Perle**' (*H. macrophylla* Hortensia Group). Raised at Friesdorf Research Station, now Landwirtschaftskammer Rheinland (Rhineland Agricultural Chamber), Germany. Mentioned in the Checklist.

'**Perle du Havre**' (*H. macrophylla* Hortensia Group) H. Cayeux 1935. France. A large, sturdy shrub, up to 2 m (6.5 feet). Flowerheads equally large, sepals serrate, usually pink. Probably lost to cultivation.

'**Pilatus**' (*H. macrophylla* Hortensia Group) Federal Research Institute for Horticulture 1960. Switzerland. Named for a mountain near Lucerne, Switzerland. Lost to cultivation.

'**Pimpernel**' (*H. macrophylla* Hortensia Group) Pieter Koek BV 2002. Aalsmeer, Netherlands.

'**Pink Fresh**' (*H. serrata*). Miyoski and Company. Japan. May be a lacecap. Mentioned in the Checklist.

'**Pink Perfection**' (*H. macrophylla* Hortensia Group) Draps-Dom 1951. Belgium. Mentioned in the Checklist.

'**Pinku Dayamonto**' (*H. serrata*) Sakamoto Seiji.

'Pinku Fantaji' (*H. serrata*) Yatabe Mototeru. Japan. Maybe an incorrect spelling of 'Pink Fantasy'.

'**Pinkupansa**' (*H. serrata*) Fukushima Massaaki. Japan.

'**Président Felix Lellieux**' (*H. macrophylla* Hortensia Group) Mouillère 1934. France. Mentioned in the Checklist.

'**Président Pinguet**' (*H. macrophylla* Hortensia Group) E. Mouillère 1911. France. Lost to cultivation.

'**Président Poincaré**' (*H. macrophylla* Hortensia Group) E. Mouillère 1914. France. Mentioned in the Checklist.

'**Primrose**' (*H. macrophylla* Hortensia Group) Mouillère 1938. France. Mentioned in the Checklist.

'**Prince Philippe**' (*H. macrophylla* Hortensia Group) Gyselinck 1967. Belgium. Mentioned in the Checklist.

'**Princess Marina**' (*H. macrophylla* Hortensia Group) H. J. Jones 1927. United Kingdom. Flowers pink. Mentioned in the Checklist.

'**Professeur A. Vézin**' (*H. macrophylla* Hortensia Group) Mouillère 1911. France. Mentioned in the Checklist.

'**Professeur Lenfant**' (*H. macrophylla* Hortensia Group). 1938. France. Corymbs large, pink. Mentioned in the Checklist

'**Professeur René Rouhaud**' (*H. macrophylla* Hortensia Group) Mouillère 1912. France. Mentioned in the Checklist.

'Pulverulenta' (*H. serrata*). May be a lacecap.

'**Puppchen**' (*H. macrophylla* Hortensia Group) F. Matthes 1925. Germany. Mentioned in the University of Dresden list.

'**Purisuburu**' (*H. serrata*). Miura Kiyomori. Japan.

'**Qing Long**' (*H. macrophylla* Hortensia Group). Chinese origin. Mentioned in the Checklist.

'**Rabuyu kissu**' (*H. serrata*). Yatabe Mototeru. Japan.

'Red Rock' (*H. macrophylla* Hortensia Group). Present in C. Esveld Nurseries, Boskoop.

'**Reine de Beauté**' (*H. macrophylla* Hortensia Group) L. F. Cayeux 1936. France. Corymbs large and compact, pink.

'**Rheingold**' (*H. macrophylla* Hortensia Group) J. Wintergalen 1920. Germany. A moderate-growing shrub up to 1.5 m (5 feet). Flowerheads bright pink. Offered by several Dutch nurseries before 1935. According to the Shamrock list, it is now lost to cultivation.

'**Richesse**' (*H. macrophylla* Hortensia Group) Lemoine 1912. France. Flowers vivid pink. Mentioned in the Checklist.

'**Rochambeau**' (*H. macrophylla* Hortensia Group) Mouillère 1918. France. A slow-growing shrub. Flowerheads crimson or even violet, becoming deep blue when fed aluminum. The sepals are rounded and entire. Flowering time is from July to September. Offered at M. Koster and Sons nursery, Boskoop, before 1935. Now lost to cultivation.

'**Roi Albert de Belgique**' (*H. macrophylla* Hortensia Group) Mouillère 1914. France. A shrub of usual size. The flowerheads are large, pinkish white or pale bluish. Sepals serrate. Also spelled "Roi Albert." Most probably lost to cultivation.

'**Ronsard**' (*H. macrophylla* Hortensia Group) Mouillère 1909. France. Similar to 'Madame Emile Mouillère' in many respects, but the flowers are blushed pink or tinted blue. A forgotten cultivar. Mentioned in the Checklist.

'**Rosa King**' (*H. macrophylla* Hortensia Group). Name doubtful. Flowers pink, midseason.

'**Rosamunde**' (*H. macrophylla* Hortensia Group) Brügger. Germany. Mentioned in the Checklist.

'**Rose Supreme**' (*H. macrophylla* Hortensia Group) Swanson 1950. United Kingdom. Synonym: 'Supreme'. Mentioned in the Checklist.

'**Rosenkavalier**' (*H. macrophylla* Hortensia Group) Versuchsanstalt Friesdorf 1968. Germany. Mentioned in the Checklist.

'**Rosengarten**' (*H. macrophylla* Hortensia Group) Dresdner Zierpflanzenbau 1992. Germany. Mentioned in the Checklist.

'**Roseomarginata**' (*H. macrophylla* Lacecap Group). Mentioned in the Checklist.

'**Rotenburg**' (*H. macrophylla* Hortensia Group) Kientzler. Germany. Mentioned in the Checklist.

'**Rotenfels**' (*H. macrophylla* Hortensia Group) Kientzler 1982. Germany. Mentioned in the Checklist.

'**Royal Purple**' (*H. macrophylla* Hortensia Group). May be present in the Shamrock collection.

'**Rubens**' (*H. macrophylla* Hortensia Group) K. Wezelenburg & Son 1936. Netherlands. Flowerheads deep pink. One of several cultivars named after Dutch painters. Probably lost to cultivation.

'**Rubin**' (*H. macrophylla* Hortensia Group) A. Steiniger 1952. Germany. Mentioned in the Checklist.

'**Rubis**' (*H. macrophylla* Hortensia Group) Lemoine 1923. France. A compact shrub, with weak branches. Flowerheads ruby red to maroon or purple. Sepals entire. Needs good care in the garden. Offered by Dutch nurseries but now lost to cultivation.

'**Ruth Mitscheck**' (*H. macrophylla* Hortensia Group) Mitscheck, Olmuetz. Germany. Mentioned in the University of Dresden list.

'**Saarbrücken**' (*H. macrophylla* Hortensia Group) A. Rosenkrantzer 1912. Germany. Mentioned in the Checklist. Lost to cultivation.

'**Sapa**' (*H. aspera*). Might be *H. aspera* subsp. *strigosa*. Sapa is a region in Vietnam, where Wynn-Jones collected wild material.

'**Satin**' (*H. macrophylla* Hortensia Group) Cayeux 1964. France. Mentioned in the Checklist. Lost to cultivation.

'**Saturne**' (*H. macrophylla* Hortensia Group) Chaubert. France. Mentioned in the Checklist.

'**Schalke 04**' (*H. macrophylla* Hortensia Group) Versuchsanstalt Friesdorf 1969. Germany. Lacks a description, but probably still in cultivation.

'**Schloss Hirschstein**' (*H. macrophylla* Hortensia Group) Dresdner Zierpflanzenbau 1991. Germany. Mentioned in the Checklist.

'**Schneekoppe**' (*H. macrophylla* Hortensia Group) Matthes 1924. Germany. Lost to cultivation.

'**Schön Rotraud**' (*H. macrophylla* Hortensia Group) J. Wintergalen. Germany. Mentioned in the Checklist.

'**Schwabenland**' (*H. macrophylla* Hortensia Group) Brügger. Germany

'**Seikai**' (*H. serrata*). Origin Japanese. Milim Botanical Garden, Korea.

'**Senyu no amacha**' (*H. serrata*). Milim Botanical Garden, Korea.

'**Shashiva**' (*H. serrata*). Mentioned in the Checklist.

'**Siegfried**' (*H. macrophylla* Hortensia Group) J. Wintergalen 1926. Germany. A medium-sized shrub, probably not more than 1.25 m (3.5 feet) high. The flowerheads are deep pink. Lost to cultivation.

'**Siegfried Glahn**' (*H. macrophylla* Hortensia Group) F. Matthes 1922. Germany.

'**Silver Lining**' (*H. arborescens* subsp. *radiata*). No description.

'**Silveredge**' (*H. macrophylla* Hortensia Group). Origin Japanese. Foliage probably variegated.

'**Skips**' (*H. macrophylla* Hortensia Group). Mentioned in the Checklist.

'**Sokoko temari**' (*H. serrata*). Milim Botanical Garden, Korea.

'**Souvenir de M. Belot**' (*H. macrophylla* Hortensia Group) E. Mouillère 1911. France. Mentioned in the Checklist.

'Souvenir de Madame Victor Raoult' (*H. macrophylla* Hortensia Group) E. Mouillère 1913. France. Mentioned in the Checklist.

'Souvenir de M. Hersant' (*H. macrophylla* Hortensia Group) E. Mouillère 1913. France. Mentioned in the Checklist.

'Souvenir de Edouard Aubert' (*H. macrophylla* Hortensia Group) Barillet 1923. France. Mentioned in the Checklist.

'Souvenir du Lieutenant Chauré' (*H. macrophylla* Hortensia Group) E. Mouillère 1911. France. Mentioned in the Checklist.

'Spätsommer' (*H. macrophylla* Hortensia Group) F. Matthes. Germany. A huge, vigorous-growing shrub with sturdy branches. Flowerheads pink. Flowering time is from August to September. Lost to cultivation.

'Splendens' (*H. macrophylla* Hortensia Group) H. Cayeux 1919 or 1920. France. A sturdy, vigorous-growing shrub with stout branches, up to 2 m (6.5 feet). The flowerheads are large, up to 20 cm (8 inches) across, bright pink or pale blue, depending on the soil. The sepals are irregularly rounded and unfringed. Offered by Dutch nurseries before the Second World War but now lost to cultivation.

'Speer' (*H. macrophylla* Hortensia Group) Federal Research Institute for Horticulture 1949. Switzerland. Mentioned in the Checklist.

'Spetchley' (*H. macrophylla* Hortensia Group). Mentioned in the Checklist.

'Spreeperle' (*H. macrophylla* Hortensia Group) H. Dienemann 1975. Germany. Mentioned in the Checklist.

'Spreetal' (*H. macrophylla* Hortensia Group) H. Dienemann 1975. Germany. Certainly related to 'Spreeperle' but also without information.

'Stardust' (*H. heteromalla*) RHS Gardens Rosemoor before 1995. United Kingdom. Never introduced.

'Stegmeyer' (*H. macrophylla* Hortensia Group) Draps-Dom. Belgium. Mentioned in the Checklist.

'Stein' (*H. macrophylla* Hortensia Group) Haller 1978. Switzerland. Mentioned in the Checklist.

'Succes' (*H. macrophylla* Hortensia Group) H. Cayeux 1920. France. Flowerheads pink, with serrate sepals. According to the Shamrock list, lost to cultivation.

'Sunset' (*H. macrophylla* Lacecap Group). Two different plants have this name, according to Dussine. One of them is a synonym of 'Grasmücke', which see. The other is a strong-growing shrub, flowerheads almost wine red to purplish rose. The ray-flowers are exceptionally large and consist of four sepals. We could not verify this.

'Susan' (*H. macrophylla* Hortensia Group) J. Kolk BV. 2002. De Kwakel, Netherlands

'Suzanne Cayeux' (*H. macrophylla* Hortensia Group) H. Cayeux 1919. France. Flowers pink. Mentioned in the Checklist.

'Synelle' (*H. macrophylla* Hortensia Group). Mentioned in the Checklist.

'Tenjou amache' (*H. serrata*).

'Thierstein' (*H. macrophylla* Hortensia Group) Haller 1982. Switzerland. According to the Shamrock list, this relatively new cultivar is no longer available.

'Thomas Stevenson' (*H. macrophylla* Hortensia Group) H. J. Jones 1927. United Kingdom. Flowers pink, sepals serrate.

'Tindonissa' (*H. macrophylla* Hortensia Group) E. Haller. Switzerland. May be spelled 'Vindonissa'. Mentioned in the Checklist.

'Trouvaille' (*H. macrophylla* Hortensia Group) Cayeux 1931. France. Mentioned in the Checklist.

'Türkenbund' (*H. macrophylla* Hortensia Group) Binz. Germany. Mentioned in the University of Dresden list.

'Urticifolia' (*H. arborescens*) Hort. Leaves more deeply serrate than those of the species. See *H. arborescens* subsp. *arborescens*.

'Van der Valk' (*H. macrophylla* Hortensia Group) 1918. Netherlands

'Vedette' (*H. macrophylla* Hortensia Group) Draps-Dom 1955. Belgium. Mentioned in the Checklist.

'Veitchii Grandiflora' (*H. macrophylla* Lacecap Group) Chaubert 1919. France. Mentioned in the Checklist.

'Vendôme' (*H. macrophylla* Hortensia Group) Mouillère 1950. France. Mentioned in the Checklist.

'Vergissmeinnicht' (*H. macrophylla* Hortensia Group) A. Steiniger 1964. Germany. Mentioned in the Checklist.

'Versicolor' (*H. macrophylla* Lacecap Group). Probably variegated.

'Victoire' (*H. macrophylla* Hortensia Group) H. Cayeux 1920. France. Flowers light pink to white. In cultivation in Netherlands before 1936.

'Vulkan' (*H. macrophylla* Hortensia Group) J. Wintergalen. Germany. Mentioned in the Checklist.

'W. A. Mowbray' (*H. macrophylla* Hortensia Group) H. J. Jones 1927. United Kingdom. Flowers pink.

'W. Bothof' (*H. macrophylla* Hortensia Group) D. Baardse 1920. Netherlands. An old Dutch variety, lost to cultivation.

'**W. D. Cartwright**' (*H. macrophylla* Hortensia Group) H. J. Jones 1927. United Kingdom: Dwarf habit. Flowers bright pink.

'**Wartburg**' (*H. macrophylla* Hortensia Group) Haller 1978. Switzerland. Mentioned in the Checklist. Lost to cultivation. Named for a castle in northwestern Switzerland.

'**Watteau**' (*H. macrophylla* Hortensia Group) Draps-Dom 1958. Belgium. Mentioned in the Checklist.

'**Wave Hill**' (*H. macrophylla* Hortensia Group).

'**Wayne's White**' (*H. macrophylla* Hortensia Group) K. Vanhoose. United States. Flowerheads snow white, aging to pink and flattened during the summer. Not available in Europe. Listed in the catalog of the Bell Family Nursery, Oregon, United States.

'**Wildegg**' (*H. macrophylla* Hortensia Group) Haller 1967. Switzerland. Mentioned in the Checklist.

'**Wizzenboss**' (*H. macrophylla* Hortensia Group). Mentioned in the Checklist.

'**Xian**' (*H. macrophylla* Hortensia Group) Eveleens 1996. Netherlands.

'**Yae hiro ken**' (*H. serrata*). Origin Japanese. Milim Botanical Garden, Korea.

'**Yasaku yae**' (*H. involucrata*).

'**Zhuni hitō**' (*H. serrata*) Milim Botanical Garden, Korea. May be an incorrect spelling for 'Juni hitō'.

References

Bean, W. J. 1970–1988. *Trees and Shrubs Hardy in the British Isles.* 8th ed. London: John Murray.

Belder, Jelena de. 1999. *Arboretum Kalmthout.* Netherlands: Terra.

Bertrand, Hélène. 2001. *Preliminary Hydrangea Checklist.* Angers, France: Institut National d'Horticulture.

Bowman, Daria P. 2000. *Hydrangeas.* New York: Friedman/Fairfax Publishers.

Bree, Rob de. N.D. Report for the Research Station for Nursery Stock, Boskoop.

Bulk, Rein, and Mark Bulk. N.D. *Bulk Nursery Catalog.* Boskoop, Netherlands.

Church, Glyn. 2001. *Hydrangeas.* Toronto, Canada: Firefly Books.

Coats, Alice M. 1992. *Garden Shrubs and Their Histories.* New York: Simon and Schuster.

Cronquist, Arthur. 1988. *The Evolution and Classification of Flowering Plants.* Bronx, New York: New York Botanical Garden.

Darthuizer Boomkwekerijen. 1994. *Darthuizer Vademecum.* Leersum, Netherlands: Darthuizer Boomkwekerijen.

Dirr, Michael. 1997. *Dirr's Hardy Trees and Shrubs.* Portland, Oregon: Timber Press.

Dussine, Alain. 2001. *Le Monde des Hortensias.* Rodez, France: Éd. du Rouergue.

Eeghen, Florentine van. 1999. *Hortensia's.* Netherlands: Terra.

Erhardt, Walter, Erich Götz, Nils Bödeker, and Robert Zander. 2002. *Zander Dictionary of Plant Names.* 17th edition. Stuttgart: Ulmer.

Federal Research Institute for Horticulture (Eidgenössische Forschungsanstalt). 1964. Annual Report. Wädenswil, Switzerland.

Haworth-Booth, Michael. 1984. *The Hydrangeas.* 5th ed. London: Constable.

Hofstede, J., and W. Hofstede. 1998. HOVARIA leaflet.

Jackson, B. D., et al. 1895– . *Index Kewensis.* Oxford University Press.

Krüssmann, Gerd. 1976–1978. *Handbuch der Laubgehölze.* Berlin: Paul Parey (translated into English, *A Manual of Cultivated Broad-leaved Trees and Shrubs,* 3 vols. 1984–1986. Portland, Oregon: Timber Press).

Laubadiere, B. de. 2000. *Hydrangeas and Hortensias.*

Lawson-Hall, Toni, and Brian Rothera. 1995. *Hydrangeas, a Gardeners Guide.* Portland, Oregon: Timber Press.

Louisiana Nurseries. 1997. *Louisiana Nurseries Catalog.* Baton Rouge, Louisiana.

Mallet, Corinne. 1993–1994. *Hydrangeas.* 2 volumes. Paris: Centre d'Art Floral.

McClintock, E. A. 1957. *A Monograph of the Genus Hydrangea. Proceedings of the Californian Academy of Sciences* 29: 147–256.

Milim Botanical Garden. 1997. Plant Lists (in Korean). Seoul, Korea.

Pauwels, Ivo, and Guy Pieters. 2000. *Hortensia en haar zusjes.* Netherlands: Terra.

Pilatowski, R. E. 1982. A taxonomic study of the *Hydrangea arborescens* complex. *Journal Series of the North Carolina Agricultural Research Service,* Paper 6582. Raleigh, North Carolina.

Rampp Jungpflanzen (nursery). 2001. *Hydrangea Catalog.* Pfaffenhausen, Germany.

Regel, Eduard A. von. 1866. *Gartenflora* 15: 290.

Royal Boskoop Horticulture Society. *Dendroflora* 38 (journal).

Sargent, Charles S. 1913. *Plantae Wilsonianae,* vol. 1. Reprint, 1998. Portland, Oregon: Timber Press.

Satake, Y., et al., eds. 1989. *Wild Flowers of Japan: Woody Plants.* Tokyo: Heibonsha Company.

Shamrock Hydrangea Collection. 1999. *Repertoire de l'Association Shamrock.* Varengeville sur Mer, France: Corinne and Robert Mallet.

Siebold, Philipp F. von, and J. G. Zuccarini. 1840. *Flora Japonica.* Leiden.

Thoby, Jean. Catalogs and lists of Pépinières Thoby. Saint-Mars du Desert, France.

Yamamoto, T. 1998. *Japanese Color Guide of Hydrangeas* (in Japanese).

Index of Hydrangeas by Common or Cultivar Name

Index of Hydrangeas by Scientific Name

Hydrangea macrophylla, Sir Harold Hillier Gardens and Arboretum.